WITHDRAWN

CAMBRIDGE STUDIES IN
ANGLO-SAXON ENGLAND

4

VISIBLE SONG

TRANSITIONAL LITERACY IN OLD ENGLISH VERSE

CAMBRIDGE STUDIES IN ANGLO-SAXON ENGLAND

EDITORS

SIMON KEYNES

MICHAEL LAPIDGE

Editors' preface

Cambridge Studies in Anglo-Saxon England is a series of scholarly texts and monographs intended to advance our knowledge of all aspects of the field of Anglo-Saxon studies. The scope of the series, like that of *Anglo-Saxon England*, its periodical counterpart, embraces original scholarship in various disciplines: literary, historical, archaeological, philological, art-historical, palaeographical, architectural, liturgical and numismatic. It is the intention of the editors to encourage the publication of original scholarship which advances our understanding of the field through interdisciplinary approaches.

Volumes published:

1   *Anglo-Saxon Crucifixion Iconography and the Art of the Monastic Revival* by BARBARA C. RAW

2   *The Cult of the Virgin Mary in Anglo-Saxon England* by MARY CLAYTON

3   *Religion and Literature in Western England, 600–800,* by PATRICK SIMS-WILLIAMS

4   *Visible Song: Transitional Literacy in Old English Verse* by KATHERINE O'BRIEN O'KEEFFE

VISIBLE SONG

TRANSITIONAL LITERACY IN
OLD ENGLISH VERSE

KATHERINE O'BRIEN O'KEEFFE

Professor of English
Texas A&M University

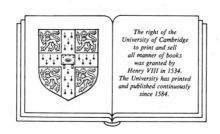

The right of the
University of Cambridge
to print and sell
all manner of books
was granted by
Henry VIII in 1534.
The University has printed
and published continuously
since 1584.

CAMBRIDGE UNIVERSITY PRESS

CAMBRIDGE

NEW YORK   PORT CHESTER

MELBOURNE   SYDNEY

Published by the Press Syndicate of the University of Cambridge
The Pitt Building, Trumpington Street, Cambridge CB2 1RP
40 West 20th Street, New York, NY 10011, USA
10 Stamford Road, Oakleigh, Melbourne 3166, Australia

First published 1990

Printed in Great Britain at
the University Press, Cambridge

British Library cataloguing in publication data
O'Keeffe, Katherine O'Brien
Visible song: transitional literacy in Old English verse.
– (Cambridge studies in Anglo-Saxon English; 4)
1. Poetry in Old English. – Critical studies
I. Title
829.1

Library of Congress cataloguing in publication data
O'Keeffe, Katherine O'Brien.
Visible song: transitional literacy in Old English verse /
Katherine O'Brien O'Keeffe.
p. cm. – (Cambridge Studies in Anglo-Saxon England: 4)
Includes bibliographical references.
ISBN 0–521–37550–9
1. English poetry – Old English, ca. 450–1100 – History and criticism.
2. Written communication – England – History.
3. Oral communication – England – History.
4. Anglo-Saxon – Intellectual life.
5. Literacy – England – History. I. Title. II. Series: Cambridge Studies in Anglo-Saxon
England: v. 4.
PR203.034 1990
829'.1 – dc20   89-77383 CIP

ISBN 0521 37550 9 hardback

CE

Contents

Plates

between pages 82 *and* 83

Figures

Preface

Writing is a technology which makes language visible. Despite the astonishing transformation involved in changing the heard into the seen, writing and reading are skills so fundamental to the conduct of life that they have become virtually transparent to us in the twentieth century (at least in developed countries). The assumptions and conditions of our own literacy are, for various historical and perceptual reasons, well hidden from us, but they must be brought to light if we are to understand the profound changes the growth of writing worked on early communities and individuals.

The present book sets out to examine one aspect of the growth of literacy in Anglo-Saxon England and its evidence in the manuscript records of Old English verse. I do not wish to argue here that any surviving verse in Old English was composed under purely oral circumstances. As the debate in the Old English scholarly community over the last thirty years has demonstrated, the circumstances for the composition of Old English verse remain an open question, and, I believe, an issue incapable of satisfactory demonstration. Precisely because the question of origin is unproductive, I do not ask it. The present book is not really concerned with composition as such, but about reception and transmission and what they may tell us about the interrelationships between 'orality' and 'literacy'. The copyists get all the lines.

My argument about the interrelationships between 'orality' and 'literacy' rests on several fundamental assumptions. First among them is that at some early point, verse in Old English was oral. From the time that Old English was first written, however, composition of verse in writing may be defined as 'literate' but only in a seriously restricted sense. The term is tendentious, since the nature and quality of that 'literacy' have yet to be established. It would be mistaken, I believe, to ascribe to the Anglo-Saxons the presuppositions and practices of our own literacy. Further, my argument assumes the possibility of one or more transitional states between pure 'orality' and pure 'literacy' and seeks to describe some of the features of an early transitional state characterized by what I shall call 'residual orality'. By this term I mean a state after the introduction of writing in a culture which nonetheless exhibits many features characteristic of 'pure' orality. And finally, I make the assumption that the special character of developing literacy before the Conquest may be described from the manuscripts of Old English and Latin verse.

In the absence of a satisfactory description of the mental conditions of individual 'literacy' in Anglo-Saxon England and of the processes involved in reading, two sets of inferences, paradoxically from written records, may provide evidence of residual orality. These inferences may be made from the development and use of meaningful space in the copying of verse and from the persistence of variance in the written transmission of texts. Considered as a mode of communication, a manuscript is a channel for transmitting a visual code. And the process of transmission requires encoding (in writing) and then decoding (in reading). As literacy develops, spatial and graphic conventions (which I term 'cues'), when added to the basic alphabetic character set, assist decoding by adding further inter-pretative signals to the text. The development and growth of these cues may be used to chart the distance of a written message from the knowledge (or possibly memory) of a potential reader. Crudely, the more sophisticated the cues, the more 'literate' the reading community, that is, the more they rely on conventional visual phenomena (rather than memory) for construc-ting or reconstructing meaning. Economy argues that such cues only appear when they are needed. By contrast, the persistence of variance (a characteristic constituent of oral transmission) in written records of verse is a conservative feature pointing backwards to orality. Since the function of writing is to *fix* a text, certain kinds of variance in the transmission of Old English verse texts strongly suggest the continuance of oral techniques of reception in the reading of verse. If I am correct, the evidence of the transmission and reception of Old English verse has consequences not only for our understanding of the literacy of the Anglo-Saxons, but our reading of the texts themselves and, indeed, their editing.

Acknowledgements

It is a pleasure to be able to acknowledge my indebtedness to a number of individuals and institutions incurred during the research for this book. The bulk of the work on the manuscripts of Caedmon's *Hymn* and on the Anglo-Latin manuscripts was made possible by a Faculty Development Leave (1984–5) from Texas A&M University and a grant from the American Philosophical Society (1984). I am grateful to Clare Hall, Cambridge, for making me a Visiting Associate in the Michaelmas term of 1984. Subsequent work in libraries in England and France was assisted by an International Enhancement Grant and a College of Liberal Arts Summer Grant from Texas A&M University (1986). Professor Hamlin L. Hill, Head of the Department of English at Texas A&M, used monies from the Ralph R. Thomas Fund to underwrite my trip to Vercelli. The Interdisciplinary Group for Historical Literary Study at Texas A&M University provided released time from teaching in 1987 and 1988, which allowed me to finish writing and, even more important, provided a forum for exchanging and testing new ideas about historical literary research.

I am grateful to have received permission to work in the manuscript collections of the following libraries: in Cambridge, the University Library, the Parker Library of Corpus Christi College, the Wren Library of Trinity College; the Durham Cathedral Library; the National Library of Scotland in Edinburgh; Exeter Cathedral Library; Hereford Cathedral Library; in London, the British Library; in Oxford, the Bodleian Library and Corpus Christi College Library; the Bibliothèque Nationale in Paris; the Biblioteca Capitolare in Vercelli; and Winchester Cathedral Library. I should like to recognize as well the particular kindness and help of Dr Bruce Barker-Benfield, Assistant Librarian of the Bodleian Library; of Canon Giuseppe Ferraris, Librarian of the Biblioteca Capitolare, Vercelli; of

Dr Timothy Hobbs, Assistant Librarian of the Wren Library, Trinity College; and of Mrs Alison Wilson, formerly Assistant Librarian of the Parker Library, Corpus Christi College, Cambridge.

For permission to publish a photograph or photographs, I should like to acknowledge the kindness of: the Bodleian Library (pl. I); the British Library Board (pls. II and III, VII and VIII); the Master and Fellows of Corpus Christi College, Cambridge (pls. IV–VIa); the Master and Fellows of Trinity College, Cambridge (pl. VIb). Ch. 2 appeared in somewhat different form in *Speculum* 62; I am grateful to the publisher for permission to reprint it here.

Nicholas Howe and Edward B. Irving read early portions of the book and made many useful suggestions. Patrick W. Conner and David N. Dumville both kindly allowed me to use and cite chapters of their forthcoming books, for which I am extremely grateful. At the invitation of Michael Lapidge, I was able to test the arguments of ch. 4 in a paper read before the Department of Anglo-Saxon, Norse and Celtic, University of Cambridge, and I benefited a good deal from the questions and comments of its faculty and students. Dr Lapidge's generous thoroughness in reading the completed manuscript has helped me clarify the arguments throughout the book and saved me from many errors. Any which remain are mine alone.

I am grateful to my friends David R. Anderson, Jeffrey N. Cox, Emily S. Davidson, Margaret J. M. Ezell and Janet P. McCann for their encouragement and help during my work on the book. Hamlin Hill provided generous moral and financial support as well as unfailing good humour. Carol Reynolds and Linda Rundell, with warm friendship, helped keep mind and body together. William Rundell not only designed the algorithm and wrote the programme to calculate the entropy of Old English, he taught me to think in new ways about entropy and information. Without his contribution, this would be a very different book. My colleague and friend, Larry J. Reynolds, always took time from his own work to listen to brainstorms about mine – and still read every word of the book as it was being written. What is good in it reflects his thoughtful and temperate criticism.

I dedicate this book to my father, Raymond F. O'Brien, whose interest in reading and misreading began this all.

Abbreviations

AIUON	*Annali, Istituto Universitario Orientale di Napoli: sezione germanica*
ANQ	*American Notes and Queries*
ASC	Anglo-Saxon Chronicle
ASE	*Anglo-Saxon England*
ASPR	Anglo-Saxon Poetic Records
BL	London, British Library
Catalogue	N. R. Ker, *Catalogue of Manuscripts Containing Anglo-Saxon* (Oxford, 1957)
CCCC	Cambridge, Corpus Christi College
CCSL	Corpus Christianorum, Series Latina
CL	*Comparative Literature*
CLA	E. A. Lowe, *Codices Latini Antiquiores*, 11 vols. and supp. (Oxford, 1934–71; 2nd ed. of vol. II, 1972
CR	Chaucer Review
CUL	Cambridge University Library
EEMF	Early English Manuscripts in Facsimile
EETS	Early English Text Society
ELN	*English Language Notes*
ES	*English Studies*
JEGP	*Journal of English and Germanic Philology*
JMH	*Journal of Medieval History*
MÆ	*Medium Ævum*
MGH	Monumenta Germaniae Historica
MLR	*Modern Language Review*
MP	*Modern Philology*
MS	*Mediaeval Studies*
NM	*Neuphilologische Mitteilungen*

Abbreviations

PBA	*Proceedings of the British Academy*
PMLA	*Publications of the Modern Language Association*
RB	*Revue bénédictine*
RES	*Review of English Studies*
SN	*Studia Neophilologica*
TCBS	*Transactions of the Cambridge Bibliographical Society*
TPS	*Transactions of the Philological Society*
TRHS	*Transactions of the Royal Historical Society*

1

Introduction

Modern readers of Alfred's translation of the *De consolatione Philosophiae* are often struck by his assimilating into the Old English version his own late ninth-century preoccupations and intellectual pursuits. The Alfredian *Consolation* is a thoroughly English work, shaped by the virtues and limitations of the native language of its translator. Alfred's temporal concerns and his desire for a coherent programme of English education based upon the translation of those Latin works 'most necessary for all men to know' define the character of the text, especially in the king's editorial comments and his simplification of Boethius's philosophy.[1] But the process of translation also took place at a level even more elemental than that of idea or syntax or word through the reduction or omission of the visual information contained in the written Latin text. The Old English text of the second redaction (that including the metres) incorporates none of the standard graphic cues, for example, capitalization, lineation, punctuation, which ensure the readability of the *metra* in the contemporary Latin manuscripts. The omission – certainly not conscious, but just as certainly habitual – of these cues is the first clue which the otherwise silent Old English manuscripts provide us for examining reading and literacy in Anglo-Saxon England.

London, BL, Cotton Otho A. vi is the unique copy of the second

---

[1] For an overview of scholarship on Alfred's *Consolation*, see M. Godden, 'King Alfred's Boethius', in *Boethius: his Life, Thought and Influence*, ed. M. Gibson (Oxford, 1981), pp. 419–24, and A. J. Frantzen, *King Alfred* (Boston, 1986), pp. 43–66 and 125–8. For the Latin sources available to Alfred, see J. S. Wittig, 'King Alfred's *Boethius* and its Latin Sources. a Reconsideration', *ASE* 11 (1983), 157–98. J. M. Bately discusses Alfred's expectations for his programme of education in *The Literary Prose of King Alfred's Reign: Translation or Transformation?* (inaugural lecture, University of London, 1980), p. 7.

redaction of Alfred's translation of the *De consolatione* (see pl. I). Ker assigns the manuscript to the mid-tenth century and considers it the work of one scribe.[2] The manuscript only barely survived the Cotton fire, and most of its leaves are so crumbled, charred and shrivelled that punctuation is difficult to detect and spacing and proportion impossible to determine. Yet despite the manuscript's unfortunate condition, it is possible to identify the textual format in the burned sections, and to distinguish other graphic cues in the later leaves.

The scribe of Otho A. vi habitually separates prose from the metres by leaving a space at the end of each discrete section of text. The section (whether prose or metre) is marked terminally by heavy punctuation (. , .), and the rest of the line is left blank. Each new section was intended to begin with a large capital, three or four lines high, but the capitals were never filled in.[3] This arrangement is the manuscript's only concession to the distinction between prose and verse, and exists, perhaps, as a consequence of the later substitution of metres for most of the original Old English prose paraphrases. As modern readers turn the leaves of this sadly damaged manuscript, they see line upon line of unrelieved text, little blank space, few capitals, and extremely light pointing. The significance of the formatting, a consequence of the text's paucity of visual information, only emerges distinctly by contrast. Were one to place alongside the Old English *Consolation* in Otho A. vi any tenth-century English copy of the Latin *De consolatione*, the difference in formatting, especially the care devoted to the spatial arrangement of the Latin text, would be immediately striking.

Perhaps the most obvious place to begin exploring the implications of the formatting of the Latin *De consolatione* is Oxford, Bodleian Library, Auct. F. 1. 15, pt 1 (see pl. II). This deluxe text of the *De consolatione* was copied at St Augustine's, Canterbury in the second half of the tenth century.[4] It is a beautiful specimen of Latin scholarly literacy. The book was designed to present both text and commentary, with space ruled for the text approximately 14 cm wide and that for the commentary 6.5 cm wide. Signes-de-renvoi in the text direct the reader to the margins for

[2] *Catalogue*, no. 167.
[3] See, for example, 35r, 40r and 46r. *The Paris Psalter and the Meters of Boethius*, ed. G. P. Krapp, ASPR 5 (New York and London, 1932), l–li, provides a table of small capitals in the manuscript.
[4] T. A. M. Bishop, *English Caroline Minuscule* (Oxford, 1971), p. 7 and pl. VII.

commentary. The *metra* are carefully set off from the prose text. Each *metrum* begins with a large ornamental green capital, and each verse within it begins with a capital in orange. Prose sections begin with a violet capital initial. The first line of each *metrum* and each prose is in capitals. *Metra* are written one verse to a line, with the exception of *metra* in dimeter, whose verses are set out in two columns.

While Auct. F. 1. 15 is unusual in the fine quality of its design and execution, it is hardly unique among English tenth-century manuscripts of the *De consolatione* in its highly visual layout. All of the surviving tenth-century copies (CUL, Kk. 3. 21, Cambridge, Trinity College O. 3. 7, Paris, Bibliothèque Nationale, lat. 6401A, 14380 and 17814) distinguish verse from prose by writing the *metra* one verse to a line and beginning each verse with a coloured capital initial.

One might dismiss the difference between the formatting of Otho A. vi and that of the Anglo-Latin manuscripts by remarking that Otho A. vi is unique in transmitting the Old English metres of the *Consolation*. However, while it may be the only surviving copy of the Old English metres, it is otherwise an unremarkable manuscript, certainly not unique in its formatting of a text with both prose and verse. The manuscripts of the West Saxon translation of the *Historia ecclesiastica* (for Caedmon's *Hymn*),[5] those of Alfred's translation of the *Regula pastoralis* (for the *Metrical Preface*),[6] those of the *Anglo-Saxon Chronicle* (for the six *Chronicle* poems),[7] to mention but a few, all transmit Old English works in both prose and poetry, but make no distinction in the formatting of verse and prose.

In contrast, throughout the Anglo-Saxon period, Latin manuscripts written in England regularly distinguished verse from prose through the use of a set of conventional visual cues.[8] That this should be so for Latin and not for Old English raises some important questions about the writing (and reading) of each language. Why, in the same centres and at the same time, did conventions for writing verse in the two languages differ so funda-

---

[5] These are: Oxford, Bodleian Library, Tanner 10; Oxford, Corpus Christi College 279; CCCC 41; CUL Kk. 3. 18.

[6] These are: Oxford, Bodleian Library, Hatton 20; CCCC 12; Cambridge, Trinity College R. 5. 22; CUL, Ii. 2. 4.

[7] That is, those poems composed in so-called 'classical' verse. The manuscripts are: CCCC 173; BL, Cotton Tiberius A. vi; Cotton Tiberius B. i; Cotton Tiberius B. iv.

[8] See O'Keeffe, 'Graphic Cues', p. 144.

mentally? What information do visual cues provide for a written text? What can the absence of these cues in Old English poetic manuscripts reveal about the nature of the literacy underlying the written verse they transmit?

In my view, the answers to these questions must begin with the understanding that a 'text' has a material reality intimately dependent on the transmitting manuscript.[9] Speaking is in essence a temporal act, and spoken communication depends on the presence of the audience before a speaker. In speech, certain aspects of meaning are time-dependent, for emphasis, clarity, surprise and suspense all depend on the speaker's modulation of his or her speech in time. When a work is written, however, its tempo no longer depends on the speaker or writer. In fact, tempo virtually disappears, because writing is language made spatial. Surprise and emphasis, and especially clarity, now depend on the transformations of temporal modulations into space. Writing thus introduces a new element of meaning into previously aural language: significant space. Irregular pauses in the stream of speech become conventionalized in writing by more or less regular spaces between 'words'.[10] Dots and marks indicate special status for portions of text; scripts and capitals indicate a hierarchy of material and meaning.[11] Literacy thus becomes a process of spatializing the once-exclusively temporal, and the thought-shaping technology of writing is an index of the development of this process.

In the hypothetical case of an originally oral poem, for example, committing the work to writing involves loss and gain – loss of interpretative performance but gain in the conservation of the poem. That loss is gradually, though never completely, compensated for by the addition of graphic cues that add information which guides interpretation. The fewer

---

[9] This approach is essentially in opposition to the distinction which Roland Barthes makes between 'work' and 'text' in his widely published 1971 essay, 'From Work to Text', in R. Barthes, *The Rustle of Language*, trans. R. Howard (New York, 1986), pp. 56–64.

[10] On the functional difference between spoken and written word, see Bäuml, 'Varieties', pp. 247–8. See also Derrida, *Of Grammatology*, pp. 30–73, esp. 39.

[11] Until M. B. Parkes's book on punctuation appears, see E. M. Thompson, *An Introduction to Greek and Latin Palaeography* (Oxford, 1912), pp. 55–64, for an overview of arrangement of text, punctuation and accents. For a convenient summary of early conventions of punctuation to mark the colon, comma and periodus, see Isidore, *Etymologiae* I.xx.1–6. P. McGurk, 'Citation Marks in Early Latin Manuscripts', *Scriptorium* 15 (1961), 3–13, discusses scribal practices for distinguishing quoted material.

the number of graphic cues in the written message, the greater the information a reader must bring to the text in order simply to read it. Non-lexical graphic cues – hierarchy of script, capitals, lineation, significant space (for division of morphemes or larger units of meaning) and punctuation – all develop as graphic analogues to oral interpretative cues. Both oral and graphic cues function to regulate the reception of the work by an audience. For early vernacular works (whether oral or written in origin), the transmitting manuscript does not merely ensure the survival of the work as a text through the operation of a technology of preservation; it actually determines conditions for the reception and transmission of the work.

The physical arrangement of a text on a page thus becomes a crucial constituent of its meaning. The less predictable a work to its reader (for verse, the less formulaic its language or the less conventional its narrative) the more necessary become graphic cues to assist its reading and decoding. In addition, the material reality of 'text' reveals the dependence of the manuscript's realization of the work upon a unique act of reception. However they may have been composed, Old English poetic works survive in manuscripts much removed from the circumstances of their composition. And as the discussion of reading and textual variance in the ensuing chapters will demonstrate, the circumstances of copying ensured that each record of a poem would be different from any other. [12] Given these features of early manuscript transmission, the usual distinction between the reality of the 'poem' (as an abstract conception to be approximated by careful editing) and its realizations in the manuscripts is illusory. [13]

An undertaking which sets out to examine the early development of literacy within a language and a culture must necessarily have as the object of its study the manuscript records. As its title suggests, this present book studies the manuscript records of Old English verse in order to explore a particular cultural moment in the history of writing – a transitional state between orality and literacy. I contend in the following chapters that the condition of literacy in Anglo-Saxon England was very different from what we understand as 'literacy' in our own society. By this statement I refer not to the numbers of individuals who might be judged to have been able to read in Anglo-Saxon England, but, more significantly, to the very practice

[12] See Sisam, *Studies*, pp. 29–44. For a defence of conservative editing in the light of scribal knowledge see Stanley, 'Unideal Principles'.
[13] See below, p. 78, n. 5.

of reading, the decoding strategies of readers, their presuppositions, visual conventions and understanding of space. My argument will be that the manuscript records of Old English poetry witness a particular mode of literacy, and examination of significant variants and of developing graphic cues for the presentation of verse (such as mise-en-page, spacing, capitalization and punctuation) provide strong evidence of persisting residual orality in the reading and copying of poetry in Old English. The first task, however, must be the definition of terms.

LITERACY: MODERN DEFINITIONS AND MEDIEVAL PRACTICE

The nature and extent of literacy in Anglo-Saxon England are issues fundamental to an understanding of early English thought. Examination of the orality underlying the Homeric poems gave rise to an explosion in our understanding of the early Greek world-view. Following the studies of Milman Parry and Albert B. Lord, Eric Havelock, for example, used the tension between entrenched orality and growing literacy to examine the nature of Greek oral consciousness.[14] Studies of the impact of literacy on a culture have extended well beyond literary criticism to include anthropology, psychology and history.[15] Incorporating the results of such studies, Walter Ong has suggested that literacy does indeed restructure consciousness but that the process is quite slow.[16] Understanding the nature of that oral consciousness and the process of modification which encroaching literacy engendered is the most important task facing current Old English scholarship. Without an accurate understanding of the consciousness which determined the contemporary reception of Old

---

[14] See M. Parry, *The Making of Homeric Verse: the Collected Papers of Milman Parry*, ed. A. Parry (Oxford, 1971) and Lord, *Singer of Tales*. See also E. A. Havelock, *Preface to Plato* (Cambridge, MA, 1963), and his *Origins of Western Literacy*, The Ontario Institute for Studies in Education, Monograph Series 14 (Toronto, 1976).

[15] See most recently Goody, *Interface*. Following Goody's lead (in *Domestication*), Scribner and Cole (*The Psychology of Literacy*, p. 236) 'approach literacy as a set of socially organized practices'. For studies of the effect of developing twelfth-century literacy, see Clanchy, *From Memory to Written Record*, and B. Stock, *The Implications of Literacy: Written Language and Models of Interpretation in the Eleventh and Twelfth Centuries* (Princeton, 1983).

[16] See Ong, *Orality and Literacy*, p. 115. See also W. J. Ong, *The Presence of the Word* (New Haven and London, 1967), pp. 53–87 and Ong, *Rhetoric, Romance, and Technology*, pp. 23–48.

English poetry, modern criticism may all too easily misread the verse which is left.

The last few years have seen much interest in the possible oral roots of Old English poetry. In the history of Old English scholarship, the subject is a relatively recent one, having taken its impetus from the work of Parry and Lord. Those arguing the orality of Old English verse have had to confront the traditional view of the canon, namely that whatever the origins and process of transmission, the versions which have been preserved are written, and therefore literate, texts. Over the years, the proponents of orality in Old English verse have attempted a variety of strategies to demonstrate their case. The simplest of these is Francis Magoun's analysis of the oral formula, in which he argued from distinguishing features of the classical Greek formula to demonstrate the orality of Old English poetry.[17] Donald K. Fry moved away from this stance by focusing on the importance of memory as a process which preserved dictated works. For him, the only demonstrably oral Old English poem is Caedmon's *Hymn*.[18] Robert P. Creed, applying Berkley Peabody's systemic approach to the classical oral tradition, judged *Beowulf* 'a copy of a recording of a performance'.[19] More recently, John Miles Foley, on the basis of comparison with Christian oral epics in South Slavic tradition, has suggested that Old English poetry shows both 'oral' character and 'literary' art.[20]

To a greater or lesser degree, these arguments depend on a crucial assumption: that the presence of formula is our assurance of the oral origin of Old English verse. That this assumption is dubious was elegantly argued in 1966 by Larry D. Benson in his much-cited study of the 'literary character' of Old English verse.[21] By using the argument that several 'literary' works had a high percentage of formulas, Benson countered the

---

[17] F. P. Magoun, Jr., 'The Oral-Formulaic Character of Anglo-Saxon Narrative Poetry', *Speculum* 28 (1953), 446–67; rpt. in *Essential Articles for the Study of Old English Poetry*, ed. J. B. Bessinger and S. J. Kahrl (Hamden, CT, 1968), pp. 319–51.

[18] On Caedmon and oral composition, see Fry, 'Caedmon as a Formulaic Poet', p. 41. On memory see Fry, 'The Memory of Cædmon', pp. 288–90.

[19] R. P. Creed, 'The *Beowulf*-Poet: Master of Sound-Patterning', in *Oral Traditional Literature*, ed. J. M. Foley (Columbus, OH, 1981), pp. 194–216. On the tests for orality, see Peabody, *Winged Word*, p. 3.

[20] J. M. Foley, 'Literary Art and Oral Tradition in Old English and Serbian Poetry', *ASE* 12 (1983), 183–214.

[21] Benson, 'Literary Character', p. 334, n. 4, argues that Old English poetry was composed within a 'lettered tradition'.

oral formulaic assertion with another: that any work which is written down is *ipso facto* literate. However, the meaning of 'literacy' behind such an assertion must be carefully scrutinized since, in the context of the debate, its use suggests that anything written down implies a fully literate consciousness in at least the composer and possibly the audience.[22] In fact, both sorts of assertions are called into question by the writings of Aldhelm, perhaps the most literate Englishman of his day. Michael Lapidge has demonstrated that Aldhelm's quintessentially 'literate' verse was composed formulaically.[23] The apparent coexistence of two modes of composition in Aldhelm's verse – formulaic and literary – makes imperative a reconsideration of the implications of the term 'literate' and its applicability in early medieval cultures.

The argument from documents is no more helpful than the argument from formulas. On the assumption that written documents imply a literate populace, J. E. Cross, examining sources and dissemination of information, has argued for the literacy of the Anglo-Saxons.[24] And with comparable persuasiveness, C. P. Wormald, also on the basis of documentary evidence, has called it into question.[25] While the debate appears to be at a standstill, examination of some of the terms and assumptions in the debate demonstrates that the issues are far from clear.

ORALITY AND LITERACY – SOME DEFINITIONS

There is little ambiguity about the meaning of the term 'orality'. In its pure sense, the word describes a state of consciousness untouched by the technology of writing. An extensive literature describes the implications of such a consciousness, and this information is the product of inferences both from written texts (i.e. Homeric poems) and contemporary oral com-

---

[22] *Ibid.*

[23] M. Lapidge, 'Aldhelm's Latin Poetry and Old English Verse', *CL* 31 (1979), 209–31.

[24] Cross, 'The Literate Anglo-Saxon', at 67–8.

[25] C. P. Wormald, 'The Uses of Literacy in Anglo-Saxon England and its Neighbours', *TRHS* 5th ser. 27 (1977), 95–114, at 113, argues that 'the traditional view of restricted literacy is substantially valid for the whole early English period'. Latin learning dominated the cultural world despite the vernacular and was the main source of literate tradition. He sees no conclusive evidence of a substantial development of literacy after Alfred. C. E. Hohler, 'Some Service-Books of the Later Saxon Church', in *Tenth-Century Studies*, ed. D. Parsons (London and Chichester, 1975), pp. 60–83 and 217–27, argues the poor Latinity of tenth-century English writers (at pp. 72 and 74).

positions (i.e. South Slavic or Xhosa poetry).[26] In his study of the psychodynamics of orality, Walter Ong describes and summarizes the primary features of oral thought and expression as additive, aggregative, redundant, conservative, agonistic, empathetic, homeostatic, situational.[27]

While it would be possible to construct a complementary list to characterize literate thought,[28] it is doubtful that any definition of 'literacy' which such a list might imply would command agreement in the Old English scholarly community. The general concord on the meaning of 'orality' is pointedly lacking for 'literacy'. The reasons for this situation are partly historical, owing to the incomplete documentary evidence left to us, and partly perceptual, owing to the peculiar nature of human perception, which obscures the very categories of intellection through which we understand the world. Insofar as we are thoroughly literate, we normally do not question our powerful visual processing of information, spatial understanding of language, dependence on sources of information external to our memories, reliance on lists as tools for analysis and categorization. Insofar as literacy is for us a defining technology,[29] we naturally assume that these fundamental conditions of our own literate thought-processes also underpin the works we value and study. In the twentieth century, man is *homo legens*.

In such assumptions lie the workings of what might be called a 'literate ideology', whose most powerful characteristic is to blind us to the visual dominance of our own thought processes. 'Ideology' in the sense I am using it is not the false consciousness of the general Marxist critique (although this kind of meaning could be usefully, if analogically, pursued), but is closer to that sense of the word which Lee Patterson defines as 'the means by and through which man gives meaning to his social world and thereby makes it available to his practical activity'.[30] Natural (and misleading)

---

[26] For an account of oral formulaic theory with particular focus on Old English, see J. M. Foley, 'The Oral Theory in Context', in *Oral Traditional Literature: a Festschrift for Albert Bates Lord*, ed. J. M. Foley (Columbus, OH, 1981), pp. 27–122.

[27] Ong, *Orality and Literacy*, pp. 31–57.

[28] Such a list of descriptors might include 'subordinative', 'analytic', 'economic', 'objectively distanced' and 'abstract'; see Ong, *ibid*.

[29] Goody, *Domestication*, p. 145, calls writing a 'technology of the intellect'. For the concept of 'defining technology', see, J. D. Bolter, *Turing's Man* (Chapel Hill, NC, 1984), p. 11.

[30] Patterson, *Negotiating the Past*, p. 54.

ideological assumptions haunt the use of the word 'literacy'. Behind its simple dictionary definition as the quality of being literate, or the ability to read a passage and answer questions on it, lies a morass of cultural assumptions and value judgements. The word itself is relatively new and came into vogue as a term in the late nineteenth century, initially in the writing of social reformers.[31] In this context, 'literacy' was a societal issue, useful or dangerous depending on one's political outlook. In fact, 'literacy' as it is used today indexes an individual's integration into society; it is the measure of the successful child, the standard for an employable adult. That 'literacy' for us connotes more than simply the ability to read is demonstrated by its frequent combination with the word 'computer'. In the phrase 'computer literacy', 'literacy' transcends reading and refers instead to an individual's knowledge of computers, competence in using them and, therefore, ability to be employed.

Whatever our assumptions may be about the conduct and meaning of literacy in our world, we must be cautious about applying them to the circumstances of earlier cultures. As Walter Ong and others have amply demonstrated, an oral world is markedly different from our own and is characterized by vastly different presuppositions and thought patterns. And in those cultures which possess some literacy but experience a heavy oral residue, the dominant power of the mind is memory.[32]

Several analyses touch on the difficulties in approaching medieval literacy with twentieth-century definitional biases. In a fundamental study, Herbert Grundmann pointed out that *litteratus* referred to an individual who could read and write in Latin (not the vernacular).[33] Using Grundmann's work as a base, Franz Bäuml extended the examination of the phenomena of medieval literacy to the vernacular, focusing in particular on the question of literate perception.[34] For Bäuml, literate perception depends 'not on the individual's ability to read and write, but on his perceptual orientation within his literate culture: the recognition of the fact that the fundaments of his culture – codified laws, the doctrine of the

[31] R. Ohmann, 'Literacy, Technology, and Monopoly Capital', *College English* 47 (1985), 675–89, at 676.

[32] Ong, *Orality and Literacy*, p. 36.

[33] H. Grundmann, 'Litteratus–Illitteratus', *Archiv für Kulturgeschichte* 40 (1958), 1–65. See also J. W. Thompson, *The Literacy of the Laity in the Middle Ages* (Berkeley, CA, 1939), p. 5: 'Literacy during the Middle Ages may be measured almost wholly by the extent of the knowledge and use of the Latin language.'

[34] Bäuml, 'Varieties', p. 239.

Church – are transmitted in writing, and his consequent reliance, if not on his own literacy, then on that of others for the acquisition of knowledge'.[35]

Grundmann and Bäuml approach the question of literacy from complementary directions. Grundmann views literacy from the perspective of individual competence; Bäuml sees it as a societal issue, affecting the literate (or non-literate) individual insofar as the existence of written records fosters a consciousness of literacy and produces advantaged and disadvantaged groups.[36] Both approaches address fundamental problems in analysing medieval literacy, but there remains the considerable difficulty of judging the extent to which a society could be termed 'literate', the extent to which 'literate' modes of thought affect the perception of an individual, and the essential nature of such 'literacy'. Bäuml's view of a socially literate perception assumes that a society becomes 'literate' at the introduction of writing. However, it avoids the problem of measuring the degree or kind of literacy possessed by an individual only at the expense of subverting the definition of literacy. Grundmann's analysis of the definition of *litteratus* clarifies the denotations and some of the connotations of the word, but brings us no closer to the character of that literacy and its perceptual consequences.

Studies of literacy in pre-Conquest England are characterized as well by these complementary approaches. As a measure of the permanent growth of literacy in society, M. T. Clanchy chooses the proliferation of documents.[37] In his introduction to the growth of literacy in post-Conquest England, Clanchy points out that bureaucratic use of documents in England before 1066 was unlikely, but notes the difficulty in determining the numbers of documents in use before the Conquest.[38] Estimates of the number of these documents vary widely and for this reason are an unreliable measure of literacy. Even if the numbers were certain, the measure of bureaucratic literacy would be unhelpful in an analysis of the impact of such restricted literacy on the non-bureaucratic individual.

M. B. Parkes distinguishes between professional and pragmatic litera-

[35] F. H. Bäuml and E. Spielmann, 'From Illiteracy to Literacy: Prolegomena to a Study of the *Nibelungenlied*', in *Oral Literature*, ed. Duggan, pp. 62–73, at 67–8.
[36] F. H. Bäuml, 'Transformations of the Heroine: From Epic Heard to Epic Read', in *The Role of Woman in the Middle Ages*, ed. R. T. Morewedge (Albany, NY, 1975), pp. 23–40, at 27; and Bäuml, 'Varieties', p. 243.
[37] Clanchy, *From Memory to Written Record*, p. 14.   [38] *Ibid.*, p. 17.

cies in the later Middle Ages,[39] and, following Parkes, Jennifer Morrish has recently argued that pragmatic literacy was important for conducting business in southern England, though standards were low, and at the same time, the nature and standards of professional literacy were substantially unaltered by the Viking wars.[40] However, the distinction between pragmatic and professional literacies leaves unanswered many questions about the applicability of analysis of literacy in Latin to literacy in the vernacular and about the usefulness of competence in copying as evidence for reading ability or for the impact of literacy on an individual. Another approach to the literacy of the Anglo-Saxons focuses on an individual figure or work. J. E. Cross argues, for example, that Ælfric exemplifies the 'associative memory cultivated by the habit of *ruminatio*'.[41] This approach infers literacy from the identification of literate sources in a writer's work, but by doing so begs the question of what the nature of that literacy might be. That such literacy requires intense processing by memory suggests that it is qualitatively different from our own experience.

Work to date on literacy in pre-Conquest England has provided much useful and important information on Latin documentary sources, but has been of limited use in the study of Old English poetry. This limitation stems in part from the notorious difficulties inherent in defining 'literacy'. Beyond that, however, lies the whole problem of evidence for the condition of literacy. Arguments from numbers of documents are not especially useful, given the small corpus of Old English poetry. And arguments from 'literary' echoes beg the question of how such echoes found their way into the poetry. Underlying the entire debate is the binary opposition implied in the use of the two terms 'orality' and 'literacy'. This use assumes that the introduction of writing destroys orality, much as if orality were some Edenic state immediately lost upon commission of the primal act of reading.[42] While early studies of oral poetry insisted that orality vanished with the introduction of writing, both Lord and Goody

---

[39] M. B. Parkes, 'The Literacy of the Laity', in *The Mediaeval World*, ed. D. Daiches and A. Thorlby (London, 1973), pp. 555–77, at 555–6.

[40] J. J. Morrish, 'An Examination of Literacy and Learning in England in the Ninth Century' (unpubl. DPhil dissertation, Oxford Univ., 1982), p. 119, notes that scribal standards for formation of letters and layout were not as high after 850 as before.

[41] Cross, 'The Literate Anglo-Saxon', p. 93.

[42] For a critique of such sentimentalism, see Derrida, *Of Grammatology*, pp. 107–40.

have recently admitted the possibility of a transitional state.[43] Walter Ong has demonstrated in the range of his works that writing only restructures consciousness over time.[44]

In the chapters which follow, I shall consider writing to be a technology. The conditions 'orality' and 'literacy' are the end points on a continuum through which the technology of writing affects and modifies human perception. The immediate consequence of such a definition is that it admits the possibility that residual orality might be encoded in early manuscripts. Indeed, considerations of the character of written Old English, the graphic conventions of the manuscripts of both Latin and Old English poetry, and the psychology of reading together suggest that such is the case.

The difficulty with the current general approach to the debate on the oral as against the literate nature of Old English poetry lies in its focus upon the literary text, as edited and printed, rather than on the manuscript or the contemporary reader. This focus can only produce an ambiguous result. The argument, when based upon the stylistics of the text (such as formula, redundancy, generative composition, type scenes), points clearly to an oral origin for the poetry, but, when based upon the dissemination of sources, points just as clearly to a literate origin. There is no way out of this dilemma without making an arbitrary decision on the relative values of the stylistic or source-based approach. There are, as well, two further difficulties. The debate has generally been argued using twentieth-century printed, edited texts as evidence and assuming only two possible, but mutually exclusive, states – orality or literacy. While these assumptions make for neat arguments, they are too simple.

The approach taken in this present book shifts attention away from

---

[43] See especially Jabbour, 'Memorial Transmission', pp. 181–2, for the traditional perception of the cleavage between written and memorial tradition. But see A. B. Lord, 'Perspectives on Recent Work on Oral Literature', in *Oral Literature*, ed. Duggan, pp. 1–24, who calls Old English Christian poems '"transitional" or perhaps "mixed"', p. 23. In 'The Merging of Two Worlds', pp. 19–64, Lord examines the impact of print culture on oral culture in the Dalmatia of the eighteenth century, Montenegro of the nineteenth century, and Yugoslavia in the early twentieth. In many ways a stimulating essay, it nonetheless assumes that the literate community which exists has *our* ideas about fixity of text and assumes a monolithic state of modern literacy rather than a developing condition. Goody argues against 'orality' and 'literacy' as binary opposites in *Interface*, esp. p. 106.

[44] Ong, *Orality and Literacy*, p. 115.

literary texts in their modern, edited and printed condition, to their historical state as manuscript texts in the linked processes of transmission and reception. Examining a work from the perspective of its transmission and its reception admits into evidence manuscript, readers, textual variance and textual fixity, and situates the work in its proper historical context. The ability of the reader and the function of the manuscript thus become the focus of study. This shift avoids the insoluble problems generated by making the demonstration of 'orality' or 'literacy' dependent upon the competence of a hypothetical composer/author, and it also avoids the problems with the validity of the stylistic or source-based approach.

Approaching the issue of orality or literacy from the perspective of the reader of the work allows examination of the conditions under which the physical text was received. It permits refinement of the argument by redefining the nature of the reader's literacy and examining a reception which takes place on a continuum from orality to literacy. Finally, such an approach allows us to examine the development of visual conventions to enhance readability in the two written languages of Anglo-Saxon England, Latin and English. Such an approach to understanding Old English poetry will require as a base some preliminary background in the psychology of reading.

PSYCHOLOGY OF READING

Cognitive psychology has contributed a great deal to our knowledge of the modern process of reading. Because reading is so complex an activity, however, it should not be surprising that at present no one explanation of the process of reading is completely satisfying, as Eleanor Gibson and Harry Levin have pointed out.[45] The following brief summary outlining the primary approaches to understanding modern reading activity both characterizes the tasks confronting a reader of Old English verse and illustrates the difficulties in constructing a model of early reading.

Models of reading can be grouped according to where they locate the critical activity of reading: at the level of identification of letter, of letter clusters or syllables, or of words. They may further be grouped by their definition of the process by which a reader translates written symbols into language. In this grouping we may distinguish models which require the

[45] Gibson and Levin, *Psychology of Reading*, p. 438.

reader to make predictions about what he or she is reading (inference models) and those which have the reader appeal to a mental lexicon for identification of words (information processing models).

The earliest model of reading focused on individual letter identification as the critical activity. Such a model suggested that word recognition depended on the serial processing of letters and their subsequent assembly into words, recapitulating in the fluent reader the letter identification of the neophyte. Using knowledge about eye movements and 'fixations' (i.e. that the eye makes only a limited number of 'fixations' per line and thus takes in several letters at a time), a rival model of reading suggests that the basic unit of reading is letter combinations. Such combinations may be simple groups or syllables, although a difficulty here lies in predicting the basis on which a reader breaks a word into syllables during a 'fixation'. The most popular current models, however, identify the whole word as the basic unit of reading. The attraction of such models has much to do with their meeting the word-superiority effects in experiments which test a reader's identification of random strings of letters as against identification of words. Such models, however, generally have problems accounting for a reader's identification of pseudo-words.[46]

If we examine models of reading from the broad perspective of the reader's role, there are basically two classes: those structured on information processing and those structured on reader inference.[47] In information-processing models, sensory input is processed in stages to produce an output. The language describing such a process deliberately reflects the computer technology from which the models take their metaphoric form. Generally speaking, a visual image (a letter, cluster or word) stimulates the brain, which then sequentially performs certain tasks, varying with the model. These may include recognizing patterns, decoding letters to phonemes, appealing to a 'lexicon' of words, or applying syntactic and semantic rules. In this sort of model, the reader's brain has a 'lexicon' and perhaps a 'codebook', and letters, syllables or words are identified by matching or decoding. The author of one highly controversial model describes well the reader's relative passivity in information-processing models; as P. B. Gough has said, 'the Reader is not a guesser. From the

---

[46] I summarize this information from the exhaustive critique of current theories of research on the psychology of reading in L. Henderson, *Orthography and Word Recognition in Reading* (New York and London, 1982), pp. 215–31.

[47] See Gibson and Levin, *Psychology of Reading*, esp. pp. 438–53 and 465–82.

outside, he appears to go from print to meaning as if by magic. But I have contended that this is an illusion, that he really plods through the sentence, letter by letter, word by word.'[48] These models are often called 'bottom-up' models, since the array of symbols on the page controls the reader's response.[49]

The opposing class of models for reading activity is based on reader-inference. In these models, the reader does not 'receive' the text but constructs the message from the text. If information-processing models work from the bottom up, inference models work from the top down.[50] Essentially, these models call for the reader to make predictions about the message at some level, or perhaps multiple levels, whether letter, cluster or word. The reader uses his or her knowledge of the language to erect and test hypotheses, and knowledge of the redundancy of the written language is critical. In these models, the reader is so active and prediction so important that one early researcher called reading a 'psycholinguistic guessing-game'.[51]

Both classes of models are open to criticism. Information-processing models are vulnerable to the criticism that they ignore a reader's knowledge of how the language works.[52] Inference models are vulnerable to questions as to where predictions are made (context, grammar, word, letter) and how they are checked.[53] Each model would appear to provide some information about reading Modern English, but neither offers a clear advantage in accounting for all reading behaviour. Together, however, their importance to a study of early medieval reading lies in their analyses of the various levels at which reading activity may take place and of the constraints on that activity.

To be economical, an information-processing model of reading at the

---

[48] P. B. Gough, quoted in Gibson and Levin, *Psychology of Reading*, p. 449.

[49] Smith, *Understanding Reading*, p. 193.

[50] *Ibid.*

[51] K. S. Goodman, 'Reading: A Psycholinguistic Guessing Game', *Journal of the Reading Specialist* 6 (1967), 126–35. A third possible class could be composed of some combination of both models, the so-called interactive models. To the extent that these models are predominantly of one or the other type, I have declined to discuss them independently.

[52] K. S. Goodman, 'The Know-more and the Know-nothing Movements in Reading: A Personal Response', *Language Arts* 56 (1979), 657–63, and K. S. Goodman, letter to the editors, *Reading Research Quarterly* 16 (1981), 477–8.

[53] Gibson and Levin, *Psychology of Reading*, p. 451.

level of words requires a lexicon based on a fixed orthography.[54] At the level of code-processing for letters or clusters (i.e. an appeal to the reader's possession of rules for phonemes), such a model requires a high redundancy in sequences of letters, or in other words, easily predictable doublets or triplets of letters.[55] The difficulty here is obvious, since a great number of entries in the lexicon or a large number of rules for combining letters into phonemes should slow recognition time. Presumably, the lower the redundancy of the message, the longer the processing. Given experiments which set off random strings of letters against words, models of information-processing actually use graphic arrays of print (i.e. significant white space) to pre-process messages into words. To the degree that this occurs, information-processing models are print- and format-dependent. And, indeed, the models presuppose that the text determines and controls the reader's response. Inference models, to be efficient, require a reader who brings a high degree of knowledge to the text. For this reason, inference models will also be sensitive to a message with low orthographic redundancy, since there is a reciprocal relationship between the level of redundancy and the knowledge needed by the reader to comprehend the message.

There are important inherent limitations in the application of these reading models to medieval reading practice. To begin with, current British and American psychological studies of reading are conducted using Modern English words.[56] Modern English has a much higher orthographic redundancy than Old English, and to the extent that the level of redundancy in Modern English is reflected in the design of such studies and the interpretation of their results, it may seriously affect the applicability

---

[54] On the principle of economy in reading, see *ibid.*, p. 482.

[55] The virtual predictability of certain combinations of letters in Modern English, notoriously 'qu' or 'ght', introduces the notion of orthographic redundancy and its great importance. As its name suggests, 'redundancy' refers to excess in a message, to those symbols which, technically, are unnecessary in the communication of the message.

[56] Studies are not conclusive on the degree to which orthography affects the level of reading ability. For discussions of cross-language reading acquisition and the 'regularity' of grapheme-phoneme correspondence, see Gibson and Levin, *Psychology of Reading*, pp. 530–1. In their examination of Vai literacy in Vai, Qur'an (Arabic) and English, Scribner and Cole (*Psychology of Literacy*, p. 132) found that 'literacies are highly differentiated. Arabic and Vai script do not trade off for each other in predicting cognitive performance, nor do they (singly or in combination) substitute for English literacy.'

of these studies to reading in Old English. A second problem arises in the restriction of these studies to print. Studies which assume the invariability of a type-fount and those which use variable founts as evidence in reaction-time experiments may have limited significance for a written language where variation among the forms of letters from different scripts are commonplace.[57] In fact, studies which focus on printed words are predicated on an assumption of regular, conventional spacing of written language and the tacit acknowledgment of the reader that words are discrete visual units. It hardly needs pointing out that such graphic conventions are not present in manuscripts of Old English.[58] In fact, the tendency to separate and combine free morphemes in written Old English raises questions about what the notion of 'word' meant to a speaker/writer of Old English.[59] A third problem is the assumption inherent in these models that the reader is fluent and silent. There is no hope of analysing the level of fluency to be assigned to the 'average' Anglo-Saxon reader. And from all indications, the process of reading in the Middle Ages involved vocalization or at least sub-vocalization.[60]

The list of caveats here is indeed formidable, but it ought not to discourage us from seeking what is usable in current psychological studies. The problems are, in the main, restricted to assumptions about language as it appears in print, about readers, and about the orthography and format of words chosen for experimental analysis.

Let me illustrate these points briefly by reference to *Beowulf*, whose manuscript state and position in the canon of Old English literature make it an ideal work against which to evaluate various difficulties in the decoding task confronting an Anglo-Saxon reader. The poem presents

---

[57] D. W. J. Corcoran and R. O. Rouse, 'An Aspect of Perceptual Organization Involved in Reading Typed and Handwritten Words', *Quarterly Journal of Experimental Psychology* 22 (1970), 526–30.

[58] R. H. W. Waller, 'Graphic Aspects of Complex Texts: Typography as Macro-Punctuation', in *Processing of Visible Language II*, ed. P. A. Kolers, M. E. Wrolstad and H. Bouma (New York and London, 1980), pp. 241–53, argues the importance of including graphic and spatial factors in a linguistic analysis of texts. Although his essay is exclusively concerned with typography, he notes the importance of visual organization in communicating meaning.

[59] See Goody, *Domestication*, p. 115, on 'word' as a variable segment of speech (from morpheme to theme) among the LoDagaa; and Scribner and Cole, *Psychology of Literacy*, p. 157, on the implications of ambiguous conversations about 'words' among the Vai.

[60] Chaytor, 'The Medieval Reader', pp. 49–56.

fairly ordinary problems in the mechanics of reading, since the manuscript in which *Beowulf* is preserved is the work of two different hands whose orthographies also differ. In terms of its composition, the poem has received equally enthusiastic claims for its inherent orality or its essential literacy, illustrated both by its pride of place in the analysis of Old English oral formulae, and by its recent treatment as a substantially revised, written work.[61] Our intuitive impression of the low orthographic redundancy of Old English (relative to that of Modern English) is statistically demonstrable for *Beowulf*.

Suppose we were to choose a model of reading the poem which operates at the level of individual letter processing, that is, where the reader deciphers one letter at a time. Because written language is orthographically redundant, it is possible to calculate the probability of the occurrence of each of the letters of the alphabet in each language, and from the probabilities calculate the predictive 'uncertainty' in any given written message. The measure of this uncertainty, termed 'entropy', is expressed in 'bits' (binary digits) of 'information', as a logarithmic function, base 2. Although entropy for single characters has generally (and correctly) been discarded as a direct measure of uncertainty reduction in the reading of Modern English, I offer it here not as a measure with its own meaning, but as an illustration of the different orthographic redundancies in the two languages.

At the level of individual letters, and given the probabilities of the occurrences of the twenty-six letters and one space character in the text, the entropy (or measure of uncertainty) of *Beowulf* is 4.18 (crudely, 4.18 bits of information per letter).[62] The higher the entropy of a message, the lower

---

[61] See, for example Niles's discussion of formula and formulaic system in his *Beowulf*, pp. 121–37, and, by contrast, Kiernan, *Beowulf and the Beowulf Manuscript*. R. D. Stevick, *Suprasegmentals, Meter, and the Manuscript of Beowulf* (The Hague and Paris, 1968) argues that there is significance in the separation of morphemes in *Beowulf*.

[62] A useful analogy here is the child's game 'Hangman'. For a basic introduction to the applications of entropy, redundancy and information to reading, see Smith, *Understanding Reading*, pp. 195–8. The estimate of the entropy of Modern English at 4.03 is generally accepted. Professor William Rundell, Department of Mathematics, Texas A&M University, devoted countless hours to writing an optimum program to calculate the entropy of Old English. His calculation of the entropy of the language of *Beowulf* uses the full text on computer tape from the Toronto Dictionary project. Because this text uses a modern printed edition, the figure for entropy could not take into account the spacing of the actual manuscript. Accounting for the manuscript spacing would

its orthographic redundancy and the higher its 'surprise'. By comparison with the standard value of the entropy of Modern English at 4.03, the single character entropy of *Beowulf* at 4.18 indicates that the 'information' (or 'surprise') conveyed in this sample of Old English is considerably higher than that for a message in Modern English.

For the sake of argument, however, we might wish to assume that an Anglo-Saxon's reading strategy avoided processing individual letters or even clusters and moved directly to words. Fig. 1, below, lists randomly sampled 'words' from *Beowulf*, and suggests the possible constraints on such a strategy regardless of whether we choose an inference model or an information-processing model.

eaðe/eðe/yðe
fah/fag
feaxe/fexe
gedryht/gedriht
gast/gæst   gæst/gist
libban/lifgan
licgan/licgean
longe/lange
maþmum/madmum
sellic/syllic
wlonc/wlanc
yldum/eldum

FIG. I Variant orthography of randomly
sampled words in *Beowulf*

Variation may occur in both vowel and consonant clusters. At two and occasionally three entries for words (even discounting variant spacing of free morphemes), a lexicon would grow very large indeed to accommodate records for possible visual matches. If we examine the manuscript itself, BL, Cotton Vitellius A. xv, for example, 156r (lines 1053–75; see pl. III), we see inconsistent word division, variable spacing, inconsistent abbreviation and infrequent punctuation. In short, the reader of *Beowulf*, and of Old English poetry in general, knew no graphic preprocessing, and

probably push the figure slightly higher. See K. O'B. O'Keeffe and W. Rundell, 'An Information-Theoretic Approach to the Written Transmission of Old English', forthcoming, *Computers and the Humanities* 24.1 (1990).

at the level of individual letters and clusters, had nowhere near the amount of orthographic redundancy taken for granted by the reader of Modern English.

This brief evaluation of the application of reading theory to *Beowulf* yields, I believe, two suggestive pieces of information. The presuppositions about graphic information and the fixity of 'word' implicit in the various models of modern reading provide an independent test of the operation of literate 'ideology', since they illustrate the extent to which spatial cues are taken for granted in our own notion of reading. More important, however, is the verification that at whatever level one wishes to examine reading activity for Old English verse, the written text is relatively rich in orthographic surprise. The implication of this statement is that a reader of Old English necessarily brought a great deal of predictive knowledge to the text to be read, precisely because the manuscripts were low both in orthographic redundancy and in graphic cues. This knowledge came from a deep understanding of the conventions of Old English verse, marked as it is by formula, generic composition and repetition, in short, by those features generally considered necessary for the successful transmission of oral poetry in non-literate cultures. Such an observation cannot be used, however, to infer an 'oral' origin for Old English verse for the reasons I have outlined earlier in this chapter. Rather, I argue in the following chapters that the nature of the Old English poetic works transmitted, the character of their manuscripts, and the record of their variance (in multiply-attested works) indicate that early readers of Old English verse read by applying oral techniques for the reception of a message to the decoding of a written text. The evidence supporting this claim traces the features of a period of transitional literacy in Anglo-Saxon culture.

THE WAY FORWARD

The following chapters analyse the manuscript records of Old English verse surviving in multiple copies in order to examine the implications of variance and to evaluate some scribal strategies for increasing visual information in the text. The presence of variant readings which are semantically, metrically and syntactically appropriate suggests a strong overlay of oral habits of transmission in the copying of Old English formulaic verse. Furthermore, the physical evidence of the writing of these poetic works – their irregular spacing of free morphemes, highly individual and sporadic capitalization and punctuation, and copying of verse without regard to length of line – argue that the visual conventions which provided necessary information for the reading of contemporary verse in Latin (for example, the writing of one verse to a line, regular capitalization and punctuation) were unnecessary for Old English. Verse in Old English was read in a different way from verse in Latin.

Chs. 2 and 3 consider in turn two very dissimilar Old English poems – Caedmon's *Hymn* and *Solomon and Saturn I* – whose single shared feature is the high number of variants in their manuscript transmissions. The evidence of formatting, variants and pointing in these poems suggests an interesting feature of a transitional state between orality and literacy, that is a scribal reading process where oral techniques of reception are used to read a written text. Chs. 4 and 5 test the observations of the previous chapters against poems with comparatively stable transmissions. Ch. 4 examines the composition and transmission of Alfred's *Metrical Preface* to his *Pastoral Care*, the substantial admixture of orality in Alfred's literacy, and the 'formulicity' (if I may be permitted to coin a word) of his brief poem. The fifth chapter argues that the dates of copying of the manuscripts of the *Chronicle* poems suggest a time within which 'formulaic' reading took place and after which it apparently gave way to a more thoroughly literate form of transmission. The final two chapters consider the significance of pointing and format in the four great codices of Old English verse.

My arguments about orality and literacy, that they exist in a continuum, that the shift from one mode of thought and reception to the other required the invention of significant manuscript space, and that literacy in Latin and in literary Old English were distinct phenomena, challenge previous assumptions about reading and writing in early medieval England. If I am correct, we must re-evaluate early 'reading' and redefine what we understand as early 'literate' thinking. Beyond that, however, a look at early writing and attitudes to writing asks that we make ourselves conscious of the mental condition of our own literacy. It reminds us of what we have gained in our own powerfully visual bias in understanding, in our abstract techniques of organizing information, and in our casual reliance on external memory aids. It reminds us as well of some things we have lost: among them the communal intimacy of spoken communication and the prodigious memory feats of those for whom mind was the only means of storing information.

2

Orality and the developing text of Caedmon's *Hymn*

The modern editorial practice of printing Old English poetry one verse to a
line with a distinct separation between half-lines distracts attention from a
well-known and important fact, that in the manuscript, Old English
poetry almost invariably is copied in long lines across the writing space.[1]
Normal scribal practice does not distinguish verses, reserving capitals and
points for major divisions of a work.[2] In manuscripts of Latin poetry,
however, quite another practice holds. Latin verses copied in England after
the eighth century are regularly transmitted in a format familiar to modern
readers: verses are set out one to a line of writing, capitals begin each line,
and often some sort of pointing marks the end of each verse. The regularity
of this distinction in copying practice and the difference in the nature and
level of graphic conventions used for verse in the two languages imply that
such scribal practice was deliberate and was useful and significant for
contemporary readers.

---

[1] There are two insignificant exceptions: the *Metrical Epilogue* to the *Pastoral Care* in
Oxford, Bodleian Library, Hatton 20, beginning at the top of 98v, is laid out in an
inverted triangle; and the commendatory verses, 'Thureth', in BL, Cotton Claudius A. iii,
31v, are similarly formatted, but in each case the arrangement of the words actually
works against the sense of the verse.

[2] See *Catalogue*, pp. xxxiii–xxxvi. The use of points and capitals in the greater part of the
corpus of Old English poetry is infrequent and irregular. For an exemplary discussion of
pointing practice in the Exeter Book, see *Old English Riddles*, ed. Williamson, pp. 12–19
and 35–48, esp. 16. A notable exception to common practice is Oxford, Bodleian
Library, Junius 11, whose half-lines are generally pointed (*Catalogue*, p. 408 (no. 334)).
Other manuscripts containing more or less regularly pointed verse are: BL, Cotton
Tiberius B. i, 112r–115v (*ibid.*, no. 191: s. xi^{med}); Oxford, Bodleian Library, Junius
121, 43v–52r and 53v (*ibid.*, no. 338: s. xi$^{3/4}$); CCCC 201, pp. 161–7 (*ibid.*, no. 49:
s. xi^{in}) and 167–9 (*ibid.*: s. xi^{med}); and BL, Cotton Julius A. ii, fols. 136–44 (*ibid.*,

23

Caedmon's *Hymn* is the earliest documented oral poem in Old English. Although the manuscripts of Caedmon's *Hymn* have been examined to analyse Old English dialects, to describe oral formulae, and to establish a text of the poem, almost no attention has been paid to the variety of ways in which the text is set out in the manuscripts which preserve it.[3] This variety of formatting and the poem's origin as an oral composition make Caedmon's *Hymn* an ideal starting point to document the existence and features of transitional literacy. Because the poem is found in fourteen manuscripts copied in England from the eighth century to the twelfth, representing two distinct circumstances for transmission (i.e. as main text or gloss) and two dialects, it provides much evidence about the transformation of a work as it passes from an oral to literate medium, about the consequent development of a text in Old English, and about the presuppositions underlying the way a text was to be read.[4]

no. 158: s. xii^med). The verse which occurs in these late manuscripts is largely translation from biblical or liturgical sources.

[3] See especially Fry, 'The Memory of Cædmon', pp. 282–93, and his 'Caedmon as Formulaic Poet', pp. 41–61. Opland, *Anglo-Saxon Oral Poetry*, examines Bede's account and understanding of the 'miracle' (pp. 112–29). Dobbie's careful study of the textual transmission provides some 'diplomatic' transcriptions of versions of Caedmon's *Hymn* (*Manuscripts*, pp. 13–42). These are broken into half-lines and are printed with modern spacing of words. I note errors in his record of manuscript punctuation below. E. Okasha, 'The Leningrad Bede', *Scriptorium* 22 (1968), 35–7, prints a diplomatic and an edited text of Caedmon's *Hymn*, as well as a plate. Her diplomatic transcription omits the space between *all* and *mehtig* in the poem. Parkes, *The Scriptorium*, p. 5 and n. 27, examines some implications of the writing of Caedmon's *Hymn* in Leningrad, Saltykov-Schedrin Public Library, Q. v. I. 18, and in CUL, Kk. 5. 16.

[4] I omit from consideration the versions of the *Hymn* in Dijon, Bibliothèque Municipale 574 (s. xii); Paris, Bibliothèque Nationale, lat. 5237 (s. xiv); and Cambridge, Trinity College R. 5. 22 (s. xiv). The first two are products of continental scribes, the last is English, but too late to be useful to this study.

In terms of simple numbers of manuscripts, Bede's *Death Song* is the most widely attested Old English poetic text, surviving in Northumbrian dialect in twelve continental manuscripts (ninth century to the sixteenth) and in thirty-three Insular manuscripts transmitting the West Saxon version (twelfth century and later). However, for evidence of the native reading and copying of an Old English poetic text, Bede's *Death Song* is unsatisfactory on several grounds. Of the many copies of the Northumbrian version, two are early (ninth and eleventh century), but all are copied by foreign scribes whose careful but mechanical copying tells us little about reading practice in Old English. The West-Saxon copies of Bede's *Death Song* descend from the same original copy (Dobbie, *Manuscripts*, p. 115), and the unanimity of these records is a tribute to the accurate copying of scribes whose familiarity with Old English is, nevertheless,

24

This study of Caedmon's *Hymn* approaches the issue of orality and literacy in Old English verse from the viewpoint of the reception rather than the composition of the work. As I argued in the previous chapter, studies focusing on the composition of Old English poetry or on the competence of the poet have provided much valuable information on orality in Anglo-Saxon England but by nature cannot be conclusive, since the presence of formulae in verse (a critical element in defining oral character) is ambiguous evidence at best.[5] The survival of some form of orality within a literate medium, however, may be gauged from the opposite quarter – the contemporary reception of the work as encoded in textual variants and textual format. If the voices are silent, perhaps the manuscripts may be made to speak.

Three assumptions underlie the argument I shall make about the manuscript evidence of Caedmon's *Hymn*. The first is that orality and literacy are 'pure' states in a theoretical sense only, and that, in fact, cultures and individuals find themselves in a continuum whose end-points are orality and literacy.[6] My second assumption is that the appearance of a work in manuscript provides no assurance that the work was conceived of as a 'text' in the modern sense or even originally written (as opposed to composed orally). My third, and perhaps most important, assumption is that the cultural movement from orality to literacy involves the gradual shift from aural to visual reception and that such a shift is reflected in the increasing spatialization of a written text.[7] The higher the degree of conventional spatialization in the manuscripts, the less oral and more literate the community.

The manuscript records of Caedmon's *Hymn* have much to tell us about the reception of this poem throughout the Old English period. In the Old English Bede, Caedmon's *Hymn* is part of the main text; in manuscripts of Bede's Latin text it is found (if at all) as a marginal gloss to Bede's Latin

---

questionable (*ibid.*). While the Insular copies of Bede's *Death Song* offer some parallel for my contentions about transmission of the *Z group of Caedmon's *Hymn* (see below, p. 40), the manuscripts of Bede's *Death Song* do not provide the rich evidence offered by Caedmon's *Hymn* for native English copying and reading in the eighth, tenth and eleventh centuries.

[5] See above, pp. 7–8.

[6] See Bäuml, 'Varieties', p. 239, on the inadequacies of the definition of medieval literacy as the ability to read and write Latin. On documents as an index of the early growth of literacy in England, see Clanchy, *From Memory to Written Record*, pp. 97 and 183.

[7] Ong, *Orality and Literacy*, pp. 117–23.

paraphrase of the *Hymn*. It survives in two dialects of Old English and in manuscripts of various date. In short, the *Hymn* offers a range of evidence sufficient for studying the formatting practices for Old English and Latin poetry over a period of time. The extralinguistic markers to examine are location of text on the page, lineation, word division, capitalization and punctuation. The differing use of these visual cues in Latin and Old English will point to differences in expectations about reading Latin, an almost purely textual language, and Old English, a living language, only newly being committed to writing.[8]

VERSE IN THE ENGLISH MANUSCRIPTS OF THE *HISTORIA ECCLESIASTICA*

From the eighth century on, Latin poetry in England was copied in lines of verse.[9] Because this technique is so commonplace to the reader of modern verse, the significance of such a shift in formatting is easily overlooked. But the developing conventions of copying Latin poetry spatially by lines of verse underlies an important step in using spatial and nonverbal cues (especially capitals and punctuation) to assist readers in their tasks. As

---

[8] On the significance of layout and punctuation in prose and poetic texts, see Parkes, 'Punctuation, or Pause and Effect', p. 130, n. 14. In 'The Influence of the Concepts of *Ordinatio* and *Compilatio* on the Development of the Book', in *Medieval Learning and Literature: Essays Presented to Richard William Hunt*, ed. J. J. G. Alexander and M. T. Gibson (Oxford, 1976), pp. 115–41, Parkes examines the integral connection of 'the structure of reasoning' and the physical appearance of books (at p. 121). Chirographic control of learned Latin is discussed in Ong, *Orality and Literacy*, pp. 112–14.

[9] Gneuss, 'Preliminary List', pp. 1–60, lists ten eighth-century manuscripts written in England which contain Latin verse. In addition to the manuscripts of the *Historia ecclesiastica* discussed below, manuscripts containing verse are: CCCC 173 (*CLA* II, no. 123; Caelius Sedulius); Vatican City, Biblioteca Apostolica Vaticana, Pal. lat. 235 (*CLA* I, no. 87; Paulinus of Nola); Leningrad, Saltykov-Schedrin Public Library, Q. v. XIV. 1 (*CLA* XI, no. 1622; Paulinus of Nola); Leningrad, Saltykov-Schedrin Public Library, Q. v. I. 15 (*CLA* XI, no. 1618; Aldhelm); and Miskolc, Zrinyi Ilona Secondary School, s.n. (*CLA* Supp., no. 1792; Aldhelm). Formatting varies from the old practice in CCCC 173 of separating verses by point to the newer practice in Leningrad Q. v. I. 15 which writes Aldhelm's *Enigmata* in lines of verse. (On the association of this manuscript with Boniface, see M. B. Parkes, 'The Handwriting of Boniface: a Reassessment of the Problems', *Beiträge zur Geschichte der deutschen Sprache und Literatur* 98 (1976), 161–79). By the tenth century, English manuscripts of Latin verse are consistently formatted in lines of verse with redundant initial capitals and points at the ends of lines.

information in a text shifts from purely linguistic to partially visual, verse becomes increasingly chirographically controlled and its formatting increasingly conventional.

Bede's *Historia ecclesiastica* contains verses in hexameters, elegiac distichs and epanaleptic distichs, each of which invites different types of spatial organization to distinguish its metrical form from the surrounding prose.[10] In their treatment of these verses, the manuscripts of the *Historia ecclesiastica* written in England thus document the incorporation of a complex set of visual cues to present Latin verse in writing. Those of the eighth century show considerable fluidity and experimentation in the formatting of verse, while the eleventh-century manuscripts (none from the ninth or tenth centuries survive) exhibit highly consistent and conservative layouts.

Five manuscripts of the *Historia ecclesiastica* written in England in the eighth century survive: Leningrad, Saltykov-Schedrin Public Library, Q. v. I. 18; CUL, Kk. 5. 16; BL, Cotton Tiberius A. xiv; BL, Cotton Tiberius C. ii; and Kassel, Landesbibliothek, 4° Theol. 2.[11] Most students of these manuscripts have assigned priority to CUL, Kk. 5. 16, which is usually dated to 737, but recently M. B. Parkes has argued cogently that the Leningrad manuscript is conceivably older and closer to Bede's scriptorium.[12] In addition to these two early Northumbrian manuscripts are the remaining fragments of Tiberius A. xiv, a mid-eighth-century copy of Leningrad Q. v. I. 18, probably also written at Wearmouth-Jarrow, and

---

[10] Those in simple distichs are: Prosper's brief epigram against Pelagius (I. 10) and the epitaphs on Gregory the Great (II. 1), Caedwalla (V. 7) and Theodore (V. 8). Bede's own hymn on Æthelthryth (IV. 20 [18]) is an epanaleptic alphabetic acrostic, and Wilfrid's epitaph (V. 19) is in hexameters. I follow throughout the chapter numbers in *Bede's Ecclesiastical History*, ed. Colgrave and Mynors.

[11] For discussions of these five manuscripts, see *CLA*: XI, no. 1621; II, no. 139, the 'Moore Bede'; Supp., no. 1703, manuscript badly damaged and fragmentary; II, no. 191; VIII, no. 1140, a fragment.

[12] *The Moore Bede*, ed. Hunter Blair, p. 28; see also P. Hunter Blair, 'The Moore Memoranda on Northumbrian History', in *Early Cultures of North-West Europe*, ed. C. Fox and B. Dickins (Cambridge, 1950), pp. 245–57, together with Wright, 'Review', pp. 110–17. Parkes, *The Scriptorium*, pp. 5–6, supports arguments advanced by Lowe, 'Key to Bede's Scriptorium', pp. 182–90. Lowe's further argument on the copying of the colophon on fol. 161 ('An Autograph of the Venerable Bede?', *RB* 68 (1958), 200–2) is disputed by P. Meyvaert, 'The Bede "Signature" in the Leningrad Colophon', *RB* 71 (1961), 274–86 and by D. H. Wright, 'The Date of the Leningrad Bede', *RB* 71 (1961), 265–73.

Kassel 4° Theol. 2, a fragmentary manuscript written in several small Northumbrian hands of the second half of the century.[13] Tiberius C. ii dates from the second half of the eighth century and is most probably southern.[14] While the first three manuscripts transmit the M-text, Tiberius C. ii and Kassel 4° Theol. 2 transmit the C-text, that version represented by all later English manuscripts.[15]

In these early manuscripts of the *Historia ecclesiastica*, verse is formatted spatially according to the complexity of verse form. Of the six poems in the *Historia*, Bede's epanaleptic alphabetic acrostic distichs on St Æthelthryth, beginning 'Alma Deus trinitas" (IV.20 [18]), is the most complex, and for these verses all the manuscripts use capitalization, lineation and punctuation to highlight alphabet, repetition and distichs. The Leningrad manuscript's treatment of these verses is instructive: as the manuscript most closely representing the practice of Bede's scriptorium, and as one illustrating the early development of Insular minuscule, Leningrad also shows early development of graphic conventions. For the verses on St Æthelthryth (100v–101v), one of the scribes (Scribe D) carefully distinguishes the visual features of the hymn.[16] A capital initial at the margin and a fresh line signal the beginning of each distich. While the two verses of the distich are run on within the column, a comma-shaped subdistinctio separates hexameter and pentameter lines.[17] The hymn ends with heavy punctuation. In a similar fashion, Tiberius A. xiv, probably a

---

[13] On Cotton Tiberius A. xiv, see *Bede's Ecclesiastical History*, ed. Colgrave and Mynors, pp. xlvi–xlvii. On Kassel 4° Theol. 2, see T. J. M. Van Els, *The Kassel Manuscript of Bede's 'Historia Ecclesiastica Gentis Anglorum' and Its Old English Material* (Assen, 1972), pp. 6–18 and 26.

[14] S. M. Kuhn, 'From Canterbury to Lichfield', *Speculum* 23 (1948), 591–629, at 613–19, and 'Some Early Mercian Manuscripts', *RES* ns 8 (1957), 355–74, at 366–8, suggests a Mercian provenance. But see K. Sisam, 'Canterbury, Lichfield, and the Vespasian Psalter', *RES* ns 7 (1956), 1–10 and 113–31, who questions his criteria. Wright, 'Review', p. 116, suggests St Augustine's.

[15] *Bede's Ecclesiastical History*, ed. Colgrave and Mynors, p. xli, follows Plummer's distinction of a C-text and a later M-text. See Plummer, *Venerabilis Baedae Opera Historica* I, lxxx–cxxxii.

[16] On the stints of the scribes, see *The Leningrad Bede*, ed. Arngart, p. 18 and Parkes, *The Scriptorium*, pp. 6–11.

[17] I have not been able to see Leningrad Q. v. I. 18 and am wary of making any argument about scribal pointing on the basis of the facsimile, especially since some repointing has been done. However, the comma-shaped point is characteristically early.

28

copy of Leningrad Q. v. I. 18, uses layout to highlight both verse form and alphabetic acrostic, beginning each distich on a fresh line with a coloured initial.

The hurried and occasionally careless scribe of CUL, Kk. 5. 16 is exceptionally careful with Bede's hymn (86v–87r). The capital initial of 'Alma Deus trinitas' is of the sort reserved for the beginnings of chapters. Each distich begins with a capital initial. The unusual care taken in spacing between the last word of a distich and the following capital initial, as well as the consistent pointing between distichs, suggests that the scribe was mindful of the visual dimension of Bede's demanding hymn. The treatment of the hymn in Tiberius C. ii shows some uncertainty over method but a clear intent to produce a visual display. To highlight the alphabetic acrostic, the scribe placed each large initial in the margin, dotting and colouring many of them. His intention seems to have been to give two column lines to each distich. However, the overrun of the last word of the prose introduction necessitated dropping each epanaleptic clause to the line below, breaking the visual symmetry. With this practice, whenever a distich ends mid-column, the scribe uses two hair-strokes to separate the completed distich from the following compressed line-end.[18] While the scribe's effort to highlight the alphabetic acrostic obscures the epanalepsis, his mixed results shows that he conceived of the distich as a visual unit.

In the eighth-century manuscripts, verses in distichs show some ambivalence in the choice of layout. The two epitaphs in bk V, those on Caedwalla (V.7) and Theodore (V.8), are useful examples. The scribe of CUL, Kk. 5. 16 writes the verses in long lines but distinguishes each verse with a capital initial, and remaining scribal punctuation marks verse length, not grammatical divisions. Tiberius C. ii employs a different format for each epitaph. In that on Caedwalla, the scribe highlights verse lines at the expense of the distich by beginning each verse line with a capital in the margin. However, in the following epitaph on Theodore, the scribe emphasizes the distich instead, beginning lines 1 and 3 in the margin. For these epitaphs, Scribe D in Leningrad Q. v. I. 18 appears to be experimenting with combinations of techniques. The first distich of Caedwalla's epitaph is written across the column, and heavy punctuation

---

[18] As a result of considerable repointing in the manuscript, each distich now appears marked by a punctus versus, but original punctuation is by medial point.

separates the two verses. Lines 3–10 each begin at the margin, and lines 11–24 revert to presentation in distich form. In the latter format, each distich begins with a capital initial; in line format, each verse begins with a capital. In the two excerpts which Bede quotes from Theodore's epitaph there is a similar ambivalence about the technique of lineation. The poem begins with a capital, and lines 1 and 2 each begin at the margin. The following two lines, however, are run on. The second set of verses, following 'ultimi hi', run on lines 5 and 6 but begin lines 7 and 8 at the margin.[19] Spacing between verses is clear, and each line of verse was apparently pointed by a distinctio.

The epitaph on Wilfrid (V. 19), in simple hexameters, shows the least complexity in graphic display. Scribe D of the Leningrad manuscript writes the first verses in long lines (though separating each verse by a sub-distinctio), but shifts method to begin verses 4 to 20 at the margin with a capital. While both Kassel 4° Theol. 2 and Tiberius A. xiv format this first epitaph in lines of verse, Tiberius C. ii distinguishes verses with capital initials only. CUL, Kk. 5. 16 distinguishes the first two lines with capital initials and terminal punctuation, but then discontinues the practice.[20]

The eighth-century manuscripts of the *Historia ecclesiastica* show a clear intention to provide visual cues to aid in reading the verses in the text. At the simplest level, this purpose is served by pointing. At its most complex, such graphic interpretation involves capitalization and the fitting of verses into the columnar lines. This practice becomes fixed in the manuscripts of the following centuries. No English manuscripts of the *Historia ecclesiastica* survive from the ninth or tenth centuries, and from the eleventh century, to my knowledge, only six manuscripts remain. In these manuscripts, layout for poetry is thoroughly consistent. The graphic representation of the poetry in the *Historia* in Oxford, Bodleian Library, Bodley 163 (s. xi[in]), is typical of the other surviving eleventh-century manuscripts: Oxford, Bodleian Library, Hatton 43 (s. xi[in]); Cambridge, Trinity College R. 7. 5 (s. xi[in]); Winchester, Cathedral Library, 1 (s. xi[1]); BL, Royal 13. C. V (s. xi[2]); and Durham, Dean and Chapter Library, B. II. 35

---

[19] Bede quotes two sections of the epitaph: the opening and the closing four lines. Kassel, Landesbibliothek 4° Theol. 2 and BL, Cotton Tiberius A. xiv both write these epitaphs out as lines of verse.

[20] The formatting for verses in I.10 and II.1 raises questions beyond the scope of this discussion; see instead O'Keeffe, 'Graphic Cues'.

(s. xi^{ex}).[21] Verses (except for the hymn in IV.20 [18]) are written across the writing space but are carefully distinguished by pointing.[22] Prosper's epigram (quoted in I.10) begins with a large red capital, and black capitals begin the next two distichs. Punctuation reinforces that structure with a low point to separate verses of the distichs and a high point as terminal punctuation for the distich.[23]

In the display typical of Bodley 163, each verse of Gregory's epitaph (II.1) begins with a red capital.[24] The pointing has been considerably altered, though originally the system must have consisted of high and low points. This practice is followed as well for the epitaphs of bk V.[25] The hymn on St Æthelthryth (IV.20 [18]), however, is written in lines of verse with the size of script reduced. Each verse begins with a red rustic capital initial.[26] Terminal punctuation for each line is a punctus versus, but the tail is in much lighter ink. The original system probably used a low point to mark the caesura and a high point for terminal punctuation. This system, by highlighting each line of verse, obscures the alphabetic acrostic which begins each distich. By the same token, the twelfth-century

[21] For Bodley 163, see Ker, *Catalogue*, no. 304; for Hatton 43, see *ibid.*, no. 326; for Winchester, Cathedral Library, 1, see *ibid.*, no. 396.

[22] The practice in the eleventh-century manuscripts of the *Historia ecclesiastica* of running verses across the writing space and using only capitals and points to separate verses is a throwback to much earlier practice, probably owing to pressures of space. In this period, manuscripts of poetry are always formatted spatially in lines of verse.

[23] Hatton 43 begins each verse with a capital.

[24] Winchester 1 points each verse, but capitalization is inconsistent. Royal 13. C. V writes the epitaph in lines of verse beginning with line 4. Durham B. II. 35 distinguishes hexameters with capital initials and separates all verses by a point on the line of writing.

[25] For the epitaph in V.7, Winchester 1 and Royal 13. C. V follow this practice. Hatton 43 points at the end of each verse but uses capitals inconsistently. The practice in Trinity R. 7. 5 is impossible to ascertain because the original punctuation has been erased. For the epitaph in V.8, Royal 13. C. V and Trinity R. 7. 5 point at the end of each line of verse. Winchester 1 capitalizes by distich, omitting the capital for line 1. Hatton 43 has a capital for *hic* only. For Wilfrid's epitaph in V.19, Trinity R. 7. 5 follows Bodley 163's practice of separating verses by marking them with high and low points. Royal 13. C. V and Hatton 43 change formats here and write the epitaph in lines of verse introduced by capital initials. Winchester 1 separates all lines by punctus versi but is inconsistent with capitals. Durham B. II. 35 formats these in lines of verse, beginning each distich with a capital initial and marking each line with a terminal point.

[26] Hatton 43 follows this practice. Winchester 1 begins each distich with a capital, writes the poem in lines of verse through 'M', and then reverts to long lines. Royal 13. C. V and Trinity R. 5. 7 begin each distich with a capital and run the verses across the space.

manuscripts examined for this study consistently write the poems in lines of verse.[27]

Although there is room for variation in the use and ornamentation of capitals, the manuscript tradition carefully distinguishes the verses in the *Historia ecclesiastica* from the surrounding prose. Pointing and capitalization mark off lines of verse, not sense- or breath-pauses. The evidence points to an awareness that Latin required extralinguistic cues to help the reader work through the verse.[28] The methods used to distinguish Latin verse were not adopted in the written record of Old English poetry. An examination of the manuscripts containing the surviving records of Caedmon's *Hymn* may suggest some reasons for this difference.

THE MANUSCRIPT RECORDS OF CAEDMON'S *HYMN*

Caedmon's *Hymn* is represented in manuscripts in two ways: as a marginal addition to the account of Caedmon's miraculous composition in the *Historia ecclesiastica* (IV.24 [22])[29] and as an integral part of the West-Saxon translation of the *Historia*. Its promotion from margin to text proper is consonant with the other modifications which the Old English translator made in the Latin text. His inclusion of Caedmon's *Hymn* necessitated as well some rearrangement of the Latin material, for example the omission of the paraphrase and Bede's apology for the Latin translation. In the context of these changes, the anonymous translator affirmed his faith in the version of Caedmon's *Hymn* which he transmitted by introducing it with the words: 'þara endebyrdnes ðis is'. An examination of the twelve Latin manuscripts in which Caedmon's *Hymn* appears offers evidence on the status of the text, the conventions of copying Old English poetry, the practices of word division and of punctuation. From these we may make inferences about practices of reading.

Dobbie divided the textual tradition of Caedmon's *Hymn* into two main lines, the *ælda/ylda* group and the *eorðu* group, which he then subdivides

---

[27] Given the number of twelfth-century English copies, I have limited my discussion to a consideration of those English manuscripts which contain Caedmon's *Hymn*. Examination of most of the other twelfth-century English manuscripts of the *Historia ecclesiastica* confirms the use of the pattern of verse presentation discussed here.

[28] See Parkes, 'Punctuation, or Pause and Effect', p. 139, on the scribe's awareness of the needs of his audience.

[29] The exception is the late manuscript, Cambridge, Trinity College R. 5. 22 (s. xiv) where Caedmon's *Hymn* has been copied into the main text.

by dialect.[30] Each of these groups has two Northumbrian witnesses, though the copies of the Northumbrian *eorðu* version are continental and too late to be useful to this study. The two Northumbrian records of the *ælda/ylda* group, Leningrad Q. v. I. 18 and CUL, Kk. 5. 16 are, however, the earliest witnesses to the text of Caedmon's *Hymn* and as such are of crucial importance.

In many ways, as records of the *Historia ecclesiastica*, CUL, Kk. 5. 16 and Leningrad Q. v. I. 18 are very different. The latter is a particularly careful copy of the text. Excepting errors in the sources quoted by Bede (and thus, probably, in the originals), editors have reported only six errors in the text of Bede's *Historia*, and these errors are minor.[31] Given the length of the *Historia*, the high accuracy of Leningrad Q. v. 1. 18 argues that it lies close to the author's draft. Apart from its accuracy, Leningrad Q. v. I. 18 is also a handsome copy of the text, and the individual work done by four Wearmouth-Jarrow scribes shows a concern for calligraphy in the manuscript as a whole.[32] The stints of the first two scribes, which supply the first eight quires, are clearly later than the work of scribes C and D, and, Parkes argues, were added to make up for loss from the original state of the Leningrad manuscript. The work of scribes C and D may, therefore, well be the oldest witness to the text of the *Historia ecclesiastica* in existence. Earlier students of Leningrad Q. v. I. 18 thought that the system of numerals in the margin, a dating device which points to the year 746, provided a *terminus a quo* for the manuscript.[33] The marks, however, are in

[30] Dobbie, *Manuscripts*, p. 48, prints a stemma. He defines four groups: for the *ælda/ylda*-text, the Northumbrian witnesses are CUL, Kk. 5. 16 and Leningrad Q. v. I. 18 (his group M-L); the West Saxon members of this group (*Z) are: Oxford, Bodleian Library, Hatton 43, Bodley 163; Oxford, Lincoln College, lat. 31; Oxford, Magdalen College, lat. 105; Winchester, Cathedral Library, 1; and Cambridge, Trinity College R. 5. 22; for the *eorðu*-text the West Saxon members (*AE) are: Oxford, Bodleian Library, Tanner 10; BL, Cotton Otho B. xi; Oxford, Corpus Christi College 279; CUL, Kk. 3. 18; CCCC 41. The peculiar witnesses, Oxford, Bodleian Library, Laud Misc. 243 and Hereford, Cathedral Library, P. v. 1 are in this group. The two continental manuscripts form the *Y group.
[31] *Bede's Ecclesiastical History*, ed. Colgrave and Mynors, pp. xxxix–xl and xliv.
[32] Parkes, *The Scriptorium*, p. 11.
[33] O. Dobiache-Rojdestvensky, 'Un manuscrit de Bède à Léningrad', *Speculum* 3 (1928), 314–21, at 318 makes this argument. Arngart revises his initial agreement with this position (*Leningrad Bede*, pp. 17–18) in 'On the Dating of Early Bede Manuscripts', *SN* 45 (1973), 47–52, where he argues that the calculations are Bede's own and thus useless for dating.

the ink of a corrector,[34] which implies that the date of the stint of scribes C and D need not be later than 746. This issue assumes particular significance, since scribe D added Caedmon's *Hymn* at the bottom of 107r.

Scribe D wrote Caedmon's *Hymn* in three long lines across the bottom margin of 107r. Whether he added it at the time of writing or at some point afterwards is impossible to determine. It is clear that he did not alter his usual arrangement of twenty-seven lines per column to accommodate the *Hymn*. Functionally, the *Hymn* is a gloss to Bede's Latin paraphrase in IV.20 [18]. The hand is Insular minuscule, and though just as precise as that in the Latin columns, much smaller. The *Hymn* begins with a capital 'N', there is no other capital, and the only point occurs after *all mehtig*.[35] The orthography and spacing of the words in the *Hymn* show characteristic attention to detail. Word division is as scrupulous as that in the Latin text. While separation of free morphemes is possible, no words are run on.

By contrast with the Leningrad manuscript, where the Latin text of the *Historia ecclesiastica* is deliberate, measured, calligraphic and accurate, that in CUL, Kk. 5 16 is hurried, uncalligraphic and inaccurate. Ornament is lacking; the scribe wrote his Insular minuscule in long lines across the writing space, leaving only very narrow margins. Punctuation is spare, and the spacing, though not cramped, is not kind to a reader. Spacing between words is about the same size as spacing between letters within words, and the Latin text often appears to be a series of undifferentiated letters. There is, however, a considerable difference between the scribe's work on the *Historia* and his execution of Caedmon's *Hymn* on the first three lines of 128v, a sort of addendum to the text of the history.[36] Like Leningrad Q. v. I. 18, CUL, Kk. 5. 16 begins with the *Hymn*'s only capital letter. The word division of the *Hymn* is actually better than that of the Latin text. The scribe runs together *nu scylun*, and splits *hefaen ricaes* and *middun geard*.

---

[34] Lowe, 'Key to Bede's Scriptorium', rejects the significance of '746' on the basis of the difference in ink. While admitting Meyvaert's arguments on the possible forgery of the colophon ('Signature', p. 286), Parkes (*The Scriptorium*, p. 26, n. 35) questions the priority of CUL, Kk. 5. 16.

[35] Dobbie, *Manuscripts*, p. 17, prints a point after *astelidae*. This point is visible neither on the facsimile (*The Leningrad Bede*, ed. Arngart) nor is it visible on the photograph of 107r which M. B. Parkes kindly showed me.

[36] See *Three Northumbrian Poems*, ed. A. H. Smith (London, 1933), pp. 20–2. Smith summarizes views of earlier scholars and accepts that the scribe of the Latin text also wrote Caedmon's *Hymn*. So too Hunter Blair, *The Moore Bede*, p. 29. Ker, *Catalogue*, no. 25, describes it as a 'contemporary addition'.

Word separations are limited to free morphemes. His orthography is highly consistent as well, although *dryctin* is consistent by correction, and the scribe varies *hefaen* with *heben*. The point which occurs after *scepen* (6b) is the only point in the text of Caedmon's *Hymn* in CUL, Kk. 5.16.

The inclusion of Caedmon's *Hymn* by the original scribes in both CUL, Kk. 5. 16 and in Leningrad Q. v. I. 18 suggests that from earliest times Caedmon's *Hymn* was considered a worthy companion to the Latin account of Caedmon's miracle. Its appearance in Leningrad Q. v. I. 18, a manuscript from Wearmouth-Jarrow very close to the author's copy, and the discipline obvious in its script, spacing and orthography speak to the care which the Old English poem was thought to merit. Equally, that it is recognized as verse, but not marked off as such by the techniques used by the same scribe for Latin verses, strongly suggests that such graphic marking was perceived as redundant. Given its scribal origin, the quality of the copy of Caedmon's *Hymn* in CUL, Kk. 5. 16, otherwise a hastily written production, argues a self-consciousness about writing the Old English verses not apparent in the Latin.

The six surviving eleventh-century English copies of the *Historia ecclesiastica* – Oxford, Bodleian Library, Bodley 163; Oxford, Bodleian Library, Hatton 43; Cambridge, Trinity College R. 7. 5; Winchester, Cathedral Library, 1 (all manuscripts of the early eleventh century), BL, Royal 13. C. V; and Durham, Dean and Chapter Library, B. II. 35 (both late eleventh century) – though broadly representative of the C-version, preserve different strands of the textual tradition.[37] Hatton 43 transmits a very accurate text, quite close to that of the eighth-century southern C-version preserved in BL, Cotton Tiberius C. ii though not a copy.[38] According to Plummer, Bodley 163 is a copy of the carelessly executed Winchester 1.[39] These two manuscripts (part of a 'Winchester' group) share alterations in the chronology of V.24 with the 'Durham' group (headed by Durham B. II. 35) but show a northern connection by the presence of Aethelwulf's poem on the abbots of a northern English

---

[37] *Bede's Ecclesiastical History*, ed. Colgrave and Mynors, p. xli. Dobbie (*Manuscripts*, p. 43) groups the texts of Caedmon's *Hymn* in these manuscripts together as the West Saxon witnesses (*Z) of the *ælda/ylda* version.

[38] The other early manuscript, Cambridge, Trinity College R. 7. 5, is sufficiently close to BL, Tiberius C. ii to suggest that it is a copy (*Bede's Ecclesiastical History*, ed. Colgrave and Mynors, p. li).

[39] *Venerabilis Bedae Opera Historica*, ed. Plummer I, cxviii–cxix. Ker, *Catalogue*, no. 396, calls them 'closely related'.

monastery.[40] Royal 13. C. V (Gloucester?) transmits a C-text which nonetheless shares some readings with BL, Cotton Tiberius A. xiv, an M-text.

All six of these manuscripts were originally copied without Caedmon's *Hymn*. Only Hatton 43, Winchester 1 and Bodley 163 contain the *Hymn*, and in each case, the copying of the *Hymn* into the *Historia ecclesiastica* was done at least a quarter-century later than the writing of the Latin text.[41] This circumstance and the wide selection of textual strands attested by the eleventh-century surviving copies suggests that Caedmon's *Hymn* did not travel integrally with the text in any one textual tradition. The addition of the *Hymn* to Hatton 43, Bodley 163 and Winchester 1 would seem to have been fortuitous.

Especially interesting is the disparity in date between the copying of the text of the *Historia ecclesiastica* in Hatton 43 (which Ker dates to xi^{in}) and that of the *Hymn* (which Ker dates to xi^2). The colour of ink for the addition is similar to that used for many corrections. The placement of the *Hymn* is interesting as well. It is written in four long lines at the bottom of 129r. The scribe has keyed the *Hymn* to the Latin paraphrase by a signe-de-renvoi and has drawn a box around the text. The location of the text here is similar to that in Leningrad Q. v. I. 18. One wonders what kind of exemplar the scribe of the addition had before him.[42]

In any event, Hatton 43 preserves the most orthographically pure text of Caedmon's *Hymn* in the *Z version, although it is later than either Winchester 1 or Bodley 163. On the basis of the textual relations between Winchester 1 and Bodley 163, Dobbie supposed that Caedmon's *Hymn* in Bodley 163 was copied from the Winchester manuscript. The independence of Caedmon's *Hymn* from the copying of the Latin text makes this supposition unlikely. Winchester 1 is a peculiar manuscript. Caedmon's *Hymn* is copied in the upper right outer margin of 81r with a signe-de-renvoi to the text. The copying was careless,[43] but apart from some

---

[40] See *Bede's Ecclesiastical History*, ed. Colgrave and Mynors, pp. xlix–li.

[41] Ker dates Caedmon's *Hymn* in Hatton 43 to s. xi^2 (*Catalogue*, no. 326), in Winchester 1 to xi^{med} (*ibid.*, no. 396), and in Bodley 163 to xi^{med} (*ibid.*, no. 304).

[42] The only surviving texts transmitting the Northumbrian dialect (and hence the earlier version) of Caedmon's *Hymn* are M-texts. At what point Caedmon's *Hymn* was added to a C-text is impossible to determine. Dobbie does note that *Z derives directly from the Northumbrian version of the *Hymn* (*Manuscripts*, p. 47).

[43] On the second line, *heri* is dotted for omission; *metoddes* has the first 'd' dotted; *heofen* has been corrected by the addition of an 'o' over the second 'e'.

orthographic differences, Winchester differs from *Z only in the substitution of *word* for *ord*. Given the copyist's carelessness, it is probable that this variant is unique to Winchester. About the text of the *Hymn* in Bodley 163 we can conclude little, save that this version has *gehwylc* rather than *gehwaes*. On this basis it can be placed confidently in the *Z group. The few letters left of the *Hymn* in the left margin of 152v survive a considerable attempt made to erase it.[44]

The copies of Caedmon's *Hymn* in the twelfth-century manuscripts show a comparable independence of the *Hymn* from the Latin text. Of the four manuscripts which transmit the *Hymn*,[45] only Oxford, Magdalen College, lat. 105 and Oxford, Bodleian Library, Laud Misc. 243, have the text in the hand of the original scribe. Ker describes the hand of the *Hymn* in Hereford Cathedral P. v. 1 as 'contemporary', and the *Hymn* in Oxford, Lincoln College, lat. 31, has been added by one of the correctors.[46]

While Magdalen 105 and Hereford P. v. 1 belong to the same textual group, that of the common text in southern England, they transmit different versions of the *Hymn*. The version in Magdalen 105 is the standard *Z text of the *ælda/ylda* group. Hereford is peculiar in transmitting a corrupt *eorðu* text, which comes either from Laud Misc. 243 or its exemplar. Laud Misc. 243 transmits a 'Gloucester' version of the *Historia*, but its text of the *Hymn*, thoroughly corrupt, derives from an *AE text (that is, it was copied from the West Saxon translation of Bede's *Historia*).

The version of the *Hymn* in this manuscript needs further examination. At issue is the nature of the transmission of Caedmon's *Hymn* in Laud Misc. 243. Dobbie favoured Frampton's conclusion[47] that Laud Misc. 243 is a transcript from memory on the basis that the appending of *halig scyppeod* at the end of the poem could not have been done by a scribe with a correct copy before him. This argument might be persuasive were it not for the other errors in the text which are of a purely graphic nature, for

---

[44] If we could know when this was done, we might learn something about the eraser's vision of the relationship between text and *Hymn*.

[45] These four twelfth-century manuscripts are only a fraction of the extant twelfth-century English manuscripts; see *Bede's Ecclesiastical History*, ed. Colgrave and Mynors, pp. xlvi–lxi.

[46] On the relationship between the text of the *History* ('Burney' group) and the additions and corrections from the 'Digby' group, see Dobbie, *Manuscripts*, pp. 88–9 and *Bede's Ecclesiastical History*, ed. Colgrave and Mynors, p. liv.

[47] M. G. Frampton, 'Caedmon's Hymn', *MP* 22 (1924), 1–15, at 4.

example, the dittography of *herian herian*, the spelling *scyppeod*,[48] and the impossible syntax caused by the omission of *ord astealde*. Despite Dobbie's assertion to the contrary,[49] it is quite possible that the transposition of *halig scyppeod* could have been made from a 'correct' copy. Such an event is far more likely than the memorial transmission of so corrupt a text, especially since the corruption violates the alliteration, the main means of aiding correct memorial transmission.

The copyist who added Caedmon's *Hymn* in Hereford Cathedral P. v. 1 reproduced the error with *scyppeod* and introduced one of his own, *drihtent*. However, he corrected the syntax caused by the missing *ord astealde* by omitting the whole phrase *swa . . . drihten* (lines 3b–4a). Once again, we see Caedmon's *Hymn* included in the Latin text by chance. The text was obviously not in Hereford's exemplar for the *Historia*, and at some point along the line either the scribe of Laud Misc. 243 or the scribe of his exemplar departed from his Latin text to use the *Hymn* from a West Saxon translation of Bede's history. The final twelfth-century manuscript to be considered, Lincoln College, lat. 31, likewise took its text of Caedmon's *Hymn* from a different exemplar. The text of the *Historia ecclesiastica* in Lincoln 31 is in the 'Burney' group of manuscripts, but it has been collated with and corrected from the 'Digby' group, from which the corrector added the West Saxon version of Bede's Death Song.[50]

The change of hand in the copying of the *Hymn* in all but Magdalen 105 and the peculiar Laud Misc. 243 suggests that the inclusion of Caedmon's *Hymn* in the eleventh and twelfth centuries is merely fortuitous. This inference is strengthened by the fact that those copies containing the *Hymn* are largely from different textual groups. No group is identifiable by the presence of the *Hymn*. Caedmon's *Hymn* did not, in fact, normally travel with the *Historia ecclesiastica*. The circumstances of its inclusion indicate that the *Hymn* appears in the *Z version as a gloss with its own discrete textual tradition. Given the various lines of descent represented by its host text, it is surprising that the West Saxon *ylda* text is in the good shape it is. That this is so argues that Caedmon's *Hymn* in the *Historia ecclesiastica* became 'textual' fairly early, that is, became a written poem in a relatively modern sense. A possible objection to this conclusion might be that the *Z

---

[48] Dobbie, *Manuscripts*, p. 41, claims that photostats indicate that the 'o' in *scyppeod* had been partially erased to make it look like an 'n'. Upon examination of the manuscript I could see no evidence of erasure or scraping. The vellum is quite smooth.

[49] *Ibid.*, p. 43.   [50] *Ibid.*, pp. 37 and 88–9.

group dates from the eleventh and twelfth centuries and thus one might expect the text to be fossilized. The best answer to this objection is an examination of the five surviving manuscripts of the West Saxon translation of the *Historia ecclesiastica*. With the exception of Oxford, Bodleian Library, Tanner 10, these are eleventh-century productions. An examination of the state of their records of the *Hymn* should demonstrate that something other than age is responsible for the fixity of the text in *Z.

There are five witnesses to the text of Caedmon's *Hymn* as it was contained in the West Saxon translation of the *History*: Oxford, Bodleian Library, Tanner 10; Oxford, Corpus Christi College 279; CCCC 41; CUL, Kk. 3. 18; and BL, Cotton Otho B. xi, now thoroughly burnt, but whose readings survive in the sixteenth-century transcript by Nowell in BL, Add. 43703.[51] The latter is useless as evidence for orthography, punctuation, spacing and mise-en-page, since Nowell was hardly photographic in his reproduction of the text. Certain readings: *ne* (for *nu*), *eorþū* (for *eorþan*), *eode* (for *teode*), *finū* (for *firum*) are clearly the visual mistakes of a sixteenth-century transcriber. However, one variant, *weoroda* (line 3a) is useful to the study of the relationships among the five manuscripts: it must be an original reading, since it is highly improbable that a non-native speaker would by accident produce a likely and grammatical variant.

Miller's examination of the manuscript tradition of the West Saxon *History* established that the West Saxon texts of the work as a whole derive from the same original translation.[52] In this light, the extensive variation shown by these copies, apart from orthographic differences, is remarkable and requires consideration. In the nine lines of the *Hymn*, *AE contains seven variations, all of which are grammatically and semantically appropriate. In the variations *nu/nu we*; *weorc/wera/weoroda*; *wuldorfaeder/ wuldorgodes*; *wundra/wuldres*; *gehwaes/fela*; *or/ord*; *sceop/gescop* we see a dynamic of transmission where the message is not embellished but where change within the formula is allowed. The variations in the *AE version are that much more startling by contrast with the record of the *Z texts. In the

---

[51] These five manuscripts are discussed in Ker, *Catalogue*: nos. 351 (s. x¹), 354 (s. xiⁱⁿ), 32 (s. xi²), 23 (s. xi²) and 180 (s. xᵐᵉᵈ) respectively. These are the main witnesses in the subdivision of Dobbie's *eorðu* group, which he names *AE. The two other witnesses in the group, the texts in Laud Misc. 243 and Hereford Cathedral P. V. 1, are too late to be considered here.

[52] *Old English Version of Bede's Ecclesiastical History*, ed. Miller I, xxiii–xxiv.

five manuscripts of this West Saxon version travelling with the *Historia ecclesiastica* there is only one non-orthographic variant, *word* in Winchester 1. How can this difference be accounted for? The likeliest explanation would be independent translation, but this has been demonstrated not to be the case on other grounds.[53] The *Z and *AE groups each descend from one original. The dating of the copies would appear to be not significant either, since the core of variables in *AE lies in the eleventh-century manuscripts, and the eleventh-century records of *Z are extremely stable. Nor is there compelling evidence that an unusual wave of scribal incompetence is responsible for the variants. There is, however, one circumstance not accounted for – the textual environment. The *Z group travels as a gloss to the Latin paraphrase in the *Historia ecclesiastica*. The *AE version, on the contrary, finds its place in the vernacular redaction of Bede's story of Caedmon. Since the only variable circumstance in the transmission of *Z and *AE is textual environment, I would suggest that the variability of text in *AE is a consequence of its environment in a purely vernacular text, a vernacular which, though written, was still heavily influenced by its earlier, purely oral condition.

When we examine the variations in the five tenth- and eleventh-century records of the West Saxon version, we see in the despair of the textual editor palpable evidence of a fluid transmission of the *Hymn* somewhere between the formula-defined process which is an oral poem and the graph-bound object which is a text. We see a reading activity reflected in these scribal variants which is formula-dependent, in that the variants observe metrical and alliterative constraints, and which is context-defined, in that the variants produced arise within a field of possibilities generated within a context of expectations.[54] The mode of reading I am proposing operates by suggestion, by 'guess' triggered by key-words in formulae. It is a method of reading which is the natural and inevitable product of an oral tradition at an early stage in its adaptation to the possibilities of writing. These five records of Caedmon's *Hymn* give evidence of a reading activity characterized by intense reader inference, where the reader uses knowledge of the conventions of the verse to 'predict' what is on the page. Variance in an oral tradition is made inevitable by the subjectivity of the speaker (and hearer), but is constrained by impersonal metre and alliteration. The

---

[53] *Ibid.*, pp. xxiv–xxvi.

[54] On the 'grammar' of formulaic composition, see Peabody, *The Winged Word*, pp. 9 and 214–15.

writing of a poem acts as a very powerful constraint on variance, and in the face of such constraint, the presence of variance argues an equally powerful pull from the oral.

The process of copying manuscripts is rarely simply mechanical. Given the normal medieval practice of reading aloud, or at least sub-vocalizing, the scribe likely 'heard' at least some of his text.[55] And copying done in blocks of text required the commission of several words or phrases to short-term memory.[56] The trigger of memory is responsible for various sorts of contamination,[57] and this is most easily seen, for example, in the importation of Old Latin readings into the copying of the Vulgate Bible. Quite another sort of memory-trigger is responsible for 'Freudian' substitutions in a text.[58] Here the substitutes, if syntactically correct, are usually not semantically or contextually appropriate.

The presence of variants in Caedmon's *Hymn*, however, differs in an important way from the appearance of memorial variants in biblical or liturgical texts. Both sorts depend to some degree on memory, but the variants in Caedmon's *Hymn* use memory not to import a set phrase, but to draw on formulaic possibility. Reception here, conditioned by formulaic conventions, produces variants which are metrically, syntactically and semantically appropriate. In such a process, reading and copying have actually become conflated with composing.[59] The integral presence of such variance in transmitting the *Hymn* in *AE argues for the existence of a transitional state between pure orality and pure literacy whose evidence is a reading process which applies oral techniques for the reception of a message to the decoding of a written text.[60] Caedmon's *Hymn* shows us neither purely literate, nor memorial transmission,[61] but a tertium quid whose function in the reading and transmission of Old English verse remains to be explored.

---

[55] Chaytor, 'The Medieval Reader', pp. 49–56.

[56] M. L. West, *Textual Criticism and Editorial Technique* (Stuttgart, 1973), pp. 20–1.

[57] On the role of memory in various sorts of textual corruption in Latin classical texts, see Havet, *Manuel*, nos. 1082–97.

[58] R. M. Ogilvie, 'Monastic Corruption', *Greece and Rome* 2nd ser. 18 (1971), 32–4; Timpanaro, *The Freudian Slip*, pp. 19–28 and 155–71.

[59] On the intrusion of oral processes into what he terms 'pre-literate written transmission' of medieval music, see Treitler, 'Oral, Written, and Literate process', p. 482.

[60] Bäuml, 'Varieties', p. 246, n. 23, notes that without functional dependence on literacy, the ability to write does not imply recognition of the fixity of a text.

[61] See Jabbour, 'Memorial Transmission', pp. 174–90. My argument is particularly in conflict with his comments on pp. 181–2.

Manuscripts	Placement of points by clause[1]							
	caelestis	creatoris	illius	gloriae	deus	extitit	tecti	creavit
Leningrad Q. v. I. 18	×		×	×	×	×	×	×
CUL, Kk. 5. 16		×				×		
Tiberius C. ii		×				×	×	×
Tiberius A. xiv	×	×	×	×	×	×	×	×
Cambridge Trinity R. 7. 5	×			×		×	×	×
Winchester 1	×	×	×	×	×	×	×	×
Hatton 43	×			×	×	×	×	×
Bodley 163	×	×	×	×	×	×	×	×
Royal 13. C. v	×	×	×	×	×	×	×	×
Laud Misc. 243	×		×	×	×	×	×	×
Magdalen 105	×	×	×	×	×	×	×	×
Lincoln 31	×		×	×	×	×	×	×
Cambridge Trinity R. 5. 22	×	×		×	×	×	×	×
Hereford P. v. 1	×		×	×	×	×	×	×

[1] The punctuation follows the last word of the clause.

FIG. 2 Pointing in the Latin paraphrase of Caedmon's *Hymn*

Manuscripts[2]	Placement of points by clause (expressed in half-lines)[1]																	
	1a	1b	2a	2b	3a	3b	4a	4b	5a	5b	6a	6b	7a	7b	8a	8b	9a	9b
Leningrad Q. v. I. 18																		X
CUL, Kk. 5. 16			X									X						
Tanner 10				X				X				X						X
CCCC 41														X				X
OxCCC 279							X											X
CUL, Kk. 3. 18					X			X				X						X
Hatton 43		X	X		X						X				X			
Winchester 1				X					X									X
Laud Misc. 243		X		X	X						X							[X]³
Hereford P. v. 1											X							[X]³
Magdalen 105		X		X	X			X			X							X
Lincoln 31		X		X	X			X		X	X							X

[1] In each case where punctuation occurs, a point follows the last word of a half-line.

[2] Bodley 163 is not considered here because it is too badly damaged to discern pointing.

[3] In Laud Misc. 243 and Hereford P. V. 1, 6b is placed at the end of the *Hymn*.

FIG. 3 Pointing in Caedmon's *Hymn*

PUNCTUATION IN THE HYMN AND ITS LATIN PARAPHRASE

To this point, the argument about the varying degrees of fixity in the text of Caedmon's *Hymn* has focused on evidence offered by textual transmission. The practices of punctuation displayed in the close Latin paraphrase of the *Hymn* and in the *Hymn* itself in the manuscripts under consideration offer a different kind of evidence to support the argument about fixity in the text, reading and visual cues.

In reviewing the evidence set out in fig. 2, which shows the punctuation of the Latin paraphrase of the *Hymn*, one cannot help but be struck by the regularity of pointing in these records. The pointing in the fullest case separates the *Hymn* into three major clauses (beginning 'nunc . . .'; 'quomodo . . .'; 'qui . . .') which are in turn subdivided. In the first case points separate the variations on the direct object, in the second and third they distinguish dependent clauses. These points are grammatical markers, and if they function as breath-pauses, they do so only secondarily.[62] The table shows unanimity in marking the main clauses, save for CUL, Kk. 5. 16, the hastily executed eighth-century M-text. The marking of objects or dependent clauses shows little variety as well.

The pointing of the Old English *Hymn* shows, on the contrary, no such uniformity. From an examination of fig. 3, several observations may be made. The only larger agreement in punctuation is a terminal point which marks off the *Hymn* as a whole. Even here, there is not unanimity, for neither CUL, Kk. 5. 16 nor, more significantly, Bodleian Library, Hatton 43 supplies terminal points.[63] Caedmon's *Hymn* divides into three main clauses (beginning 'nu . . .'; 'he . . .'; 'þa middangeard . . .'). The first contains three variations on the direct object (or on the subject in versions without *we*) and the subordinate *swa* clause. The second is a simple main clause with a variation on the subject. The third is a complex sentence with OSV structure and nested variations on subject and object. Of all the records of the *Hymn* under consideration, only Tanner 10 provides a consistent grammatical pointing terminating each main clause. As might be expected, the *AE group shows great variety. One might note especially the difference in pointing between CUL, Kk. 3. 18 and its probable

---

[62] On the various practices of pointing for verse and prose, see Parkes, 'Punctuation, or Pause and Effect', p. 130, esp. n. 14. On the possible functions for pointing, see below, pp. 151–3.

[63] Dobbie, *Manuscripts*, p. 39, incorrectly prints a terminal point.

exemplar. The later manuscript clearly added points to separate the variant objects, but pays no attention to the full stop wanting after *onstealde*. The *Z group shows, predictably, both a higher incidence of punctuation and a higher incidence of agreement within itself. The system of punctuation in Hatton 43, in many ways the best record in the group, is similar to that in the Latin paraphrase of the *Hymn*. Hatton 43 divides the *Hymn* into two statements, *nu . . . astealde* and *he . . . aelmihtig*, though the final point is missing. These statements are further divided, the first by object variant and the dependent *swa* clause. The second separates two variants on the main clause, both depending on *gesceop*. This scheme is followed by Magdalen College, lat. 105 (with terminal punctuation); Lincoln College, lat. 31 adds points after *bearnum* and *scyppend* while omitting the point after *drihten*. Winchester 1, Laud Misc. 243 and Hereford P. v. 1 are predictably idiosyncratic.

There are several issues here, and these are best examined in Dobbie's manuscript groups, beginning with the last, *Z. Just as an examination of mise-en-page and textual descent in *Z established the high degree of fixity in the text, so its frequent use of punctuation as an extralinguistic signal confirms the impression of transition from the subjectivity of the speaker to the objectivity of the graph committed to vellum. Yet the Old English records show a high variability in pointing as compared with Latin records of the paraphrase copied during the same period.

*AE shows an idiosyncracy in punctuation consonant with the variability it shows in the transmission of the *Hymn*. While pointing in Tanner 10 can be analyzed as 'grammatical', such a pattern is lacking in the other three extant *AE records. Most interesting are the relationships between Oxford, Corpus Christi College 279 and CUL, Kk. 3. 18. Whether Kk. 3. 18 is a copy of the Oxford manuscript's exemplar, or of the manuscript itself, we see in the Cambridge manuscript some influence of later trends in pointing verse.

The group consisting of CUL, Kk. 5. 16 and Leningrad Q. v. I. 18 stands apart from the West Saxon versions in several ways. Its antiquity, its closeness to Wearmouth-Jarrow, the exquisite care lavished on its copying (even for the hurried CUL, Kk. 5. 16) make the record which it transmits supremely important. These records show systems of pointing in Latin and Old English at variance with one another. Even discounting CUL, Kk. 5. 16 as a careless copy, and hence of little use for argument, we have the testimony of Leningrad Q. v. I. 18 where the Latin text and Caedmon's *Hymn* are both written by one scribe. The copy of Caedmon's

Hymn in the Leningrad manuscript is a very careful and correct record in the same way as the text of the *Historia ecclesiastica* is careful and correct. Yet the pointing of the Latin paraphrase is copious while the pointing of the Old English poem is limited to a purely formal terminal point. The points, so useful in Latin, are missing precisely because they were thought redundant in Old English, unnecessary either for scansion or sense. In the early copies of the *Hymn*, the omission of pointing, a visual cue for decoding, is a powerful indication of the still strongly oral component in the *Hymn's* transmission and reception.

The records of Caedmon's *Hymn* show that the status of the *Hymn* as text and the degree of fixity of the text depend on the environment of the *Hymn*, whether Latin or Old English. When the *Hymn* travels as 'gloss' to the *Historia ecclesiastica*, the text is subject to little variation, while those records of the *Hymn* which are integrated in the West Saxon translation of the *History* show a high degree of freedom in transmission. Examination of the conventions of lineation and punctuation in Latin and Old English poetic texts within the *History* demonstrate a considerable variation in conventions for each language. Both lineation and pointing for poetry are necessary extralinguistic cues which assist the reader in decoding the Latin text. These conventions are uniformly applied. The Old English *Hymn*, however, is never displayed graphically by metrical line, nor does punctuation distinguish lines or half-lines, nor does it act consistently as a marker of grammatical divisions.[64]

This examination of the transmission and reception of Caedmon's *Hymn* has several implications for the larger understanding of literacy in Anglo-Saxon England and for our own reading of Anglo-Saxon poetic works. The differing level and nature of extralinguistic cues in Latin and Old English implies that Caedmon's *Hymn* was read with different expectations, conventions and techniques than those for the Latin verses with which it travelled. Techniques of reading Old English verse which allowed the incorporation of 'formulaic' guesses into the written text represent an accommodation of literacy, with its resistant text, to the fluidity of the oral process of transmission. The evidence suggests that for Caedmon's *Hymn*, at least, an oral poem did not automatically become a fixed text upon writing and that under certain conditions the 'literate' reception of Old English verse retained a substantial element of oral processes.

[64] In the late manuscripts of Old English verse, points are used to mark half-lines; see below, pp. 185–6.

3

Speech, writing and power in *Solomon and Saturn I*

'It would be properly generous to the poets to attribute these deviations from the classical style to corruption of the manuscripts . . .'

(Menner, *Poetical Dialogues*, p. 15)

'Now, *Pater-noster*, clom!'

The Dialogues of Solomon and Saturn have suffered the sort of obscurity in Old English studies which oddities in the canon of literature generally do.[1] While there has been some modest interest in *Solomon and Saturn II* as literature, and, quite recently, in the prose text copied with it, the dialogue known as *Solomon and Saturn I* has received short shrift.[2] Modern scholarship, it would seem, concurs with Chaucer on the ludic (and

---

[1] Greenfield and Robinson, *Bibliography of Publications on Old English Literature*, pp. 270–2, list eighteen separate items under 'Studies', beginning with Kemble's historical introduction of 1844. A review of the bibliographies in *Anglo-Saxon England* (3 [1973] to 17 [1989]) yields some eleven more. The overwhelming number of these are textual notes, and most are concerned with *Solomon and Saturn II*.

[2] The most recent edition of the prose in CCCC 422 is G. Cilluffo, *Il Salomone e Saturno in prosa del Ms. CCCC 422*, *AIUON* 23 (1980), 121–46. The prose of a related tradition of dialogue is edited by J. E. Cross and T. D. Hill, *The Prose Solomon and Saturn and Adrian and Ritheus* (Toronto, Buffalo and London, 1982). On *Solomon and Saturn II* as literary art, see J. Dane, 'The Structure of the Old English *Solomon and Saturn II*', *Neophilologus* 64 (1980), 592–603. T. A. Shippey pronounced *Solomon and Saturn I* 'a witness to the eclectic nature of Anglo-Saxon learning, but unapproachable in present terms' (*Old English Verse* (London, 1972), p. 62) and excluded it from his edition and translation of *Poems of Wisdom and Learning*. Apart from attempts at textual reconstruction, the only recent critical studies of *Solomon and Saturn I* are J. P. Harmann, 'The Pater Noster Battle Sequence in *Solomon and Saturn* and the *Psychomachia* of Prudentius', *NM* 77 (1976), 206–10, which proposes the *Psychomachia* as a general source, and G. Kellermann and R. Haas, 'Magie und Mythos', pp. 387–403, which argues, to the contrary, that the poem shows native Germanic traditions through a Christian perspective.

47

ludicrous) aspects of using the Pater Noster as a charm, just as it seems to concur with him in mistrusting the acuity of scribes.[3] This disregard for *Solomon and Saturn I*, engendered as much by a scholarly aversion to 'superstition' as by an editorial reflex which seeks the 'authorial' over the actual manuscript text, has, unfortunately, obscured evidence about the fascinating interplay of orality and literacy which gave rise to the poem.

Caedmon's *Hymn* is a bench-mark poem for the canon of Old English literature. Whatever other poetry there may have been, the *Hymn* is our earliest surviving work, whose beginnings (we have been assured) were oral, despite the happy irony of its preservation in writing. It is much celebrated, much studied, widely anthologized and, as a result and a cause of these practices, deemed archetypal and canonical. *Solomon and Saturn I* is precisely the obverse of Caedmon's *Hymn*. Its origin and date are obscure (though quite probably late and almost surely a product of writing) and its subject arcane. One version of the poem is twenty times the length of Caedmon's *Hymn*, a fact perhaps partially responsible for the poem's modern unpopularity. Despite the important differences between them, both Old English poems preserve in their transmission evidence of transitional literacy in the formulaic reading which their variants imply and in the conventions of formatting the manuscripts display. For *Solomon and Saturn I* evidence of the interplay of orality and literacy manifests itself in three ways: conceptually, in the language and thought of the poem; textually, in the double transmission of the poem with variants; and graphically, in the spatial arrangement of the written poem. These features, which inform and determine the transmission of *Solomon and Saturn I*, demonstrate that the 'formulaic' transmission exemplified in Caedmon's *Hymn* is not confined to originally oral verse.

SPOKEN WORD/WRITTEN WORD

Solomon and Saturn I presents itself as an oral event, a dialogue in which Saturn asks Solomon to enlighten him about the power of the Pater Noster. The opening lines describe both the object of Saturn's quest and his dissatisfaction with his own knowledge:

[3] See, for example, 'Chaucers Wordes unto Adam, His Owne Scriveyn', in *The Works of Geoffrey Chaucer*, ed. F. N. Robinson, 2nd ed. (Boston, 1957), p. 534 or *Troilus and Criseyde* V.1793–8 (*ibid.*, p. 479).

swylce ic næfre on eallum
þam fyrngewrytum   findan ne mihte
soðe sam[n]ode.   Ic sohte þa git
hwylc wære modes   oððe mægenþrymmes,
elnes oððe æhte   ⟨oððe⟩ eorlscipes,
se gepalmtwigoda   Pater Noster.
Sille ic þe ealle,   sunu Dauides,
þeoden I[s]raela,   ðritig punda
smætes goldes   and mine suna twelfe,
gif þu mec gebringest   þæt ic si gebrydded
ðurh þæs cantices cwyde,   Cristes linan,
gesemeð mec mid soðe   (7b–18a)[4]

Saturn has searched the books of Libya, Greece and India but has not achieved his desire, for the truth he seeks was not collected in those ancient writings. He desires not simply to *know* the power of the Pater Noster, but beyond that, to *experience* it.

The nature and object of Saturn's quest have occasioned a certain editorial discomfort, especially because of the manuscript's problematic hapax legomenon *ge brydded*.[5] Menner reads *gebrydded* (from *gebryddan*), translating 'shaken, overawed'.[6] Dobbie emends to *gebryrded*, and following Grein accepts 'incited, inspired' as a contextually suitable translation.[7] In both cases, the editors reject as inappropriate the violence implicit in the

---

[4] 'Such things I could never find truly gathered in all the ancient writings. I have sought further what the palm-twigged Pater Noster may be, of what spirit or virtue, of what power or possession or of what supremacy. I will give you all, son of David, lord of Israel, thirty pounds of refined gold and my twelve sons, if you will bring me to the point that I may be terrified by the speaking of that song, Christ's rule, if you satisfy me with truth.' References to both *Solomon and Saturn I* and *II* are to *Poetical Dialogues*, ed. Menner. Menner's edition of *Solomon and Saturn I* provides facing texts for that portion of the poem transmitted in the two manuscripts: CCCC 422 (*Catalogue*, no. 70, s. x^med) and CCCC 41 (*Catalogue*, no. 32: s. xi¹).

[5] I discuss the two manuscripts of *Solomon and Saturn I* below, pp. 67–8. Damage to the first page of CCCC 422 leaves CCCC 41 as the only witness to the first twenty-nine lines of the poem.

[6] *Poetical Dialogues*, ed. Menner, p. 106. In rejecting the common definition of this hapax as 'terrified', Menner argues (unconvincingly, I believe) that a translation 'if thou bringest me to the point that I am terrified by the Pater Noster', is out of keeping with the sense of *gesemeð* in line 18a.

[7] *The Anglo-Saxon Minor Poems*, ed. Dobbie, ASPR 6, 161.

standard gloss, 'frightened, terrified'; but in so doing they misinterpret – in my view – the context and content of the poem as a whole.[8] Saturn's quest is not simply an intellectual journey. In context, for him to know the power of the Pater Noster is to be acted upon (a recognition implicit in the passive construction of line 16b and in the double use of *mec* as the object of Solomon's action [lines 16a and 18a]). The dialogue between the two wise men is a contention, as is the companion dialogue *Solomon and Saturn II*, and the verbal encoding of struggle, even violence, is symptomatic of oral culture. Assuming that the anomalous lines 170–8 are associated with *Solomon and Saturn I*, the poem ends with a statement of Solomon's victory and Saturn's pleasure in submission.[9] It is in submission that he is to be reconciled to the truth (line 18a: 'gesemeð mec mid soðe'). The verbal and physical manifestation of power in the poem and the conceptual relationships among power, speech and writing which these imply are the subjects of inquiry here.

In *Solomon and Saturn I*, the power of the Pater Noster manifests itself in physical terms, and in a mode deeply revelatory of the poem's synthesis of oral and literate understanding. The poem hypostasizes the Pater Noster, conceptualizing it as a material being (with clothing, weapons and jewels), but unlike the simple allegorical treatment of the Pater Noster in the accompanying prose dialogue (in CCCC 422), the physical projections of the Pater Noster in *Solomon and Saturn I* are the individual letters composing the written prayer. The *power* of the prayer, anatomized in the poem, comes to be known through its physical state as a written object, but this power can only be *used* by one who speaks or sings the prayer. With three exceptions, the order of letters in the poem follows their arrangement in the Latin prayer, a structure reflecting both respect for the syntactic order of the words and a probable written tabulation of letters antecedent to

---

8 See Bosworth and Toller, *An Anglo-Saxon Dictionary*, p. 377, where *gebryddan* is glossed as 'to frighten, terrify'. F. Holthausen, *Altenglisches etymologisches Wörterbuch*, 2nd ed. (Heidelberg, 1963), p. 37, glosses *bryddan* (*brygdan*) as 'erschrecken'. C. W. M. Grein, *Sprachschatz der angelsächsischen Dichter*, rev. J. J. Köhler (Heidelberg, 1912), p. 75, glosses *gebryddan* as 'terrere, obstupefacere'.

9 The opening of *Solomon and Saturn II* situates the poem as a contest: 'Hwæt, ic flitan gefrægn on fyrndagum / modgleawe men' (179–80a). I discuss the problem of lines 170–8 below, pp. 68–9. On the agonistic tone, verbal conflict, verbo-motor behaviour and the noetic role of the bizarre characteristic of orally based thought, see Ong, *Orality and Literacy*, pp. 43–5 and 68–71.

the composition of the poem.[10] The poem thus situates itself conceptually within two oppositions: the one between power and knowledge about it, the other between speaking and writing.

The mode of conceptualizing the Pater Noster in speech and writing which *Solomon and Saturn I* exhibits has numerous filiations in early English thought. That writing itself is powerful was acknowledged in various ways in the literature of Anglo-Saxon England. A ready, intellectual context for this understanding of writing is offered by the seventh-century Isidore of Seville in the discussion of 'letters' in his massive *Etymologiae*.[11] In this treatment of writing, Isidore observes:

Litterae autem sunt indices rerum, signa uerborum, quibus tanta uis est, ut nobis dicta absentium sine uoce loquantur. (Verba enim per oculos non per aures introducunt.) Vsus litterarum repertus propter memoriam rerum. Nam ne obliuione fugiant, litteris alligantur. In tanta enim rerum uarietate nec disci audiendo poterant omnia, nec memoria contineri.[12]

Much is going on beneath the surface of this explanation. Isidore sees letters as concrete entities. (Presumably they are letters insofar as they are actually fixed physically on the page.) But letters do not make up words, but rather are *signs* of words, for they only point to, but are not, the words themselves.[13] For Isidore, words are still predominantly sound-defined.

[10] *Solomon and Saturn I* is only partially attested in CCCC 41, and only the first three letters (written simply as Roman characters) survive. In CCCC 422 the letters are written both as Roman characters and as runes, with the following exceptions: N lacks an accompanying rune and O appears to be missing (line 108a); I is missing (line 123a) as is B (line ?137); H lacks an accompanying rune (line 138a). Thus of seventeen possible letters the manuscript transmits fourteen.

[11] On the popularity of the *Etymologiae* in England (at least as evidenced by surviving manuscript records), see below, ch. 6, note 22.

[12] Isidore, *Etymologiae* I.iii.1–3. 'Letters . . . are the disclosers of things, the signs of words, in which there is such power that the speech of those absent is spoken to us without voice. (Indeed they introduce words by the eyes and not by the ears.) The use of letters was invented for the memory of things. For lest they fly into oblivion, they are bound by letters. Indeed, in so great a variety of affairs, everything could not be learned by hearing nor held in memory.'

[13] Analysing the traditional 'logocentrism' and 'phonocentrism' of the Western understanding of the relationships among truth, speech and writing, Jacques Derrida writes: 'If, for Aristotle, for example, "spoken words (*ta en tē phonē*) are the symbols of mental experience (*pathēmata tes psychēs*) and written words are the symbols of spoken words" (*De interpretatione*, I, 16a 3) it is because the voice, producer of *the first symbols*, has a relationship of essential and immediate proximity with the mind. Producer of the first

51

Were they not, his subsequent definition of 'verb' ('a sign of the mind by which men mutually demonstrate their thoughts by speaking') and his etymology ('it is so called because it sounds by beating (*uerberato*) the air') would make no sense.[14] Thus his fascination with letters lies in their power (*uis*) to transform sound into sight. This power speaks (*loquantur*) the speech (*dicta*) of those absent and does so without a voice (*{sine uoce} per oculos non per aures*).

Isidore comprehends writing visually as a technology of memory, despite retaining an aural notion of word. Letters owe their existence to the need to aid memory, for neither hearing nor memory is sufficient to take in the great variety of things. Interestingly, Isidore's argument here is the opposite of Socrates's position in Plato's *Phaedrus*, where Socrates maintains that writing destroys memory.[15] For Isidore, information which might otherwise vanish, is bound (*alligantur*) by letters. But every technology exacts its price. The power to preserve is gained at the cost of the intimacy of words. Through writing, words, divorced from oral source and substance, are conveyed by silence and absence. Writing becomes a technology of alienation.

The implications of Isidore's understanding of the mechanics of writing are played out in one of Aldhelm's *Enigmata*, whose solution is 'Alphabet':

> Nos decem et septem genitae sine uoce sorores
> Sex alias nothas non dicimus annumerandas.
> Nascimur ex ferro rursus ferro moribundae
> Necnon et uolucris penna uolitantis ad aethram;
> Terni nos fratres incerta matre crearunt.
> Qui cupit instanter sitiens audire docentes,
> Tum cito prompta damus rogitanti uerba silenter.[16]

---

signifier, it is not just a simple signifier among others . . . The written signifier is always technical and representative. It has no constitutive meaning' (*Of Grammatology*, p. 11).

[14] 'Verbum dictum eo, quod uerberato aere sonat, uel quod haec pars frequenter in oratione uersetur. Sunt autem uerba mentis signa, quibus homines cogitationes suas inuicem loquendo demonstrant' (I.ix.1).

[15] *Phaedrus*, 275, in B. Jowett, *The Dialogues of Plato*, 4 vols. (New York, 1892) I, 278.

[16] *Aldhelmi Opera*, ed. Ehwald, p. 112 (*Enigma xxx*). 'We were born seventeen voiceless sisters; we say that the six other bastards are not to be counted in our number. We are born of iron – and we die once again by iron – or of the feather of a bird flying swiftly in the sky. Three brothers begot us of an unknown mother. Whoever in his eagerness

The seventeen sisters make up the original letters of writing, while the six bastards are letters which later became used in the Latin alphabet. These details Aldhelm got straight from the *Etymologiae* (I.iv.10–15), but the metaphorical development is all his own. In fact, this poem concentrates most of the metaphors which fixed the attention of Anglo-Latin riddlers on written language. The letters of Aldhelm's poem are voiceless, but for the person thirsting to *hear* learning (*audire*), the sisters offer ready (*cito prompta*) words in silence. The poem emphasizes the immediacy of the words as writing collapses time and space to offer knowledge which is desired *instanter* and *cito*. The cost is silence.[17]

Aldhelm's *enigma* on letters has another metaphor common to the Anglo-Latin riddle tradition. The letters have their birth and death from iron. The word he uses, *ferrum*, signifies many things: iron, a sword, an iron implement and metaphorically, the stylus and the scraping tool used for erasure. In one word he conjures up notions of birth and death, productivity and destruction. This combination of productivity and violent destruction reappears in riddles on the implements used in writing, where the implements suffer in becoming useful.[18] Not only do these implements endure painful transformations, they are themselves ignorant. Eusebius's 'pen' (no. xxxv) is ignorant, yet produces wisdom. His 'book wallet' (no. xxxiii) though full of wisdom, is ignorant, and though wisdom comes from its mouth (*ore*), it cannot take wisdom in. Aldhelm's 'bookcase' (no. lxxxix), stuffed with books, can learn nothing from them. Though dead, it has innards which are pregnant (*praecordia gestant*) with volumes it

wishes earnestly to hear our instruction, we quickly produce for him silent words.' *Aldhelm: the Poetic Works*, trans. M. Lapidge and J. L. Rosier (Cambridge, 1985), p. 76.

[17] The image of the silent word haunts the Anglo-Latin enigmatists. In Eusebius's *enigma* on letters (vii), the letters speak loudly, but make no sound ('Et licet alta loquamur, non sonus auribus instat'). His riddle on parchment (xxxii) focuses on the silent word. When it was skin, the parchment had no voice to produce words, but in its transformed state produces words without voice. Alive it never spoke, dead it gives answers: *Variae Collectiones Aenigmatum I*, ed. F. Glorie, pp. 217 and 242.

[18] In one riddle on parchment (Tatwine, no. v), skin is despoiled by a robber only to be shaped into a field by an artisan. A pen (Tatwine, no. vi) reports that an enemy deprived it of its original nature. Once flying in air, now it is constrained by three fingers. Aldhelm's pen (no. lix) once graced a pelican; Eusebius's quill (no. xxxv), now confined to earth, once flew in the skies. See *Variae Collectiones Aenigmatum I*, ed. Glorie, pp. 172, 173, 455 and 245.

can never enjoy. The written object is dead; the written message is passive and can only invite use.

The Anglo-Latin riddle writers inherited a vocabulary for writing and a corpus of dead metaphors from Latin writers before them.[19] The images of violence, however, are to the best of my knowledge an English contribution to the Latin *enigma* tradition, and the metaphors of sad transformation, common to these *enigmata*, appear as well in the Old English riddle tradition on writing.[20] The use of mouthless speakers, dead lifegivers, dumb knowledge-bearers, clipped pinions – all metaphors of loss – reflect an Anglo-Saxon understanding that speech itself is not a *thing*, but that writing, as it alienates speech from speaker, transforms living words into things. The technology which preserves also kills.[21] And these new things which preserve thought are themselves vulnerable in a new way.[22]

These Anglo-Saxon meditations on the differing power and vulnerability of speech and writing offer a context for the tension in *Solomon and Saturn I* between spoken word and written word. Delight in the possibilities of writing and gratitude for its ready conservation of knowledge are tempered by expressions of discomfort and loss associated with the painful transformations which writing requires. But the tension in *Solomon and Saturn I* between spoken and written operates at an even more elemental level than in the *enigmata*. The spoken word in the dialogue derives its force (both in the uttering of the Pater Noster and in the instructing of Saturn) from the agonistic verbal performance characteristic of oral cultures. In the oral world, knowledge is gained and displayed in verbal struggle.[23]

---

[19] E. R. Curtius, *European Literature and the Latin Middle Ages*, trans. W. R. Trask (Princeton, 1953), pp. 312–15, esp. 313.

[20] See Exeter Riddle 60, 'Reed-Pen', on the contradictions of wordless speech.

[21] Such a perception underlies the danger which Ælfric (following Augustine) suspected in the untutored reading of 'letters': they are devoid of the spirit. See *The Homilies of the Anglo-Saxon Church*, ed. B. Thorpe, 2 vols. (London, 1844–6) I, 186. See also *In Iohannis Evangelium Tractatus CXXIV*, XXIV.2, CCSL 36 (Turnhout, 1954), 244–5.

[22] For example Exeter Riddle 95, '?Book' ('?Bible') and, of course, Riddle 47, 'Bookmoth'.

[23] Ong observes that 'writing fosters abstractions that disengage knowledge from the arena where human beings struggle with one another. It separates the knower from the known. By keeping knowledge embedded in the human lifeworld, orality situates knowledge within a context of struggle': *Orality and Literacy*, pp. 43–4.

The relationship between spoken words and written words recapitulates the relationship between subject and object. The charge which Derrida imputes to philosophers of language from Socrates to Saussure, that they privilege spoken language as the logos and relegate written language to a mediate role, is equally applicable to *Solomon and Saturn I*.[24] In the contention between them, Solomon is the figure of wisdom, the one who comprehends the secret of the Pater Noster. Saturn is a learned man, though deficient in wisdom. It is hardly coincidental, therefore, that the references to book-learning in the poem are all made by Saturn. In his opening remarks, he claims that he has 'boca onbyrged' (2a) and 'larcræftas onlocen' (3a). Further, he says, he has studied the history of India, and commentators have interpreted for him stories in a great book. The words *istoriam* (4a) and *treahteras* (5a), both Latin loan-words, intimately connected to literacy, underscore the learning of the Chaldean prince, 'bysig æfter bocum' (A 61a), who continues to seek for knowledge, betrayed by *fyrngewrytum* (8a), which do not contain what he desires.

The wisdom of Solomon, by contrast, is associated not with reading but with speaking. Saturn has acknowledged that the power of the Pater Noster lies somehow in the words of the canticle (*ðurh þæs cantices cwyde*, 17a), and Solomon affirms that the individual who does not know how to praise Christ through *ðone cantic* (24a) is no better than a dumb animal. *Cantic* is no mere figure of speech, for the poem emphasizes that the Pater Noster is the actual speech of Christ, in which lies its power. It is *cwyde* (17a; *Godes cwide*, 63a, 84b and 146a), *cantic* (17a, 24a and 49a), *organ* (33a and A 53a; B 53a, *organan*). As the speech of Christ, articulation of the Logos, the Pater Noster has greater power than scriptures:

> Forðan hafað se cantic   ofer ealle Cristes bec
> widmærost word: he gewritu lǽreð,
> stefnum steoreð   and him stede healdeð
> heofona rices   heregeatewa wigeð.   (A 49–52)[25]

As the prayer teaches scripture (as audience or object?), the meaning of *word* shades into 'power'. And Saturn's query in reply, 'How is this song cultivated in the memory?' ('Ac hulic is se organ ingemyndum / to

---

24 Derrida, *Of Grammatology*, p. 30.
25 'Therefore this song has beyond all Christ's books the most celebrated words: it teaches scripture, guides the voices, and will hold a place for them in the heavenly kingdom; it wears war-gear.'

begonganne', A 53a–54a), locates the conflict between writing and speech: access to the power of the Pater Noster is through the voice.

> And se ðe wile geornlice   ðon*e* Godes cwide
> singan soðlice   and hine siemle wile
> lufian butan leahtrum,   he mæg ðone laðan gæst,
> feohtende feond,   fleonde gebrengan   (A 84–7)

> And se ðe wile geornlice   þon*e* godes cwide
> singan smealice   and hine symle
> lu[f]ian wile butan leahtrum,   he mæg þone laþan gesið,
> feohtenne feond,   fleonde gebringan   (B 84–7)[26]

Given the correct spiritual state, the singing of the Pater Noster is the trigger which activates the power of the prayer and puts the fiend to flight. When juxtaposed, the two records of the poem, with their semantic, syntactic and metrical variations, manifest the irruption of oral thought-processes into the written transmission of the text, a phenomenon I will consider more fully below. Both versions agree, however, in reading *singan*.[27] This understanding of the activating power of speech is developed further in the long version in CCCC 422, where Solomon, having described the impressive properties of the Pater Noster, restates the observation:

> Mæg simle se Godes cwide   gumena gehwylcum
> ealra feonda gehwane   fleondne gebrengan
> *ðurh mannes muð.*   (146–8a [my italics])[28]

Power comes from the speech of the mouth. The devil, however, is a writer who inscribes on a man's sword deadly letters to weaken its force:

> Awriteð he on his wæpne   wællnota heap,
> bealwe bocstafas,   bill forscrifeð,
> meces mærðo.   (161–3a)[29]

[26] 'And whoever will diligently sing God's speech truly (B, 'accurately') and will, without sins, continually praise him, may put to flight the hateful spirit (B, 'companion'), the warring fiend.'

[27] See also lines 166a–167a on the necessity of singing the Pater Noster to ensure the power of a sword.

[28] 'For every man, God's speech, through the mouth of a man, is always able to put to flight every one of the devils.'

[29] 'He writes on his weapon a multitude of fatal letters, dire characters, he inscribes the sword, inscribes the sword's glory.'

These are the letters of death whose effect can only be countered by reciting the Pater Noster. The opposition which this distinction implies should not be overdrawn. All writing is not evil any more than all speech is good. Against the *bealwe bocstafas* must be arrayed the letters of the Pater Noster.

The letters composing the Pater Noster are singularly martial entities. Their equipment includes a golden goad (P), flint (R), whips (N and O), bright spears and whips (Q and U), sharp spears, arrows, fire (F and M), and pointed twigs and silver whips (H [B?]), with which they inflict various kinds of (presumably satisfying) mayhem on fiends. The dual purpose in the violence of the letters is to send the devil back to hell and to silence him. And so, for example, R, *bocstafa brego* (99a),[30] after shaking the fiend by the hair and breaking his legs sends him back to hell, to seek out a dark retreat in the narrowest of kingdoms. Similarly, L and C so injure him *ðæt he on hinder gæð* (126b).

The activity of S fixes the relationship between power and speech:

> Ðonne .[rune].S. cymeð,   engla geræswa,
> wuldores stæf,   wraðne gegripeð
> feond be ðam fotum,   læteð foreweard hleor
> on strangne stan,   and stregdað toðas
> geond helle heap.   Hydeð hine æghwylc
> æfter sceades sciman;   sceaða bið gebisigod,
> Satanes ðegn   *swiðe gestilled.*   (111–17 {my italics})[31]

By smashing his face and causing his teeth to scatter throughout hell, S, letter of glory, not only sends the fiend into hiding, but in a triumph of power *silences* Satan's fiend. Depriving the enemy of speech, accomplished explicitly as well by G in a related formula, *nearwe stilleð* (133b), and implicitly by T in stabbing the devil's tongue (94b), deprives him of power. The silencing of the devil is thus accomplished by the speaking of the Pater Noster. And herein lies the crux of the double understanding of writing, letters and speech in the poem. Speaking the words of the prayer (a notion implicit in an oral mentality) invokes its power, which the poem conceptualizes as being situated in its letters (a notion suggesting a literate mentality). *Godes cwide* is scripture fully useful through man's speech.

---

[30] Cf. *bealwe bocstafas* (line 162a), the writing of the devil.

[31] 'Then S, chief of angels, letter of glory, comes, grips the hostile enemy by the feet, smashes his face against a hard rock, strews his teeth over the host of hell. Each one hides himself behind the bloom of shadows. The enemy is overcome, Satan's thegn thoroughly silenced.'

The writing of the letters of the Pater Noster involves us in a curious hybrid of speech and silence. In CCCC 422 the letters composing the prayer (except for N and H) are written in paired runic and Roman letters (see pl. IV). Reading both aloud would disturb the metre in many half-lines, because it would require inserting an additional stressed monosyllabic noun. For example, the a-verse, *ðonne hiene on unðanc .rune.R.* can only admit pronunciation of either *rad* or 'r'.[32] Similarly, the alliteration and metre of the c-verse, *ðonne .rune.S. cymeð* can only be preserved if the letter *s* is pronounced with a vocalic alliteration and the rune-name, *sigel*, is not.[33] It is difficult to avoid concluding that one set of letters must be silent, and the preponderance of evidence suggests that the runes are the silent, visual additions.[34] The runes in *Solomon and Saturn I* certainly do not function in the same fashion as the runes in Cynewulf's 'signatures', where they act both as signs of words with grammatical, metrical and alliterative significance and as letters spelling out another word.[35] It is not possible to ascertain whether the runes are 'authorial' or scribal, particularly since the runes do not appear in CCCC 41.[36] Their appearance in CCCC 422, in any event, adds another stratum to the meaning of the poem, where the Pater Noster is silently spelled out in what were esoteric, powerful characters.[37]

There is a striking difference between the treatment of the Pater Noster in *Solomon and Saturn I* and its appearance elsewhere in the three Pater

---

[32] Menner, *Poetical Dialogues*, p. 112, observes that the names for the Roman letters require long vowels. In fact his reading of line 93a as a D-type is only possible if one letter remains unarticulated.

[33] The letters in lines 127a and 108a also require the pronunciation of the Roman letter values to supply vocalic alliteration. See Menner, *Poetical Dialogues*, p. 113.

[34] The suggestion of Kellermann and Haas, 'Magie und Mythos', that the rune-names are significant for interpretation and are owing to poetic intent (p. 392) is thus difficult to support. See Sisam, review of Menner's *Poetical Dialogues*, p. 35. The shapes of the letters have no apparent connection with the force or weapons predicated of them. Only two letters are alluded to by shape: C and G are described as *geap*.

[35] See *The Old English Rune Poem: a Critical Edition*, ed. M. Halsall (Toronto, 1981), p. 19.

[36] Sisam, review of Menner's *Poetical Dialogues*, p. 35, considers CCCC 41 to be the manuscript closer to the 'original' because it omits the runes.

[37] See, for example, the West Saxon translator's Old English rendering of Bede's *litteras solutorias* (*HE* IV.22, ed. Colgrave and Mynors, p. 402), as *alysendlecan rune*; cited in R. W. V. Elliott, 'Runes, Yews, and Magic', *Speculum* 32 (1957), 250–61, at 250.

Noster poems in the surviving canon of Old English verse. *The Lord's Prayer I* is an eleven-line, literal translation of the Pater Noster. Written in long lines with no punctuation save the characteristic heavy terminal marks to signal the end of the poem, it is found in a short run of brief religious verse between the two sections of Riddles in the Exeter Book (122r).[38] The other two treatments of the prayer, *The Lord's Prayer II* in CCCC 201 and *The Lord's Prayer III* in Oxford, Bodleian Library, Junius 121, are more sophisticated, conceptually and visually.[39] Both treatments present the Latin verses of the prayer as visually distinct from the Old English 'gloss'. In CCCC 201, the scribe uses red and green capitals alternately to begin Latin and Old English passages. In Junius 121, the Latin verses of the prayer are rubricated. Both poems offer Latin words and Old English 'meanings'.

While these three treatments of the prayer are designed to make the Pater Noster comprehensible and accessible, *Solomon and Saturn I* does precisely the opposite. The prayer is spoken (or written) about, but its words are never uttered (or written); its power is described but not called forth. The poem achieves this end by opposing writing with speech. In written silence the prayer is conserved, its effects perhaps physically concentrated,[40] and its language hidden from Saturn, the pagan prince. While Saturn is told of the power, he is not given access to the powerful words, for letters, finally, are the signs of words not the words themselves.

Solomon and Saturn I testifies to the deeply felt power of the spoken word. But it also speaks to a consciousness which accords writing its own power: to objectify, to hold, to fix, to hide. How these powers are realized in the written transmission of the poem is the subject of the following section.

---

[38] On the punctuation of the Exeter Book, see below, pp. 158–64.

[39] Ker, *Catalogue*, pp. 82 and 412 dates the relevant portion of CCCC 201 to xi^{med} and of Junius 121 to xi^3. On the punctuation and visual effects of verse in these manuscripts see below, ch. 7, n. 72.

[40] A number of Old English charms require the individual to carry on his person specific written characters. At least one, *Wið Lenctenadle*, in *Anglo-Saxon Charms*, ed. F. Grendon (New York, 1909), p. 99 [D9], requires these letters to be carried in silence. Numerous charms require the singing of the Pater Noster in addition to other ritual actions. *Wið Ælfsogoþan* requires a written charm to be recited, dipped into a drink to be consumed by the affected person, and the Pater Noster and Credo to be recited thereafter.

MANUSCRIPT TRANSMISSION

The transitional literacy informing the thought behind *Solomon and Saturn I* shapes the written transmission of the poem as well. The sixty-three lines of *Solomon and Saturn I* for which there are two manuscript records (lines 30–94a) display a large number of variants. Of these, the twenty listed in fig. 4 may be considered substantive. A sampling of these variants was considered by Kenneth Sisam in his essay on the transmission of Old English verse.[41] He concluded that the variants in *Solomon and Saturn I* (as well as those which he examined in the two versions of *Soul and Body*, *Daniel* and *Azarias*) were by nature distinct from those found in the transmissions of Latin texts: 'But as compared with the variants in classical texts, they show a laxity in reproduction and an aimlessness in variation which are more in keeping with the oral transmission of verse. An editor who has these passages in mind will not regard the integrity of a late manuscript as axiomatic.'[42]

Two points in these observations command agreement, that the modes of transmitting Old English and Latin verse appear to differ and that variation is a hallmark of oral transmission. The imputations of 'laxity' and 'aimlessness', however, must give pause, particularly as they are predicated of 'oral transmission'. A literate ideology underlies the implicit judgement in this passage on the relative values of literate and oral transmission and lies behind the cautionary statement following – that the 'integrity' of most surviving manuscripts is suspect.[43] Sisam's use of the term 'integrity' tells us that manuscripts are judged by faithfulness to a hypothetical authorial version, and that manuscripts which can be regarded as lax are impeachable witnesses. The index of 'laxity', it would seem, is variance.

The significant variants which the two records of *Solomon and Saturn I* exhibit are remarkable even by their number.[44] Both manuscripts have a

---

[41] Sisam, *Studies*, pp. 32–4.

[42] *Ibid.*, p. 34.

[43] Sisam (*ibid.*, p. 35) dismisses the testimony of Caedmon's *Hymn*: 'Here the conditions of transmission are abnormal, and again it is unsafe to rely on the evidence.'

[44] I have employed 'significant variant' as a temporary category to denote those pairs of variants which are productive of some sense, that is, which are not immediately identifiable as mechanical or visual errors. 'Substantive' variants, however, describe a somewhat smaller class of pairs which can be defended as true alternatives and as evidence of the 'formulaic' reading characteristic of the transmission of Caedmon's *Hymn*. Establishing such a class requires eliminating those variations productive of weak readings.

	CCCC 422	CCCC 41
32b	feoh gestreona	fyrn ge streo / na
35a	unge lic	unge sibb
44a	dream	dry
52a	heofona rices	heofon / rices
56a	scyldig*um*	scyldu*m*
59a	ge menge∂	geond menge∂
60b	dreose∂	dreoge∂
62b	hædre	hearde
65b	god spel secgan	god spellian
73a	he ahie∂e∂	*hege* hege hide∂
75	he *is* modigra middangearde	heis mo/digra middan/geardes
76	sta∂ole strengra ∂on*ne* ealra stana gripe	sta∂ole / he is strengra / þone ealle stana / gripe
78b	dumbra	deadra
82a	wyrma ‗elm	wyrma wlen co
83a	on westenne	westen es
85a	so∂ lice	smealice
85b	7hine / siemle wile	7hine symle
86a	lufian butan leahtrum	lui/an wile butan / leahtru*m*
86b	gæst	gesi∂
92b	him	‗‗‗‗
92b	fylge∂	læte∂ [expunging dots, filgi∂ written above]

FIG. 4 Significant variants in *Solomon and Saturn I*

number of visual errors, characteristic of written transmission.[45] They also display ordinary orthographic and grammatical differences.[46] Discounting these, however, there are nevertheless the twenty variants summarized in fig. 4, many of which are lexical. These variants form the core of the evidence which suggests that *Solomon and Saturn I*, like Caedmon's *Hymn*, displays participatory copying and 'formulaic' reading. The issue here is

[45] See Havet, *Manuel*, esp. nos. 1082–97. Neither CCCC 422 nor CCCC 41 is immune from visual errors: CCCC 41 is prone to omit individual words (e.g. at lines 62a, *neah*, and 64a, *leaf*), but CCCC 422 omits an entire line (67). The scribe of CCCC 41 writes and catches a dittography (at line 72a); that of CCCC 422 misreads an 'f' for an 's' at line 41b. The examples could be multiplied.

[46] See Menner, *Poetical Dialogues*, pp. 3–4.

certainly not to demonstrate that in every pair both members are equally attractive – that would be at best a quixotic enterprise – but rather to examine in the nature of each variance the marriage of oral and literate processes which produced its variants, and to question the implications of an editorial method which would privilege one variant reading over another.

The significant variants of *Solomon and Saturn I* (that is, excluding orthographic differences and simple mechanical errors) are most simply analysed in three categories: lexical, grammatical and syntactic. The grammatical and syntactic categories of variant generally produce readings which are semantically and syntactically acceptable but which are metrically unequal. Three pairs from fig. 4 exhibit grammatical variance. In the pair composing 65b, *godspel secgan* (422) / *god spellian* (41), the reading in CCCC 41 is the weaker version and only marginally acceptable.[47] The variance in 83a, *on westenne weard* (422) / *westenes weard* (41), yields a metrically deficient a- or e-verse in CCCC 41.[48] The final example of grammatical variance occurs at 52a, *heofona rices* (422) / *heofon rices* (41). In CCCC 41, *heofon-* is written at the end of the column, and it is entirely possible that the variant before us is a simple product of an eyeskip rather than a grammatical substitution. However, *heofonrices*, producing semantic and syntactic sense, still qualifies as a grammatical variant, which is, nonetheless, syllabically deficient (since both syllables of the head-word are short).

The two cases of syntactic variance also involve formal difficulties. In the variants of lines 75–6, the readings of both manuscripts are syntactically, semantically and metrically sound,[49] but 76a in CCCC 41 does not conform to the classical shape of the half-line, since the beginning of the independent clause is not coincident with the beginning of the metrical unit.[50] The other instance of syntactic variance occurs in the word order of lines 85b–86a. CCCC 422 reads *7hine / siemle wile lufian butan leahtrum.* CCCC 41 reads *7hine symle luilan wile butan / leahtrum.* Menner breaks the

---

[47] Compare *Daniel* 657b, 'godspellode'.

[48] But compare 'Babilone weard' in *Daniel* 104b, 117a, 209b, 228b, 448b, 460b, 487b and 641b (cf. 'Babilonie weard', 167b).

[49] With line 76a, *staðole he is strengra*, compare (metrically) Exeter Riddle 40 (K–D), lines 92a, *mara ic eom ond strengra*, and 105a, *mara ic eom ond fættra*.

[50] Mitchell, *Old English Syntax* II, §3960, lists exceptions for noun, adverb and adjective (but not independent) clauses.

line at *symle* to preserve alliteration on the first stave in 86a, but it is unlikely that the copyist conceived of the break there. Although the spacing of the record in CCCC 41, written as it is across and down the margins of the West Saxon *Ecclesiastical History*, provides no positive evidence of metrical division, the scribe did press the first three letters of the infinitive into the line, breaking the word in the process. The order in CCCC 41 (with the infinitive following *symle*) suggests that the scribe was reading 85b as a variant on the preceding half-line with its infinitive dependent on *wile* in line 84a. The manuscript reading *luilan* increases the difficulty in interpreting the evidence. CCCC 422 has *lufian*, on the basis of which reading Menner emends CCCC 41. But at some point in the transmission of the poem, quite possibly in the copying of CCCC 41, a visual or mechanical error occurred in the omission of the 'f' of *lufian*. Ignoring, for the moment, the consequences to the following half-line, one might equally well scan 85b with *lufian*, for the metrical results are only slightly less satisfactory than the reading in CCCC 422. After these adjustments, 86a becomes a weak a-verse with alliteration on the second stress.[51] As with the previous example of lines 75–6, the syntactic variation in 85b–86a produces an awkward metrical consequence.[52]

While both grammatical and syntactic categories of variant offer useful information about the consequence of participatory copying, the last category, lexical variants, offers information which is most intriguing. Because they can all be claimed to produce some degree of sense, I included, in preliminary fashion, thirteen variants in this category, three of which (in 56a, 73a and 92b) are properly suspect. These may be disposed of fairly quickly.

The variation in 56a *scyldum* (CCCC 41) / *scyldigum* (CCCC 422) is composed of two readings which are syntactically, metrically and semantically acceptable, though in this case CCCC 41 appears to have the more pleasing reading. Because *scyldigum* can be argued to be a mechanical error, it is best not to include this pair in the count of 'formulaic' lexical variants.

---

[51] Or in A. J. Bliss's theory (*The Metre of Beowulf* (Oxford, 1958)), a 'light verse' (p. 62, §69), perhaps similar to *Beowulf* 1013a, *bugon þa to bence*.

[52] The obvious assumption behind this statement is that the half-line with the 'better' metrics transmits the 'better' reading, but this is not necessarily to say that it is an 'authorial' reading. It would be possible to argue (though incapable of proof) that the 'better' reading was the product of deliberate editing.

More straightforward as the consequence of visual errors are the other two pairs, occurring in 73a and 92b. In 73a, *hungor he ahieðeð* (CCCC 422) / *hungor hege hege hideð* (CCCC 41), by a correction of an obvious mechanical error the first *hege* in CCCC 41 has been underlined for deletion in the same ink as the text of the poem. The resulting reading, *he gehideð*, is metrically and syntactically acceptable, but semantically peculiar. The reading *gehideð* may be partially the product of a 'ð' mistaken for a 'd'. The last of the three, the variation in 92b, *7him on swaðe fylgeð* (CCCC 422) / *7 onswaðe læteð* (CCCC 41), also contains a scribal correction. The scribe of CCCC 41 dotted *læteð* for omission and wrote *filgið* above it. The omission of *him* is quite probably the result of an eyeskip.

The remaining ten pairs of variants are truly alternate readings between which there is no clear choice.

35a *ungelic* (422) / *ungesibb* (41): semantically, metrically and syntactically acceptable. *Ungelic* appears in five other contexts, usually with the adjective in first position.[53] *Ungesibb* is elsewhere attested in Exeter Riddle 9.8a as a dative singular.

44a *dream* (422) / *dry* (41): syntactically and metrically acceptable, but in context neither makes much sense, though *dry* marginally more. The half-line probably ought to be read as a variation on and specification of the preceding *blod*.

60b *dreoseð* (422) / *dreogeð* (41): syntactically, metrically and semantically acceptable. Both words are fairly common.

62b *hædre* (422) / *hearde* (41): syntactically, metrically and semantically acceptable. While *hearde* is well attested as an adverb, *hædre* is only elsewhere attested in the sense 'oppressively' once (*Resignation* 63a).

78b *dumbra* (422) / *deadra* (41): syntactically, metrically and semantically acceptable.[54]

82a *and wyrma {w}elm* (422) / *wyrma wlenco* (41): syntactically acceptable and metrically so by the addition (or subtraction) of *and*. Among the fantastic terms of this litany, neither *welm* nor *wlenco* can claim pride of place.

85a *soðlice* (422) / *smealice* (41): syntactically, metrically and semantically acceptable. *Smealice* is somewhat more precise (specifying that the Pater Noster must be sung *accurately*), but the word is otherwise unattested in verse.

86b *gæst* (422) / *gesið* (41): syntactically, metrically and semantically acceptable. For *gæst*, compare *Soul and Body II*, 110b and *Guthlac* 361b. For *gesið*, compare *Daniel* 661b and *Juliana* 242a.

[53] See *Genesis* 356b and 612b; *Daniel* 112a; *Wulf and Eadwacer* 3; *Metres of Boethius* XX.33a.

[54] See Sisam, *Studies*, p. 34.

The remaining two examples are best considered at length because they focus attention on issues touched on in the consideration of the previous eight pairs. We begin with 32b, one of whose elements is a hapax: *feohgestreona* (CCCC 422) / *fyrngestreona* (CCCC 41). Both readings are syntactically, semantically and metrically acceptable. *Fyrngestreona*, however, is unique, while *feohgestreona* is well attested.[55] Should the fact of the hapax be troubling? The *Concordance to the Anglo-Saxon Poetic Records* lists some eighteen compounds with *fyrn-* as first element, and of these, eleven are only attested once. If the occurrence of these compounds may be considered representative of their use in Old English verse then *fyrn-* was clearly a popular morpheme with which to build nonce-words. A similarly problematic pair occurs at 59a: *gemengeð* (CCCC 422) / *geondmengeð* (CCCC 41). While *geondmengeð* is a hapax, *geond-* is a highly popular affix.[56]

Can the principle of *difficilior lectio potior* give any guidance?[57] Clearly *fyrngestreona* is the rarer reading, but just as clearly compounding with *fyrn-* is common. *Feohgestreona* is well-attested, but numbers of attestations open the reading (once again on the principle of *difficilior lectio*) to the charge of 'scribal' trivialization. When the argument is stated in these terms, and given the background of the previous eight pairs of variants, it becomes apparent that certain editorial rubrics for deciding correct readings, which developed historically in the editing of classical texts and which have as presuppositions 'classical' models of authorship, have only limited use in the editing of early vernacular works. Because 'classical' texts are attributable to authors and may have enjoyed a comparatively stable (and, by inference, a comparatively literate) transmission, they are amenable to the fiction of an 'authorial' text. Anonymous vernacular poems, composed and copied in a period of early literacy (by this I mean the transitional literacy which the variants of Caedmon's *Hymn, Solomon and Saturn I, Soul and Body I and II* and Exeter Riddle 30a and 30b encompass), are not so amenable and form another class of realized

---

[55] As *feohgestreon* in *Andreas* 301b and *Juliana* 42b; as *feohgestreona* in *Elene* 910a and *Juliana* 102a.

[56] See Bessinger, *Concordance*, p. 437, for compounds which affix *geond*. For metre compare (among others) *Wanderer* 51b and 60b; *Juliana* 399b; *Metres of Boethius* XXX.15b.

[57] On the use of the principle of *difficilior lectio potior*, see Patterson, *Negotiating the Past*, p. 95. See also J. E. Cross, 'The Poem in Transmitted Text – Editor and Critic', *Essays and Studies* 27 (1974), 84–97, at 85.

texts.[58] The mode of existence for such works is far from the Romantic concept of the poem as the fixed expression and product of an author's genius. These anonymous compositions, whether of oral or literate origin, nonetheless share the oral poem's hallmark of never being the same twice. Written transmission may diminish the range of variance, but the records of these poems demonstrate that the reading and writing of the scribes still bore the imprint of oral reception.

By printing the two versions of *Solomon and Saturn I* on facing pages, Menner avoided the problem of choosing a base text for that section. But Dobbie used the older manuscript as a base text, supplementing its first thirty lines from CCCC 41. From an historical perspective this choice fashions an interesting monster whose head and torso are certainly orthographically and probably lexically at odds. Indeed, if the rate of significant variance in the sixty-three surviving doubly attested lines (1:3 lines) held for the first thirty (CCCC 41 and the now mutilated first page of CCCC 422), there would be some nine or ten significant differences between the two versions. One must conclude that Menner's is the more historically accurate account of the available evidence for *Solomon and Saturn I*. Dobbie's redaction of the poem obscures the evidence of the poem's early mode of existence.

Given the three possible categories of significant variance, the limitation of substantive variants to lexical alternatives is instructive. The poet and performer have active roles in producing and reproducing oral verse. The audience, in receiving such performances, remember, approve or disapprove, but their participation is essentially passive. The scribe, in receiving the text, is a special case of audience, and as reproducer of text is a special case of performer. His performance as a 'formulaic' reader is thus always at odds with his normally passive reception as copyist, and muddles often

---

[58] R. M. Liuzza, 'The Texts of the Old English *Riddle 30*', *JEGP* 87 (1988), 1–15, provides a scrupulous account of the variants in the two versions of Exeter Riddle 30. He suggests (at p. 14) that the scribe be viewed as an 'editor' and 'shaper' of Old English poetry. The variants he cites also support the case I have been making for *Solomon and Saturn I*. For an analysis of the variants of the two versions of *Soul and Body*, see P. R. Orton, 'The OE "Soul and Body": A Further Examination', *MÆ* 48 (1979), 173–97, who attempts to demonstrate that 'a single written text is the ancestor of both surviving witnesses' (p. 194). His essay is a persuasive rebuttal of A. [Jones] Gyger, 'The Old English *Soul and Body* as an Example of Oral Transmission', *MÆ* 38 (1969), 239–44. See also D. Moffat, 'The MS Transmission of the OE *Soul and Body*', *MÆ* 52 (1983), 300–2.

arise from the conflation of the two roles of language-producer and visual-reproducer. Truly formulaic reading is no more consciously produc-tive of variance than oral performance. In formulaic reading (the hybrid of 'literate' and oral reception), the relative passivity required of a reader/ copyist (as against the activity of a poet or performer) almost guarantees that any modifications other than simple lexical substitution will leave traces of change. Grammatical or syntactic alteration may have wide repercussions within a clause. Simple lexical substitution is the change least likely to affect surrounding context because it is generally containable to the half-line.

VISUAL MEANING: TEXT AND SPACE

Solomon and Saturn I, as it is realized in its two manuscript records and read in the context of the other dialogues, both confirms and extends the conclusions of ch. 2. The poem is preserved in two dissimilar manuscript environments. The earlier manuscript, written on two imperfect quires of the mid-tenth century, and now preserved in a composite volume (CCCC 422), presents both verse dialogues of Solomon and Saturn, separated by a prose dialogue, as main texts.[59] The later manuscript, CCCC 41, transmits part of *Solomon and Saturn I* (ninety-three full verses and a fragment of the next) in the margins of a West Saxon translation of Bede's *Historia ecclesiastica*.[60] The manuscript history of this peculiar poem thus recapitulates, at least in part, one of the circumstances of the transmission of Caedmon's *Hymn*, although in a delightful reversal, the lengthy *Solomon and Saturn I* finds itself as the marginalized addition to the Old English *History*, in which Caedmon's *Hymn* travels as part of the main text. Considered together, these manuscripts are a study in the visual information available to a reader of Old English verse, both through their use of graphic cues and their treatment of space.

CCCC 422 presents a number of difficulties in the physical and interpretative reading of the Solomon and Saturn material. The first of these is the physical difficulty of deciphering the writing on the first leaf. This leaf was sadly mistreated at various points in its history. As an outside cover, pasted down, stained, rubbed and treated with reagents, it is now

[59] Ker, *Catalogue*, no. 70 (s. x^med).
[60] On pp. 196–8 of the manuscript. Ker, *Catalogue*, no. 32, dates the hand to s. xi[1] or xi^med.

mostly unreadable.[61] In every practical sense, CCCC 41 is the sole witness to the first twenty-nine verses of *Solomon and Saturn I*. The three dialogues of Solomon and Saturn in CCCC 422 are copied into two quires of eight, the first lacking a leaf after p. 12, the second lacking presumably conjugate leaves 3 and 6.[62] The first and second dialogues, though distinct as verse and prose, appear to run together. With the exception of the increase of lines (from twenty-three to twenty-four) on pages 7 to 12, there is no distinction between the presentation of prose and verse in this part of the manuscript.[63] On p. 6, line 12, in the middle of the manuscript line, following *cyme* (169b), the prose begins. It is in no way distinguished from the preceding or following verse, beginning with a simple capital 'S' (the same size as other internal capitals) and following a single medial point. This fact presents a second, interpretative problem. Leaf 7, now missing from the first quire, presumably continued the prose dialogue and contained at least the opening of the half-line 170a (in Dobbie's numeration). But the fragmentary state of the prose dialogue prevents us from drawing any conclusion about the relationship between *Solomon and Saturn I* and the prose dialogue which the scribe joined to it.

The third dialogue in the manuscript, a verse composition, *Solomon and Saturn II*, begins on p. 13 of the present manuscript, that is, on the recto of the original eighth leaf of the first quire. The first seven lines of this leaf present a third interpretative difficulty, since the connection of the anomalous verses in these lines with either the first or second poetic dialogue is problematic. The scribe's arrangement of prose and verse lies at the heart of the question of where the nine lines of verse at the top of p. 13

[61] Page, 'A Note', p. 36. For a list of ill-treated pages, see Menner, *Poetical Dialogues*, p. 2, n. 5.

[62] Menner's conjecture, *Poetical Dialogues*, pp. 1–2, supported by Ker, *Catalogue*, p. 120.

[63] It is unclear why the scribe increased the number of lines per page to twenty-four. The missing leaf 7 effectively blocks any kind of inferential reconstruction of events. It does not seem likely that he was trying to join up with an already existing second quire, given the seven manuscript lines of verse preceding the opening of the second poetic dialogue. It is possible that the scribe hoped to arrange his material in order to place the initial capitals of the second poetic dialogue at the top of p. 13 and thought he might squeeze the rest of the matter on p. 12. Although Ker (*Catalogue*, p. 120) reports that the two quires are written in twenty-three lines save for pp. 7–13, I was unable to see more than twenty-two long lines on p. 2.

belong. Dobbie makes the conservative decision to print the verses after the main body of *Solomon and Saturn I*, simply indicating a hiatus in the place of the prose section. Menner, following Vincenti, assigns the lines in question to the conclusion of *Solomon and Saturn II* (following line 496), placing heavy significance on the presence of the half-line *forcumen and forcyŏŏed* (198a) in both the opening of *Solomon and Saturn II* and in the anomalous nine lines.[64] Although Menner confirms his editorial decision by noting that the repetition of these words makes a tidy conclusion, they are indeed all too tidy.

There are serious problems with the moving of these lines, not the least of which is the violence which it does to the manuscript's order of texts. The simple repetition of a half-line is insufficient evidence on which to claim some sort of lexical or stylistic (or dialectal!) similarity, especially given current knowledge about the use of oral formulae in the composition of verse. One might note that in both instances the half-line alliterates with *Caldeas*. Since *Solomon and Saturn II* breaks off at the bottom of p. 26, it is likely that this poem originally extended to at least part of a third quire. The assembly of works suggests that the scribe undertook to copy a collection of Solomon and Saturn materials, but that *Solomon and Saturn I* and the prose dialogue were either one work or had been copied together previously by the same individual. The scribe of CCCC 422 seems unperturbed by the generic distinction between verse and prose, and his performance treats the two as one text. Perhaps they ought to be considered as one.

The companion texts to *Solomon and Saturn I* in CCCC 41 locate the poem in another interesting visual and intellectual context. Unlike the *Z, *Y, and M-L records of Caedmon's *Hymn*, whose marginal status is due to the conception of the poem as a gloss to the Latin text, the record of *Solomon and Saturn I* in CCCC 41 has no intrinsic connection with the main text of the manuscript. Its probably fortuitous appearance on pp. 196–8 of the manuscript coincides with Bede's description of the apostasy of Sighere and the East Saxons.[65] And so, by a splendid graphic accident, the account of

---

[64] That is, *forcumen and forcyŏed* in line 176a (503a). A. R. von Vincenti, *Die altenglischen Dialoge von Salomon und Saturn* (Leipzig, 1904), p. 64. Shippey, *Poems of Wisdom and Learning*, p. 102, follows this order as well.

[65] 'Then they began to restore the heathen temples which previously had been abandoned, and they worshipped idols and prayed as if through those objects they might be protected from destruction and mortality.' See *The Old English Version of Bede's Ecclesiastical History*, ed. Miller I, 250 (III.22).

the East Saxons' return to devil worship – 'þa ongunnon hi þa hergas edniwan ðaþe ærfor / lætene wæron 7 deofolgyldworþodon 7 gebædon / swaswa hiþurh þasþing mihton frāþā wale 7 frā / þære deadlicnesse gescylde beon' – is physically framed and contained by Solomon's recounting of the power of the Pater Noster against demons (see pl. V). The other marginal texts with which the poem was copied also comment on the intellectual context of *Solomon and Saturn I* and the interests of its collector/copyist. In various blank spaces and in the margins of the *History*, the individual who copied *Solomon and Saturn I* also copied a number of masses and liturgical prayers (in Latin), six homilies in Old English, charms in both languages, and, especially interesting in light of the content of *Solomon and Saturn I*, the 'Sator' formula.[66] The latter, written in the right margin of p. 329, is positioned between two Latin prayers. The formula is written on two lines following a cross, and the words are separated by points. It is curious that the formula was not visually arranged (there is ample room in the margin), particularly since its charm lies in its graphic dimensions. The appeal of 'Sator' as an acrostic palindrome is obvious, but it is immeasurably enhanced by the origins of its words: its power derives from its composition as a series of permutations on the letters of 'Pater Noster'.[67] In CCCC 41, *Solomon and Saturn I* and 'Sator' are the visual reflexes of the *sygegealdor* of the charms in the marginalia of that manuscript.[68]

MEANING AND VISUAL CONVENTIONS

The central tension of *Solomon and Saturn I* lies in the opposition of speaking and writing both as modes of discourse and as means to power. Writing holds the power of memory, but exacts the price of silence. This double bind is ironically epitomized in the physical impediments to

---

[66] Following a cross, the words of the formula are arranged: 'SATOR . AREPO . TENET . / OPERA . ROTAS .' For a discussion of the connection between 'Pater noster' and the Rotas-Sator Square see K. Aland, 'Der Rotas-Sator-Rebus. Seine Diskussion in der Korrespondenz Franz Cumont-Hans Lietzmann und in der Zeit danach', in *Corona Gratiarum: Miscellanea Patristica, Historica et Liturgica Eligio Dekkers*, 2 vols. (Bruges, 1975) II, 285–343.

[67] See E. J. Sharpe, 'The Old English Runic Paternoster', in *Symbols of Power*, ed. H. R. E. Davidson (Cambridge, 1977), pp. 41–60 and 162–5, at 59.

[68] See 'A Journey Charm', 6a (Dobbie, *Minor Poems*, pp. 126–8), copied on pp. 350–3 of CCCC 41.

reading owing to the present condition of CCCC 422 and by the interpretative difficulties owing to the ambiguous formatting of the scribe. These are problems for modern scholarship precisely because the manuscripts are visually poor in information and because we do not possess the information which a contemporary reader could bring to the texts. Just as the poem conceptually joins oral and literate mentalities, it graphically embodies, in its material existence as *realized* texts, two transitional states in the development of significant visual space. These may be seen most easily in the formatting of dialogue and in the use of punctuation.

Formatting

The variability of format in CCCC 422 suggests that the scribe changed and developed his practice as the writing of the manuscript progressed. The text of *Solomon and Saturn I* opens on the first line of the first folio with the rubrics (which R. I. Page has partially recovered) 'S..VRN(V)S.. HWÆT'.[69] The size and array of these letters accord with the scribe's approach to capitalizing the first half-line of *Solomon and Saturn II* (p. 13, line 8). Here, a blank space (the rest of line 7 after the closing three words and terminal points of the anomalous verses) in combination with a full line of capitals, 'HWÆT.IC.FLI.TAN.GEFRÆGN.', signals the opening of the new work.[70]

Although his signals for beginning a text are relatively conventional, in the course of copying *Solomon and Saturn II* the scribe took a fresh approach to formatting dialogue and was not altogether consistent in his application. He moves from his practice in *Solomon and Saturn I* and in the prose dialogue, where he simply began the names 'Solomon' and 'Saturn' with a

---

[69] Page's last reading on the damaged p. 1, 'he.fdu. o..' ('A Note', p. 37), indicates that CCCC 422 contains no more at the beginning of the poem than CCCC 41 preserves. The initial capital 'S' of the dialogue, written in the left margin, is approximately three spaces high. The rest of the visible capitals are about one space high and extend across the line. 'HWÆT' is visible on the right side almost flush with the right margin (the ruling is not visible, but letters seem to stop there).

[70] In the right margin he combines as well a triangle of three points followed by a virgule. The initial capital 'H' is approximately three spaces high (around 20 mm) and the remaining capital letters are a full line high (averaging 6 mm between horizontal rulings).

capital initial, and in *Solomon and Saturn II* arranges the identifying statements with an eye to setting them off from the verse text proper.[71]

His approach to writing the two names of the prologue of *Solomon and Saturn II* suggests that this new method of highlighting the speakers in the dialogue is his own innovation rather than the arrangement in his exemplar. To begin the name 'Salomon', he wrote a large capital 'S' in the left margin (two ruled spaces high). He wrote a small capital Caroline 's' within the margin several lines below (for 'Saulus', line 190a) and immediately resumed the text. In this move he duplicates his practice in the previous verse and prose dialogues. Whatever he may have written on p. 14 is irrecoverable, after being scraped off and replaced by a twelfth-century formula for excommunication. However, in the original text on p. 15, the scribe follows his new practice by beginning each identifier at the left ruling with the capital initial in the margin. He highlights the statement *SATURNUS CVÆÐ* by writing a large capital 'S' in the margin (two ruled spaces high) and the rest of the statement in small capitals, about half a writing-space high. Rather peculiarly, he has positioned the small capitals not on the ruling but in the middle of it. For the next dialogue-marker he capitalizes 'Salomon' in the same fashion but writes *cwæð* in regular minuscules.[72]

The range of variations which he introduces into his practice is illustrated on p. 16. The first *Saturnus cuæð* is in capitals as above. The following *Salomon cuæð* is in capitals with the second 'o' of 'Salomon' diamond-shaped and set off by dots. The two words are separated by a point as well. The following three instances of *Saturnus cwæð* (that is to the bottom of p. 17) only receive a large capital initial 'S', while 'Salomon' receives a full run of capitals.[73]

As fanciful as this mode of capitalization may seem, there are trends within it which suggest a deliberate and meaningful pattern. The scribe's practice on p. 13 extends his method of distinguishing speakers in *Solomon*

---

[71] For example, in *Solomon and Saturn I*, when the beginning of either character's name occurred at the left margin, he wrote the capital 'S' in the initial column, but he made no effort to do this by design. In the prose dialogue, he capitalizes as well the initial letters of written numbers.

[72] This strategy of highlighting the identifying statements by placing them at the margin cost him space. He makes a faint attempt to fill in very empty lines with modest series of 'x's. See p. 15, line 23, for example.

[73] In the fashion of *Solomon and Saturn I*, only larger. Compare an average size of 11–12 mm for *Solomon and Saturn II* with 5–6 mm for *Solomon and Saturn I*.

and Saturn I and in the prose dialogue, where he regularly identified speakers by beginning names with a capital initial. His capitalization on p. 15, however, implies that he then conceived a new practice. Although he initially used capitals to separate the identifying phrases from the verse speeches, after a number of such capital arrays, he reserved capitals for the name 'Salomon' only, ornamenting the second 'o' of the name on occasion. That this shift in practice occurs in the middle of the second poetic dialogue suggests that the new capitalization is the scribe's own and not necessarily taken from his exemplar.

While both names of the contestants are emphasized to set off the identifying statements, Solomon's name receives the greater prominence. Through a graphic display, the scribe has chosen throughout to emphasize the name of the winner of the contest. The power and prestige of Solomon are thus encoded visually in the material text, and the inequality between the contestants reinforced. Significantly, this practice reappears in the record of *Solomon and Saturn I* in CCCC 41, even though the circumstances of writing the poem (compressed across and down the outer margins of the *History*) made capitals somewhat of a luxury because they required space.

The scribe begins 'Saturnus' at the outer left corner of p. 196 with a capital 'S' slightly more than twice the size of the minuscule letters. The following 'A' is a small capital, and the rest of the letters are normal minuscules. The other instances of 'Saturnus' follow a capital initial with normal minuscules. The name 'Salomon' (after 20b), however, not only receives a large capital initial, but the next four letters are written in small, distinctive capitals followed by a decorative mark of abbreviation over the 'M'. The next 'Salomon' (after 38b) is even more extravagant, with 'M' written as a rune. The third and final 'Salomon' (after 62b) is written in a mixture of capitals and exaggerated minuscules.[74] The visual distinction awarded to the name 'Salomon' as against the name 'Saturnus' is the only unusual feature in the writing of the poem in CCCC 41. That it appears at all in a text copied within the confines of a margin is curious and suggests that the practice had graphic significance for the scribe.

---

[74] It is unlikely that the rune in 'Solo(M-rune)' was meant to be read independently as 'mon', since in all three cases of the word, there is a bar above the letters indicating that the graph signifies an abbreviation.

Pointing

In contrast to the graphic congruity in their use of capitals in the two versions of *Solomon and Saturn I*, the manuscripts display very different pointing practices. The scribe of CCCC 422 regularly uses two grades of punctuation, an inverted triangle of points (I include here the triangle of points with an added virgule following) and a simple medial point. There is no hierarchy, however, to predict the appearance of the triangle or the augmented triangle.

In *Solomon and Saturn II* the triangle of points (in its several manifestations) regularly appears as a marker before the names of the contestants in the dialogue. There is an element of the mechanical about the use of the inverted triangle before a capital 'S' – hence the two probable miscues of this punctuation before simple names.[75] The use of the inverted triangle of points before the names of contestants coincides with its use to mark the end of lengthy statements, and in three instances the triangular points conclude a statement *within* the speech of a contestant.[76] The scribe's use of these triangles, which may be duplicated at the end of a blank line, is idiosyncratic. His use of simple points, however, is fairly conventional: they mark numerals and runes, set off an ornamental letter within an array of capitals, terminate a row of capitals, and signal the end of a line of writing. Because points are fairly rare in this verse dialogue, the two 'grammatical' uses (at 225b to separate an independent clause from a subordinate clause and at 319a before a small capital in a series) are surprising.

The pointing of *Solomon and Saturn I* in CCCC 422 is roughly similar. There are fewer instances of 'Solomon cwæð' or 'Saturnus cwæð' in this dialogue, but the generalizations in *Solomon and Saturn II* for the inverted triangle and the simple point hold fairly well: the inverted triangle marks off statements, but the point is used more frequently, generally to separate independent clauses either with or without following small capitals.[77] On

---

[75] That is, before those at 182a and 189b.

[76] In addition to its use before the names of the contestants, the triangle of points occurs at: 203b/204a (before a small capital 'w'); 381b/382a (before a small capital 'н'); 402b/403a (before a small capital 'ð' in the margin); and at the end of a row of capitals.

[77] The triangle appears following: 38b (before 'Salomon'); 52b (before 'Saturnus'); 160b, 165b, 174b (all separating independent clauses, in conjunction with a capital); 178b (present end of the poem). The single point appears following: 62b (before

average, not counting points separating runes or numerals, *Solomon and Saturn I* in CCCC 422 is pointed at a rate of about 10 per cent.

The sharp difference between the pointing of *Solomon and Saturn I* in the two manuscripts, is most likely a consequence of the later copying of CCCC 41. The greater number (though not the location) of points in the later manuscript is consistent with the evidence of the eleventh-century records of Caedmon's *Hymn*. Excluding numerals or runes, CCCC 422 uses only three points to CCCC 41's fifteen in the sixty-three lines they transmit in common. For this portion of *Solomon and Saturn I* common to both manuscripts, CCCC 422 points at a rate of 5 per cent while CCCC 41 points at 24 per cent. CCCC 41 uses a simple point exclusively, and while it occurs only at the b-line, the punctuation is not metrical in nature. Generally speaking, the points mark statements, mostly independent clauses, and approximately half of these occur before capitals.[78] The use of capitals as visual markers in the two records of *Solomon and Saturn I* is, however, closely similar. From this fact, I infer that the increased use of pointing in CCCC 41 marks the development of conventional pointing as further useful visual information in the writing of a text.[79] In neither manuscript, however, is pointing used as a convention which distinguishes the line of verse graphically, and its use in the text might be termed expressive rather than analytic.[80] Points in *Solomon and Saturn I* interpret the text and are the writer's visual analogues of the speaker's drop in voice.

Examination of the graphic display in the two records of *Solomon and Saturn I* indicates the degree to which the manuscripts of the poem are poor in visual information. There are few visual instructions available for the reader, and those there are – capital displays, initial capitals and points –

'Salomon'); 132b, 145b, 149b, 154b, 157b (all separating independent clauses, in conjunction with a capital); 117b, 126b (separating independent clauses); 136b (anomalous, perhaps intended to mark an independent clause); 113b (mid-half-line); 121b (end of page); 169b (before the beginning of the prose dialogue).

[78] The frequency of points in *Solomon and Saturn I* (CCCC 41) matches the general frequency in the narrative poems of the Exeter Book (see below, pp. 160–2) and the scribe's usage is conventional for individual letters and abbreviations.

[79] It is doubtful that the pointing of *Solomon and Saturn I* in CCCC 41 is substantially the original work of the scribe. Variations in the pointing of the other Old English texts he copied suggests that he simply copied the punctuation before him.

[80] Pointing practice appears to have changed radically between the dates for the copying of CCCC 422 and of CCCC 41. This difference in the use and significance of pointing in Old English poetic manuscripts forms the subject of chs. 5 and 6.

are highly variable. The displays of capitals in the writing of the contestants' names reinforce a conceptual point (about the relative power and prestige of the speakers) more prominently than a syntactic one. Because their use is generally expressive, these graphic cues are not predictable, and for this reason they are of only modest help in decoding the text. Their presence may demonstrate the perception that they are useful, but their use is strongly marked by the expressive subjectivity of a speaker.

CONCLUSIONS

Caedmon's *Hymn* and *Solomon and Saturn I* could not be farther apart in their origins, histories, intellectual presuppositions or circumstances of transmission. They do, however, share one important characteristic: the writing of their verses, reflected both in numerous appropriate variants and in minimal graphic aids for decoding, demonstrates strongly that the poems called forth 'formulaic' guesses as an essential part of reading activity. The presence of such variants in *Solomon and Saturn I* (and in *Soul and Body* and Exeter Riddle 30) suggests that 'formulaic' reading was a possible response to formulaic verse whatever its mode of composition. The extraordinarily high number of variant readings which are syntactically, semantically and contextually appropriate suggests that at least some scribes 'participated' in the heavily formulaic texts they received and transmitted. As they read familiar formulas, they naturally and quite unconsciously substituted other alliterating words which were also metrically correct. In this way, their written transmission of texts with traditional diction became the literate analogue of oral transmission by performers and poets.

4

The writing of the *Metrical Preface* to
Alfred's *Pastoral Care*

Literate ideology has been responsible for several peculiar notions about the reading and writing of Old English verse. Among them is the notion that the impact of modern literate cultures and practices on former oral cultures is a useful measure of the impact of *early* reading on *early* oral cultures.[1] Another is that Alfred could write simply because he had learned how to read.[2] And yet another is a smuggled aesthetic value judgement which simplistically opposes 'living formulaic language' to the 'parroting of formulaic tags'. Thus, where the *Beowulf* poet (we must presume) 'thought like an oral poet' because he 'var[ied] verse-length phrases within a vast interlocking network of formulaic systems', a poet, such as the translator of the *Metres of Boethius*, who 'used a number of formulaic tags', had to have been literate, *because his verse is poor*.[3] There is, I believe, at least one scenario where the poet who produced the Old English Metres could have been illiterate: he might have been asked to turn the prose translations of the *metra* into verse, had them read to him (just as prose was read to Caedmon) and then redacted them as verse – admittedly weak verse, but verse nonetheless.[4] We will never really know because no historian such as Bede recorded his procedure; the poet's name is lost to us and the manner of his work is shrouded in silence.

---

[1] See Lord, 'The Merging of Two Worlds', pp. 19–64, who examines the impact of print culture on oral culture.
[2] See Benson, 'Literary Character', p. 335.
[3] Niles, 'Formula and Formulaic System', pp. 410–11.
[4] Caedmon appears to have been given a limited passage of material, which he then turned into verse overnight: '. . . praecipientes eum, si posset, hunc in modulationem carminis transferre. At ille suscepto negotio abiit, et mane rediens optimo carmine quod iubebatur

77

Literate ideology is to blame for another difficulty in our understanding of the condition of medieval reading. This difficulty arises from the Platonic abstraction of the modern edited text, be it optimist or recensionist, which presents us with a remade, often hybrid, work, stripped of its context, its spatial arrangement and its points.[5] The brilliant and indispensable philology which produced the edition we study today nonetheless privileges an *idea* of composition over actual, *realized* texts which medieval readers had to hand. By 'realized' text, I mean the poetic work as it appears in manuscript, the word, in fact, made thing. But the cost of privileging the *idea* of composition comes high and is nothing less than the actuality (and, as a consequence, a crucial part of the history) of the work which we hope to understand. This problem is particularly acute when the work in question is shaped by a participatory tradition of reading and reproducing poetic texts. A truly historical perspective, however, requires us to know the realized texts in order to come to know the readings of the work before us.

In the present discussion, it is necessary to disentangle 'literacy', a word which refers to a condition of living within a society and a technology, from

conpositum reddidit' ('bidding him make a song out of it, if he could, in metrical form. He undertook the task and went away; on returning next morning he repeated the passage he had been given, which he had put into excellent verse', *Bede's Ecclesiastical History*, ed. Colgrave and Mynors, pp. 418 and 419). E. G. Stanley expresses the view that few Old English poets could be considered 'geniuses': 'Unideal Principles', p. 256.

[5] Writing of the impossibility of divorcing a text from the social conditions of its reception McGann observes that 'an author's work possesses autonomy only when it remains an unheard melody. As soon as it begins its passage to publication it undergoes a series of interventions which some textual critics see as a process of contamination, but which may equally well be seen as a process of training the poem for its appearances in the world' (*Critique of Modern Textual Criticism*, p. 51). The opposing, traditional view of 'text' is usefully defined by Boyle ('Optimist and Recensionist', p. 273): 'The object of an edition, however, is not solely to recover a text from the witnesses. Rather it is to uncover a textual tradition by which to see beyond the text encased in that tradition to that text as it was before it was launched on the devious path of variation by the present witnesses.' On the problem of choosing variants in a highly variable tradition, see F. Masai, 'Principes et conventions de l'édition diplomatique', *Scriptorium* 4 (1950), 177–93, at 181. On the importance of codicological environment, see F. C. Robinson, 'Old English Literature in its Most Immediate Context', in *Old English Literature in Context*, ed. J. D. Niles (Cambridge, 1980), pp. 11–29. See also Mitchell, 'The Dangers of Disguise', pp. 385–413.

'reading' and 'writing', words which refer to an individual's ability to decode written language to spoken and spoken language to written. The separation of condition from praxis helps to clarify the fact that literacy is not a single phenomenon, but rather multiple phenomena which are place- and time-specific. And since my interest is in the nature of reading in Anglo-Saxon England, the word 'text' in this chapter refers not to some abstract form of the *Metrical Preface*, but to the concrete evidence for its written existence. Such a point of reference gives us an entrée into the history of the *Metrical Preface* from its generation through its realizations in the manuscripts left to us.

In ch. 2, treating the developing text of Caedmon's *Hymn*, I argued that the essential interconnection between the composition and the trans- mission of the *Hymn* lay in the number and nature of the variants in the manuscript records. The many metrically and syntactically appropriate variants in the extant records of this poem demonstrated that the reading and copying involved in its written transmission had a substantially oral component. Under these circumstances, transmission becomes a part of the process of composition.[6] The variants in the lengthy *Solomon and Saturn I* argue that similar cases may be made for *Soul and Body I* and *II* and Exeter Riddles 30a and 30b.[7] While Caedmon's *Hymn* is our clearest record of a purely oral composition, the scholarly acceptance of its intrinsic orality is based less firmly on analysis of the nature or number of the formulae in the *Hymn* than on Bede's authoritative account of its author's illiteracy and of its miraculous occasion of composition.[8] We have likewise been influenced in our reception of another brief text by a Latin writer's account of that text's author, although in this case the influence is in quite another direction. The *Metrical Preface* to the *Pastoral Care* was composed under circumstances far different from those of Caedmon's *Hymn*. If not a miracle, the poem is a wonder in its own right, produced by a king distinguished by

---

[6] See Treitler, 'Oral, Written, and Literate Process', p. 482.

[7] Bede's *Death Song* and the *Leiden Riddle* both offer textual variations which are beyond the scope of this study, because their records are either very late or are the product of copying by continental scribes.

[8] On the accepted orality of Caedmon's *Hymn* and the dependence of that judgement on Bede's account, see, for example, F. P. Magoun, Jr., 'Bede's Story of Caedmon: The Case History of an Anglo-Saxon Oral Singer', *Speculum* 30 (1955), 49–63, at 49, and Fry, 'Caedmon as a Formulaic Poet', pp. 42–5.

learning as well as by arms. And it is Asser's account of Alfred's learning and love of books which has led us to judge, perhaps too readily, the literate composition of this poem.[9]

Like Caedmon's *Hymn*, the *Metrical Preface* to Alfred's translation of the *Regula pastoralis* is transmitted in multiple records spanning the centuries from Alfred's reign to the end of the Old English period. But the circumstances of their transmissions are critically different. Caedmon's *Hymn* found itself included in as many manuscripts by accident as it found itself an integral part of the transmitting text. Within its several lines of descent, it enjoys many distinctive variants. The text of the *Metrical Preface*, by contrast, travels only and always with the Old English translation of the *Regula pastoralis*, presents few problems of editing, and appears, compared to Caedmon's *Hymn*, *Solomon and Saturn I*, *Soul and Body*, and Exeter Riddle 30, remarkably stable. This comparative lexical stability, with its illusory suggestion of thoroughly 'literate' scribal habits, invites a further look at the facts of manuscript transmission.

The two axes of its existence, both the composition and the transmission of the *Metrical Preface* to the *Pastoral Care*, ask consideration in some detail, for the facts of this poem's generation contain much information on the questions of contemporary verse composition, of reading, and of the development of a text in its graphic dimensions. The number of copies, their textual descent and their geographic and temporal distribution give scope for some inferences about deliberate improvements, unconscious changes, and the use of graphic cues as aids to reading the text.

SPOKEN, WRITTEN AND READ: FORMULAE AND COPYING

Any discussion of the mode of composition for the *Metrical Preface* to the *Pastoral Care* necessitates taking on several difficult theoretical issues involved in the relative orality or literacy underlying any poetic work in Old English. If it is not possible to use repeated formulae as an index of oral composition, neither is it possible to claim that the *Metrical Preface* is a 'literate' work simply because it speaks about books and writing and was composed by a man who knew how to read. That the *Metrical Preface* is a

---

[9] See *Asser's Life of King Alfred*, ed. Stevenson, chs. lxxvii–lxxix. For an historical introduction and translation, see Keynes and Lapidge, *Alfred the Great*, pp. 9–110.

verse composition farther along the oral-literate continuum than Caed-mon's *Hymn*, is an eminently supportable claim; that the *Metrical Preface* is a purely literate composition, however, is a claim that will not withstand scrutiny.

The Evidence of Alfred's Literacy

The record of Alfred's reading which Asser presents is a highly complex one, made more difficult by Asser's cut-and-paste chronology and his hagiographic portrayal of Alfred's commitment to writing and the 'liberal arts'. [10] In a series of four chapters early in the biography, Asser recounts (not without censure of Alfred's parents) that Alfred remained ignorant of letters until his twelfth year or later ('usque ad duodecimum aetatis annum, aut eo amplius, illiteratus permansit' (ch. xxii), although he listened to and memorized English poetry. Immediately following is the charming story of Alfred's memorizing his mother's book of verse that he might gain it as a prize. The condition of the prize was that the winning brother would have to 'intelligere et recitare' the book. But the evidence of this little story is vexing. The Latin reads: 'Tunc ille statim tollens librum de manu sua, magistrum adiit et legit. Quo lecto, matri retulit et recitauit.'[11] Since the story is meant to illustrate Alfred's great desire for knowledge even though illiterate, *legit* cannot mean 'read' (since Alfred at this point could not), but must mean something like 'study'.[12] Similarly, *recitare* in this context cannot mean 'read aloud', but clearly means 'recite by memory something contained in a book'.

In the following chapter, Asser recalls that Alfred afterwards (*post hæc*) learned the psalms for the hours and numerous prayers and had them gathered in a little book. How long afterwards this was, Asser does not indicate, but Alfred's habit of carrying this book everywhere suggests that

[10] Any doubts about the authenticity of Asser's *Life* were put to rest by D. Whitelock, *The Genuine Asser*, The Stenton Lecture 1967 (Reading, 1968), pp. 18–21.

[11] *Asser's Life of King Alfred*, ed. Stevenson, ch. xxiii: 'Then immediately taking the book up in his hand, he went to his teacher and studied it. When it was learned, he returned to his mother and recited it.'

[12] Keynes and Lapidge point out (*Alfred the Great*, p. 239, n. 48) that *et* may be a copying error for *qui*, in which case Alfred's teacher read the book. But the following *lecto* makes this translation unlikely, since it would imply that Alfred learned the contents the moment his teacher read the book. It may, however, be an indication of the connection in Asser's or the copyist's mind between reading and studying.

at this point he could read. It does not suggest, however, that he could write, since the Latin – 'quos in uno libro congregatos in sinu suo . . . circumducebat'[13] – indicates merely that the psalms and prayers had been committed to writing, but not by whom. One cannot overlook the possibility that Asser's repeated accounts of Alfred with books (chs. xxiii, xxiv, lxxvi, lxxvii, lxxxi, lxxxvii, lxxxviii and lxxxix) have an iconographic purpose, since they lack for the most part specific chronological detail.

In ch. xxiii Alfred is clearly illiterate. In ch. lxxvi, with no chronological mooring, Asser relates that Alfred, despite the press of war and state affairs, was accustomed to recite material from English books ('Saxonicos libros recitare'). In an immediately following parallel construction, Asser adds that Alfred also especially learned English poems by memory ('maxime carmina Saxonica memoriter discere'). We do not know the identity or content of these 'Saxon' poems. As in ch. xxiii, however, Asser gives us some important information here. Although ch. lxxvi (whenever in Alfred's life this may have occurred) seems to imply that he could read English, it very clearly makes the point that Alfred regularly committed English verse to memory. And *discere*, with its underlying meaning of being *told* something, strongly suggests that his learning of verse was done aurally, especially given Asser's earlier statement that Alfred learned and memorized English poetry by hearing it.[14]

It is not necessary to press this point, however, in order to appreciate the amount of aural learning which Asser records as part of Alfred's continuing adult education. After Alfred had assembled his great teachers, Werferth, Plegmund, Athelstan and Werwulf, he had one or another of them read aloud continually, and by this method, we are told, he gained some knowledge of almost all books: 'quapropter pene omnium librorum notitiam habebat' (ch. lxxvii). Asser explains that at this point Alfred was unable to understand this material on his own and that he was unable to read ('Non enim adhuc aliquid legere inceperat': ch. lxxvii). Given the phrase 'Saxonicos libros recitare' in the previous chapter, and the clearly temporal narrative marker heading ch. lxxvii, which describes the arrival

---

[13] *Asser's Life of King Alfred*, ed. Stevenson, ch. xxiv: 'which gathered in one book . . . he would carry about in his hand'.

[14] *Ibid.*, ch. xxii: 'Sed Saxonica poemata die noctuque solers auditor, relatu aliorum saepissime audiens, docibilis memoriter retinebat' ('But he was a careful listener to English poems by day and night, and hearing very often what was performed by others, held it easily in his memory.').

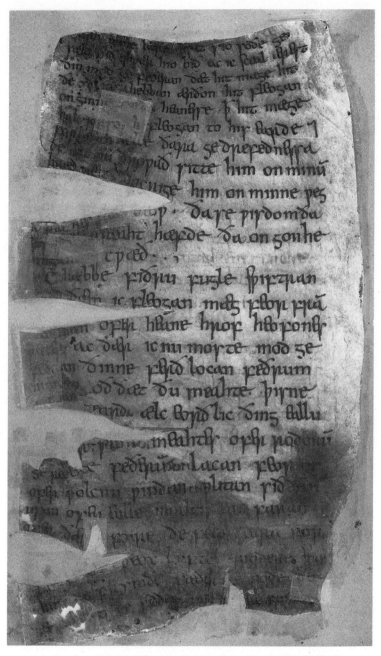

I London, British Library, Cotton Otho A. vi, 87v (Alfred's
translation of the *De consolatione Philosophiae*)

ratione caret · Nam si uti corporum languor ita ui ti
ositas quidam est quasi morbus animorum · cum aegros
corpore minime dignos odio · sed potius miseratione
iudicemus · multo magis non insequendi sed miserandi
sunt · quorum mentes omni languore atrocior urget
improbitas ·

QVID TANTOS IVVAT EXCITARE MOTVS ·
Et propria fatum sollicitare manu
Si mortem petitis · propinquat ipsa
Sponte sua uolucres nec remoratur equos;
Quos serpens leo · tigris · ursus aper ·
Dente petunt · idem se tamen ense petunt;
An distant quia diffidentque mores
Iniustas acies et fera bella mouent
Alternisque uolunt perire telis;
Non est iusta satis saeuitiae ratio;
Uis aptam meritis uicem referre ·
Dilige iure bonos & miseresce malis;

HIC EGO VIDEO INQVAM QVAESIT L FELICITAS VEL MISE
ria · in ipsis proborum atque improborum meritis
constructa · sed in hac ipsa fortuna populari · non
nihil boni maliue inesse ppendo; Neque enim sapi
entum quisquam · exul · inops · ignominiosusque · eo ·
malit · potius quam pollens opibus · honore reueren
dus · potentia ualidus · in sua pmanens urbe florere;
Sic enim clarius testatiusque sapientiae tractatur

II Oxford, Bodleian Library, Auct. F. 1. 15, 57v (*De consolatione Philosophiae*)

þe laðe ⁊þone annan heht golde

dan þone ðe grendel ær mane acwealde

swa he hyra ma wolde nefne him witi

god wyrd forstode ⁊ðæs mannes mod

god eallum weold sumena cynnes swa

nu git ded forþan bið andgit æghwær

selest ferhðes fore þanc fela sceal ᵹe

bidan leofes ⁊laþes seþe longe her on

ðyssum win dagum worolde bruceð þær

wæs sang ⁊sweg samod ætgædere fore

heal fdenes hilde wi san gomen wudu

greted gid oft wrecen · ðon heal gamen

hroþ gares scop æfter medo bence mæ

nan scolde finnes eaferum ða hie se

faer begeat hæleð healf dena hnæf

scyldinga in fres wæle feallan scolde

ne huru hilde burh hetwan þorfte ·

eotena treowe unsynnum weard be

loren leofum æt þam hild plegan beadnum

⁊bordwum hie on ᵹe byð hwurfon gare

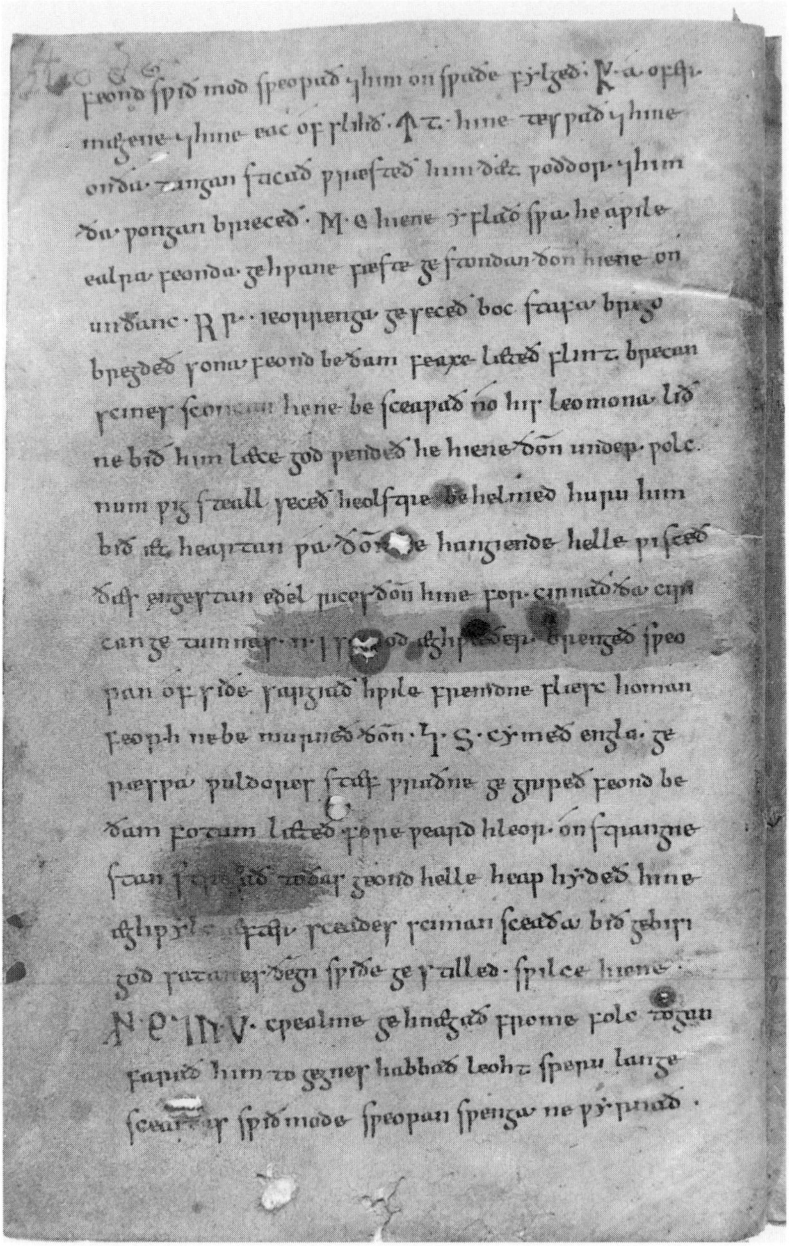

IV Cambridge, Corpus Christi College 422, p. 4 (*Solomon and Saturn I*)

V Cambridge, Corpus Christi College 41, p. 198 (*Solomon and Saturn I*)

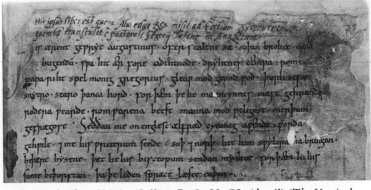

VIa Cambridge, Corpus Christi College 12, 3v (detail) (*The Metrical Preface* to Alfred's *Pastoral Care*)

VIb Cambridge, Trinity College R. 5. 22, 72r (detail) (*The Metrical Preface* to Alfred's *Pastoral Care*)

VII London, British Library, Cotton Tiberius A. vi, 32r (*The Battle of Brunanburh*)

VIII London, British Library, Cotton Tiberius B. i, 141v (*The Battle of Brunanburh*)

of his teachers (*at tunc*), we can only reconcile these phrases in one of two ways: either *legere* must be understood in a restricted sense (as Keynes and Lapidge suggest) as reading Latin, or *recitare* must be understood as referring to the general recitation of material found in books (which Alfred had previously had read to him) and not simply to reading aloud (as in ch. xxiii). In either case, Alfred's education here is aural.[15]

For all his emphasis on the king's continuing interest in learning and in educating his children and others at court, Asser nowhere indicates that Alfred was himself able to write, even though the biographer records that Alfred's children were taught to read *and* write (ch. lxxv). In fact, Asser's account of the famous *Enchiridion* shows that he (that is, Asser) himself copied the passages which Alfred directed: 'Cui, cum me, ut quanto citius illud scriberem, urgeret, inquam: "placetne tibi, quod illud testimonium in aliqua foliuncula segregatim scribam?"'[16] Asser then prepared a quire and in a short while filled it with passages Alfred chose. Eventually, the *Enchiridion* grew to the size of a 'psalter' (ch. lxxxix).

The two crucial scenes balancing Alfred, books and knowledge require further examination. In the first scene Alfred acquires knowledge by memorizing a book of verse, *illectus*, we are told (is this 'attracted' or 'seduced'?) by the beauty of the initial letter. The representation of Alfred is metonymic here, for the letter stands for the book, and Alfred is presented as a materialist. Alternatively, in the attempt to learn the book, Alfred becomes his own text. In either case Asser appears uncomfortable and devalues the king's achievement. Perhaps, as verse in English, the knowledge acquired by memorization was not good enough. In fact, Asser's delicacy about the verb 'to read' suggests that reading (in Asser's eyes) was to be done in Latin.

The second scene reveals less about Alfred than it does about Asser. Asser's acutely limited notion of literacy in this account has little to do with reading *per se* and much to do with Latin as the hieratic language of power. In Asser's view, the mother tongue needs no interpretation, and so in the first scene Alfred simply received the book from his mother's hands. In the climactic scene, however, conducted in the 'father' tongue, Alfred

---

[15] See also *ibid.*, ch. lxxxviii, for Asser's description of his own reading to Alfred.

[16] *Ibid.*, ch. lxxxviii: 'When he pressed me to write it out as quickly as possible, I replied, "Would it please you if I were to write the passage separately on another sheet?"'

receives instruction as Asser's pupil. [17] Asser's concept of his own power lies in his ability to read and write Latin and to guide the growth of his pupil. In Asser's account, the king's words come through Asser's mouth. Through Asser's writing, *Asserius de rebus gestis Ælfredi* at this point is actually an autobiography of *Asser* – his text, book, writing and ideology. And where is Alfred in this account? A man and a king at a transitional moment in the shift from orality to literacy, he does not write but orders Asser to do it for him. Alfred *wordum weold*.

Alfred's presumed inability to write is no reflection on the extent of his learning. After all, according to Einhard, Charlemagne, despite great learning in Latin and Greek, rhetoric and dialectic, could never master writing. [18] It is, however, an important reminder that Alfred's modes of acquiring and remembering information were essentially and primarily aural/oral. [19]

Formulaic Systems in the Metrical Preface

That Alfred could read is clear enough from Asser's evidence; that Alfred's little poem was committed to writing close upon its composition is a reasonable inference from the manuscript tradition. But the close analysis of Asser's language in his biography prohibits the commonly held

---

[17] The distinction between 'mother' tongue and 'father' tongue, where 'father' tongue is applied to Latin as the sex-linked language of the Middle Ages (and later) is Walter Ong's. See Ong, *Orality and Literacy*, pp. 112–15. See also his *Rhetoric, Romance and Technology*, pp. 113–41 and *Fighting for Life: Contest, Sexuality, and Consciousness* (Ithaca, NY and London, 1981), pp. 119–48.

[18] Asser was acquainted with Einhard's biography of Charlemagne and used its phrasing at several points (Keynes and Lapidge, *Alfred the Great*, p. 254, n. 139). He must have been aware, therefore, that Charlemagne could never master writing. As Einhard points out, Charlemagne came to the task too late in his life. See *Éginhard: vie de Charlemagne*, ed. and trans. L. Halphen, 4th ed. (Paris, 1967), p. 76 (ch. xxv): 'Temptabat et scribere tabulasque et codicellos ad hoc in lecto sub ceruicalibus circumferre solebat, ut cum uacuum tempus esset manum litteris efficiendis adsuesceret; sed parum successit labor praeposterus ac sero inchoatus' ('He also tried to write, and used to keep tablets and blanks in bed under his pillow, that at leisure hours he might accustom his hand to form the letters; however, as he did not begin his efforts in due season, but late in life, they met with ill success' (*The Life of Charlemane*, trans. S. E. Turner (Ann Arbor, MI 1960), p. 54)).

[19] By Bäuml's classification ('Varieties', p. 246), he was closer to quasi-literate than fully literate.

assumption that Alfred could write, and consequently, the associated inference that the *Metrical Preface* was composed 'pen in hand' is not allowable from the evidence we have. This is hardly to suggest that King Alfred was a 'singer'; that is unlikely in itself, and there is no evidence of longer narrative poems to temper its unlikelihood.[20] The open question of Alfred's writing, however, asks us to re-examine some of the assumptions and conclusions which have been made about the writing of the *Metrical Preface*.

In his admirable essay, which has been provoking response for the last twenty years, Larry Benson estimates that about 59 per cent of the *Metrical Preface* was 'formulaic'.[21] His survey of formulae (done without the help of the Bessinger and Smith *Concordance*) is necessarily suggestive, not complete. Since his definition of what qualify as relevant formulae is overly loose (allowing in evidence half-lines without similar metrical, syntactic or lexical content), his list actually obscures Alfred's use and adaptation of formulae from elsewhere in the corpus of Old English verse.[22]

A stricter definition of relevant formulae in the corpus is needed to clarify Alfred's generation of poetic formulae. I have therefore analysed the half-lines in the *Metrical Preface* within the larger context of formulaic systems in the corpus, generally following Anita Reidinger's redefinition of Fry's formulation of 'system'.[23] Only those lines which match Alfred's half-lines metrically and syntactically and which contain one or another of the stressed lexical items are allowable as evidence. This evidence divides into three main categories: (1) half-lines which are exactly duplicated elsewhere in the corpus (repeated formulae); (2) half-lines, with metrical

---

[20] Opland, *Anglo-Saxon Oral Poetry*, p. 156, correctly discounts legends of Alfred as a minstrel.

[21] Benson, 'Literary Character', p. 335, n. 8.

[22] For example, he includes different metrical types under the same formula, e.g., listing *Christ* 63b (b-verse) as an analogue of *Metrical Preface* 3b, a c-verse; and he allows as evidence half-lines with no semantic connection, e.g. *Andreas* 1424b *læston woldon* as an analogue of *Metrical Preface* 16b, *læste cuðon*.

[23] By traditional formulae I mean those half-lines which are found identically in other contexts throughout the canon. In distinguishing 'traditional formulae' from 'system', I use A. Riedinger's definition in 'The Old English Formula in Context', *Speculum* 60 (1985), 294–317, at 305: 'A system is a group of verses usually sharing the same metre and syntax in which one word, usually stressed, is constant and the other stressed word or words may be varied to suit the alliterative and/or narrative context.' Clearly, a 'traditional formula' would be a subset of a system. For earlier definitions of 'system', see D. K. Fry, 'Old English Formulas and Systems', *English Studies* 48 (1967), 193–204, at 203, and Niles, 'Formula and Formulaic System', p. 399.

and semantic conformity, containing at least one constant stressed word (lines with high lexical congruence); (3) half-lines, with metrical and syntactic conformity, having similar semantic content (lines with low lexical congruence). For the sake of completeness, a fourth category, half-lines with no known congruence, may be added, but it has only one member, *adihtode* (4a) (see the appendix to this chapter, pp. 96–107).

Examination of these categories provides information not only on Alfred as a poet but on the poem itself as the object of transmission. Because the copying of the poem is integral to the process of its realization, its formulae must be understood not merely as phrases memorable to poets, but also as phrases whose conventional and familiar shape would affect reading and copying, particularly in the 'formulaic' reading I have traced in Caedmon's *Hymn* and in *Solomon and Saturn I*. In the discussion which follows I consider the formulae and systems in the visual conventions of the modern edited text. Such a consideration is a practical preliminary to examining the various articulations of the poem in the manuscript records.

Four half-lines make up the first (and least interesting) category, repeated formulae. Most prominent among these are *dryhtnes cempa*, found also in *Guthlac* 727b, 901b and *Phoenix* 452b, and *rodra wearde* found in *Genesis* 169b.[24] *Rodera weard* (or an orthographic variant of it) forms the lexical freight of half-lines in *Genesis* 1b, 2119a, *Christ and Satan* 611a, *Christ* 134b, 222b and *Metres of Boethius* xi.20b. There are, as well, many half-lines in the corpus with the structure genitive + *cempa* or *weard*. Similarly, the half-line *ofer sealtne sæ* occurs in *Christ* 677a.[25] Bessinger and Smith's *Concordance to the Anglo-Saxon Poetic Records* reveals numerous combinations of *sealtne* with *mere*, *mersc* and *wæg*, as well as combinations of *sealt* with *ypa* and *sæstreamas*. The combination of *sealt-* with *sæ* in the other half-line is also common. Line 7a, *ðurh sefan snyttro* appears in *Christ* 442a, and *on sefan snyttro* in *Andreas* 1165a and *Elene* 382a. *Sefan* commonly alliterates with *snyttro* in the other half-line.

The second category, high lexical congruence, contains fifteen half-lines, each of which can be demonstrated to be part of a frequently occurring formulaic system in the larger corpus. In this category, Alfred demonstrates his ability to use conventional formulaic systems. One example of this formulaic type is *Metrical Preface* 9b, *romwara betest*. Half-lines with its structure (*romwara* + noun [nom. sg.]) occur in *Elene*

[24] *Rodra weardes* is found in Riddle 13, 7b.

[25] In *Metres of Boethius* xix.16a the formula occurs as *on sealtne sæ*.

62a, 129b and *Metres of Boethius* I.34a and IX.3a. The operative terms in 13a, *suð and norð*, appear widely as the alliterating parts of half-lines in *Widsið, Beowulf, Genesis, Daniel, Christ, Phoenix* and *Solomon and Saturn II.* The half-line *sendan meahte* (15a) is part of a formula structured by *sendan* + a modal in pret. 3 sg. (See *Christ* 129b, *Resignation* 24b, *Descent into Hell* 27b, *Psalm CVII.* 8, 4b.)[26] Line 3a, *iegbuendum*, belongs to a vast system in which the shared lexical item occupies the second stressed position: *X-buendum*. The most frequent formula within this system is *eorðbuendum*, a fact whose significance will emerge in examination of the text in Cambridge, Trinity College R. 5. 22.

The phrase *þis ærendgewrit* (1a), not surprisingly, appears nowhere else in the corpus, although *ærendgewrit*, a word Alfred also uses in the *Prose Preface*,[27] appears in *sende ærendgewrit* in *Metres of Boethius* I.63a. And *mærðum gefrægost* (10b) appears in *Metres of Boethius* XX.2b, *mærþum gefræge*. In fact, a fair number of phrases from the *Metrical Preface* appear in identical or similar versions in the *Metres of Boethius*.[28]

The greatest number of half-lines which exhibit low congruence with formulaic systems in the canon occur in the last part of the poem, 11a–16b. For this part, where the speaking book explains the circumstances of its translation and copying, Alfred was hard put to find analogous *traditional* formulae dealing with the matters he discusses so pointedly in the prose preface. His solution, in many cases, is to collapse two systems together. One example will clarify this practice. Line 13b reads *heht him swelcra ma.* Although there is no directly comparable system elsewhere in the canon, Alfred achieved his line by reforming two related systems, representatives

---

[26] In the same category are lines 5b, *ryhtspell monig* and 7b, *searoðonca hord.* The pattern for 5b is dissyllabic compound + *monig*. A partial listing of instances of this pattern includes: *Genesis* 1766a; *Maxims I* 15a; *Panther* 50b; *Ruin* 23a; *Beowulf* 776a, 838b, 1510b; *Metres of Boethius* I.3b. The pattern of 7b, *searoðonca hord* (genitive compound + *hord*), appears in *Christ* 1055a and *Psalm L* 151b.

[27] *King Alfred's West-Saxon Version of Gregory's Pastoral Care*, ed. H. Sweet, 2 vols., EETS os 45 and 50 (1871–2) I, 3 line 15.

[28] These are: *MP* 1a/*MB* I.63a; *MP* 2a/*MB* XIX.16a; *MP* 5b/*MB* I.3b; *MP* 9a/*MB* XI.20b; *MP* 9b/*MB* I.34a, *MB* 9:3, *MB* XXX.4b; *MP* 10b/*MB* XX.2b; *MP* 13a/*MB* X.13b. The *Regula pastoralis* was probably Alfred's first translation, and scholarly opinion places the translation of the *De consolatione Philosophiae* as his second. It is generally agreed that the Boethian *metra* were first translated into prose and that the verse version was made from the Old English prose; see D. Donoghue, 'Word Order and Poetic Style: Auxiliary and Verbal in *The Metres of Boethius*', *ASE* 15 (1986), 167–96, at 167.

of which are *heht his engel gan* (*Andreas* 365b) and *swa hit beorna ma* (Riddle 60, 16b), to provide him with a half-line conveying both command and a genitive noun + *ma*. At least one measure of Alfred's poetic ingenuity is the difficulty of reading we see witnessed in the realized texts.

The Manuscripts of the Metrical Preface

Four manuscripts survive which transmit complete texts of the *Metrical Preface* to the *Pastoral Care*: Oxford, Bodleian Library, Hatton 20; CCCC 12; Cambridge, Trinity College R. 5. 22, fols. 72–158; CUL, Ii. 2. 4. Two other manuscripts, badly burned in the Cotton fire, also once transmitted the *Metrical Preface*: BL, Cotton Tiberius B. xi + Kassel, Landesbibliothek Anhang 19 and Cotton Otho B. ii.[29] Junius's transcript of Tiberius B. xi (Oxford, Bodleian Library, Junius 53) provides a version of the *Metrical Preface* with variants from Otho B. ii and Hatton 20. Because Junius 53 is a post-medieval transcript, I have excluded it from discussion.

Dorothy Horgan has done a great deal to clarify the textual history and manuscript relationships of the surviving records of Alfred's translation of the *Regula pastoralis*. On the basis of certain scribal errors in Hatton 20, she infers that no extant copy derives from that manuscript (H); and her examination of south-eastern variants shared by Cambridge, Trinity R. 5. 22 (T) and CUL, Ii. 2. 4 (U)[30] leads her to suggest a 'common ancestor' with an archetype, perhaps, from Canterbury.[31] She further contrasts the common ancestor of T and U, a manuscript updated lexically and syntactically, with CCCC 12, a backward-looking, deluxe tenth-century copy with apparently archaized spellings.[32] These larger generali-

---

[29] These six manuscripts are described in Ker, *Catalogue*: nos. 324 (written 890–7); 30 (s. x²); 87 (s. x/xi); 19 (s. xi³/⁴); 195 (written 890–7); 175 (s. x/xi) respectively.

[30] 'U' is the siglum adopted by Horgan in her study of the textual transmission of the translation, 'The Relationship between the OE MSS', pp. 153–69. I use her sigla throughout. Dobbie's standard edition of the verse (ASPR 6) inexplicably omits the version of the *Metrical Preface* in CUL, Ii. 2. 4 (U). F. P. Magoun, 'King Alfred's Letter on Educational Policy According to the Cambridge MSS', *MS* 11 (1947), 113–22, notes the omission, but does not print the version. In the essay which follows, I discuss the relationship of the copy in U to the rest of the copies of the *Metrical Preface* in order to discuss the significance of its low lexical variance. This low lexical variance contrasts remarkably with the high variance in the patterns of pointing for each record of the poem.

[31] Horgan, 'The Relationship between the OE MSS', pp. 156–7.

[32] Horgan, 'The Lexical and Syntactic Variants', p. 221.

zations about the text of the translation offer some useful information about the descent and copying of the *Metrical Preface.*

Despite notable errors in the copying of the *Pastoral Care* in Hatton 20, at least by Scribe 1, the version of the *Metrical Preface* appears so clean that Dobbie used it without emendation for his edition of the poem, limited his editorial work to modernizing word division, capitalization and punctuation, and to providing an apparatus. The apparatus, unfortunately, is incomplete and misleading – incomplete since it lacks readings from U, and misleading since it notices word division in the manuscripts only in the case of an orthographic variant. My argument supplements the information in Dobbie's apparatus by examining the permissible graphic variants in the records of the *Metrical Preface* to illustrate the variations a reader had to cope with even in lexically stable texts.

While Hatton 20 is datable with unusual precision to 890–7, and is certainly the manuscript which Alfred had sent to Worcester, the precise place of its copying is less certain.[33] According to Ker, the manuscript was annotated by a hand of s. xi[in] (Wulfstan's hand?) as well as by the 'tremulous' hand.[34] Marks inserted by the 'tremulous' hand are easy to detect. There are, as well, a large number of points in black ink, which appear to have been inserted later and which often coincide with marks in CCCC 12, a manuscript at Worcester by the thirteenth century. When I examined the manuscript in both daylight and artificial light, the only marks of punctuation I could accept as genuine were the comma-shaped or wedged points which begin midway up the height of a low letter.

The *Metrical Preface* in Hatton 20, copied on 2v11–20, begins with a large capital initial thorn and is written in long lines across the writing space. There are two other capitals: The 'F' in *Forðæm* (8a) and the 'S' in *Siððan* (11a), which appear to divide the text into three statements.

---

[33] Parkes ('Palaeography of the Parker Manuscript', p. 160, n. 4) believes that the bifolium containing Alfred's letter 'may have been copied' at Winchester and added to the text of the translation, probably copied at Worcester. But if Ker is correct that the main scribe, after finishing his work, later wrote the *Metrical Preface* on the second verso of the bifolium, we are presented with the serious question: where did the exemplar of the *Metrical Preface* come from? See also Sisam, *Studies*, pp. 144–5, who, on the basis of the mismatched heading to the *Prose Preface* in BL, Cotton, Tiberius B. xi and in CUL, Ii. 2. 4, believes that the 'inclusion in the book itself of Alfred's famous letter to his bishops was an afterthought, made possible by the interval necessary to produce enough copies of the text' (p. 145).

[34] Ker, *Catalogue*, p. 385.

Within each statement are mentioned the achievements of an individual associated with the history of the *Regula pastoralis*. The first of these is St Augustine, who brought the text to England. The second is Gregory, whose authorship of the *Regula pastoralis* illustrated his spiritual gifts. The third is Alfred, whose translation and orders for making the book, the verses imply, were prompted by the weak Latinity of the clergy. Such graphic division seems quite remarkable, until we recall that the stop before *Forðæm* and its capital initial actually interrupts the lines devoted to Gregory. The points and capitals give us the text we have, to be sure, but we cannot discount the possibility that their placement before adverbs may have been mechanical rather than critical.

The only marks of punctuation which can be considered original occur (not coincidentally) before the interior capitals and thus reinforce the divisions noted above. These comma-shaped points occur following 7b (*hord*) and 10b (*gefrægost*), and heavy punctuation (:7 :7) ends the poem.[35] Aside from spacing, the only mark which sets these lines apart from the preceding prose preface is the initial capital thorn. No aspect of formatting – neither capitalization, pointing nor layout – distinguishes verse from prose. The quality of the copy, its close association with the king, who ordered it for Worcester, and the self-consciously literary verses, in which the volume is made to speak of Alfred's orders to 'writers' for copies, all argue that the presentation of verse in the *Metrical Preface* is neither casual nor accidental. 'Literary' or otherwise, Old English verse did not share the graphic hierarchy of Latin verses.

Two other early manuscripts of Alfred's translation contain the *Metrical Preface*: CCCC 12 and Cambridge, Trinity College R. 5. 22.[36] While these manuscripts are not far apart in date, they realize the text in significantly different fashions.

CCCC 12 is a deluxe copy of the *Pastoral Care*, but is in a slightly unfinished state, with chapter-headings and many capital initials having been omitted. The original mark of punctuation is a wedged point, in the black ink of the text, placed even with the line of writing. Its characteristic shape is the same as the scribe's dot over a 'y'. Occasionally a correctly

[35] There are possible light points after *Agustinus* (1b); *brohte* (2b); *ðorfton* (15b); and *læden-* (i.e. mid-word, 16a).

[36] Ker dates CCCC 12 (*Catalogue*, no. 30) to the second half of the tenth century, noting a Worcester connection by the presence of glosses in the 'tremulous' hand. The Trinity manuscript is somewhat later, dated to s. x/xi (*Catalogue*, no. 87).

shaped point appears whose ink may have flaked or faded. Terminal punctuation for chapters is :7 (a colon and a hooked comma). At least one other punctuator besides the 'tremulous' hand has been through the manuscript, and there are some small, dark, ill-shaped points throughout.

The *Metrical Preface* in CCCC 12 (3v11–4r1) follows the *Prose Preface* and is in turn followed by a list of chapter headings (see pl. VIa). Its only capital is an initial red eth in *ðis*. The verses contain seven original points and a terminal point (:7).[37] The 'tremulous' hand added a point in brown after 15a, and there are, as well, two erased points after 9b and 13b, whose origin is unclear. Of these, the only point occurring after an a-line precedes an '7'. It seems reasonable to infer from this information that the scribe preferred to point after a b-line, but it is also clear that he only provided such marks 50 per cent of the time. When viewed as a static array, the arrangement of points appears to follow neither a syntactic nor a metrical pattern. However, when considered as the product of a planned process, the points can be seen to have been positioned so as to mark what the scribe may have conceived as statements. In this process, the scribe pointed when he perceived a statement to have been concluded, even though in one case this left him with an outrageous fragment of left-over modifiers (9a–10b). Such an explanation would account for all but the point following 11b (*aelflfred cyning*), whose location eludes understanding. And the erased points at 9b and 13b may well represent errors perceived by the scribe and subsequently corrected. If this explanation is valid, then the record of the *Metrical Preface* which CCCC 12 transmits provides a different reading of the verses than does the record in Hatton 20, one perhaps process-oriented, although lexically the two records are very close.[38]

The scribe who wrote the *Metrical Preface* in Trinity College R. 5. 22 produced yet another, and a highly idiosyncratic, reading. The *Metrical Preface* begins with a large red capital thorn (72r), and there is one other capital in the poem, a black initial 'S' in *Seððan* (11a), before which the scribe placed a high point (see pl. VIb). The *Metrical Preface* here is more

---

37 These points occur following 2b, 5b, 7b, 8b, 10b, 11b and 12a. The point after 13b is highly questionable.

38 The scribe was not especially careful with separation of words. It is interesting to note that the 'tremulous' hand, though familiar with Old English, found the separations and joins difficult, and marked the text to divide the words 'correctly'. This habit may indicate the degree of information needed to be supplied by native speakers/readers.

heavily pointed than that in CCCC 12, and even less predictable.[39] Original points occur after both a- and b-lines, but also occur in the middle of three half-lines: within 12a, 13a and 14a. Placement of points cannot be satisfactorily accounted for by postulating either a syntactic or a metrical system.

The serious anomalies begin with 11a. Put another way, the scribe's difficulties only start in that part of the poem which he has defined as a separate section by placing a high terminal point after 10b and beginning 11a with a capital 'S'. This portion of the poem contains several difficult and atypical half-lines, prominent among them being 11a, 12b and 14a. Beginning with 11a the scribe writes continuously 'Seððan me on englesc ælfræd cynincg awende'. There are at least two ways to understand how the scribe was reading these lines. The first is a 'metrical' explanation. The *me* which follows *Seððan* is a variant reading. Both Hatton 20 and CCCC 12 read *min*. However, study of the formulaic systems upon which Alfred was drawing shows that this pronoun is an anomaly in that position, and so either the scribe of Trinity or of his exemplar supplied the expected accusative form.[40] The scribe provided no point between 11a and 11b which might indicate where he understood the caesura to be. If we are to understand the point after *awende* as a metrical statement, then the scribe must have understood *ælfræd* as part of 11a, which is technically possible if the line is read as hypermetric.[41] Such a reading leaves *cynincg awende* as the following half-line, and although metrically possible, it lacks appropriate alliteration.[42] It also leaves *worda gehwilc* as 12a, unsatisfactory but possible, supported analogously by several readings from the *Metrical Psalms*.[43] There is, as well, a conceivable metrical explanation for the point

[39] The scribe points following: 1b, 2a, 2b, 3a, [4a], 4b, 6a, 6b, 7a, 7b, 8b, 9a, 10a, 10b, 12a [mid-half-line], [12a], 13a [a punctus elevatus at mid-half-line made by adding a later virgule to the original point], 13a, 14a [mid-half-line], 14a, 15a, 15b and 16b. All points are placed in the middle of the line of writing save the point following 10b, which is a full distinctio preceding the capital 'S'. The preface concludes with a simple terminal point. Several letters in red have been erased following *cupon* (72r9).

[40] CUL, Ii. 2. 4 also reads *me*. Since both T and U share a common ancestor (Horgan, 'The Lexical and Syntactic Variants', p. 221), it is possible that this variant stems from the ancestor. It is also possible that both T and U independently supplied the much more common accusative form.

[41] Compare *Beowulf* 2996b. See Pope, *Rhythm of Beowulf*, p. 125.

[42] A similar half-line occurs in *Andreas* 538b (*cyninc wyrðude*), but it is a rare form.

[43] See, for example, *worda þinra*, *Paris Psalter* CXVIII.15, line 2b, CXVIII. 32, line 1b, CXVIII.138, line 4a, CXVIII. 160, line 1b; and *worda æghwylc*, *Paris Psalter* CXVIII. 167, line 2b.

following *sende* (13a). Line 12b is technically poor, since it places *writerum*, the word carrying alliteration, in secondary position. The scribe promotes *writerum* to first stressed position by adding *sende* to the half-line. Once again, the scribe avoids pointing the caesura, obviously because no metrically acceptable arrangement of what remains of the line is possible. But again, in 13b he fills out a peculiar b-line by adding a verb, this time *brengan* from 14a.

There is an alternative explanation for what is going on in the pointing of these lines. The scribes of both Trinity R. 5. 22 and CUL, Ii. 2. 4 write a capital initial for *Siðð an*, which suggests that the capital was in their common ancestor. However, unlike his colleague, the scribe of Trinity places a high point before the capital, a choice which implies that the scribe considered there to be a clear break between what preceded and what followed the combination of capital and point. In fact, if we ignore for a moment what we know to be the case, namely that 11a–16b are indeed verse, the scribe appears to have pointed these lines as prose, very much in agreement with his practice of pointing in the translation of the *Regula pastoralis*, where he points by clause. In any case, the scribe's comprehension of the metrical scheme wavers when Alfred's verse becomes less traditional. Where it is highly traditional, the scribe of Trinity has no difficulty with it. This explanation is beautifully illustrated by a variation which he alone introduces into the text: for *iegbuendum* (3a) in all other records, Trinity reads *eorð/ bugendu{m}*. Of the many possible variations on the system X(x)-*buend/a/e/ra/um*, by far the most common in the corpus of extant verse is *eorð buendum*.[44] The scribe of Trinity has given us the kind of syntactic and metrically appropriate variation which we have seen to be prominent in the records of *Caedmon's Hymn*, *Soul and Body* and *Solomon and Saturn I*.

CUL, Ii. 2. 4 is the last of the manuscripts which transmit the *Metrical Preface*. It shared a common ancestor with Trinity College R. 5. 22, as an analysis of their common variants in the translation of the *Regula pastoralis* has indicated,[45] but CUL, Ii. 2. 4 exhibits some independence from the Trinity manuscript in its transmission of the *Metrical Preface*, and the scribe is certainly much closer to the pointing practice of CCCC 12 than to that in Trinity R. 5. 22. The scribe writes a large, careful squarish script, which

---

[44] I count twenty-nine instances listed in the *Concordance to the Anglo-Saxon Poetic Records*, ed. Bessinger and Smith.

[45] Horgan 'Lexical and Syntactic Variants', pp. 213–21.

Ker attributes to the third quarter of the eleventh century and places 'almost certainly at Exeter'.[46] The *Metrical Preface* begins after a space following the end of the *Prose Preface* on 6v. The text begins with a large, initial capital eth in faded orange, and there are two other capitals, a small black capital 'A' for *Agustinus*, and a much larger black capital 'S' for *Siððan*. The only mark of punctuation is a point placed slightly above the line of writing. Although a post-medieval hand has provided an interlinear gloss for the prose and poetic prefaces, there seems to have been no contemporary Anglo-Saxon meddling with the text. The points are all scribal.

There are eight points within the *Metrical Preface* and a terminal point. While the scribe seems to prefer pointing after the b-line (2b, 5b, 7b, 9b, 10b and 16b), he points as well at 12a (before $_7$?) and at 13a, all of which puts his pointing closer to that of CCCC 12 than Trinity College R. 5. 22. However, to complicate matters, the scribe points after *sende* in mid-line (13a), and although the point is slightly crowded, it is nonetheless original. This is, however, the only pointing anomaly which CUL, Ii. 2. 4 shares with Trinity R. 5. 22. Although both manuscripts agree against Hatton 20 and CCCC 12 by reading *beþorftan* for *þorftan*, CUL, Ii. 2. 4 agrees with Hatton 20 and CCCC 12 by reading *egbugendum* where Trinity reads *eorðbugendum*.[47] CUL, Ii. 2. 4 has its own peculiarities, however. It adds *for þam he* to the beginning of 13b and omits *Gregorius* (6a).

CONCLUSIONS

The *Metrical Preface* is most widely known in Dobbie's 1942 edition in the Anglo-Saxon Poetic Records. With its imposition of modern presuppositions about the meaning of space, the purpose of graphic cues, the nature of 'word' or even of 'text', it gives us a readable text, although it does not give us Alfred's composition, nor even that of Hatton 20. Its redaction of the *Metrical Preface* gives us a text *we* can read, but hides from us the manuscript records, at once both objects for reading and evidence of the process. We should, I believe, want more than that.

The text of a poem exists in actuality only when realized in writing. For the *Metrical Preface* there are four such early realizations extant, and each presents an individual version and a reading. Why is Hatton 20 not enough

---

[46] *Catalogue*, no. 19.

[47] The shared reading *beþorfton* probably stems from the 'edited' ancestor of T and U. See Horgan, 'Lexical and Syntactic Variants', pp. 215–16.

for us? The pragmatic, editorial answer is that the full range of manuscripts shows us errors, or potential for error, in copying. The more important, contextual, answer lies in our current interest in the signs of literacy. The apparent lexical stability of the *Metrical Preface* is only one feature of the poem in the context of its culture. A reading of the four manuscripts together shows us in Trinity's *eorðbugendum* the impress of the same oral 'reading' which made such a mark on Caedmon's *Hymn*. The scribal variations and hesitancies in these manuscripts reveal unease with Alfred's hybrid formulae, indicative in turn of disappointed scribal expectations. We can also see that the visual cues in the manuscripts, particularly capitals and points, did not travel with this Old English poem but are, rather, signs of individual reading. A poem is both the product of thought and the producer of thought. To understand it in its fullest historical dimensions requires not only study of the circumstances of its composition but study as well of those means by which it acts in the world, its realized texts. Their visual information encodes important evidence of the nature of medieval literacy.

APPENDIX

Formulaic systems in the *Metrical Preface* to Alfred's *Pastoral Care*[1]

I REPEATED FORMULAE

2a: ofer sealtne sæ
　　x (x) sealtne X

ofer sealtne sæ	3 Chr 677a
on sealtne sæ	5 MB 19 16a
ofer sealtne mersc	1 Exo 333b
on sealtne mersc	5 P106:33 2a
geond sealtne wæg	1 Dan 322b
þurh ?sealtne ?weg	2 And 1532a [MS þurh scealtes sweg]
on sealtne wæg	3 Whl 27b
ofer sealtne mere	6 Mnl 103a[2]

---

[1] The short titles for Old English poems are those used in Bessinger and Smith, *Concordance to the Anglo-Saxon Poetic Records*, pp. xiii–xv. Punctuation marks are used to mean the following: a semi-colon (;) separates individual poems in a list, while a comma separates line numbers within an individual poem (e.g. 1 Gen 25a; 4 Bwf 414a, 1015b). A pipe (¦) indicates that those citations listed after the pipe show some variant spelling from the form attested in the left column. A slash (/) distinguishes among the appearance of cases. For example:

> drytnes domes/e/as　　3 Chr 1021a; 3 Phx 48a ¦ 1 Gen 2573a/ 4 Bwf 441a/ 1 Gen
> 　　　　　　　　　　　　2584a ¦ 1 Dan 32a, 744a; 1 Xst 505a, 553a

Dryhtnes domes appears in 3 Chr 1021a, 3 Phx 48a and 1 Gen 1573a, but the latter exhibits a different spelling (here *drihtnes*). *Dryhtnes dome* appears in 4 Bwf 441a only, and *dryhtnes domas* is attested by the last five, once again with a difference in spelling. The comma separates multiple line references within a single poem (e.g. 1 Dan 32a, 744a).

[2] Semantic matrix: it is interesting to note the collocations of *sealtne* with *sæ* outside the confines of the formula: 1 Exo 333b alliterates *sealtne* with *sæwicingas*; 1 Dan 322b alliterates it with *sæfaroða*. Outside this system, *sealt*( ) and *sæ*( ) or *sæ-* are collocated frequently: *salte sæstreamas* 2 And 749a and *sealte sæstreamas* 2 And 196a (*sæ* is undisputed, *streamas* is an emendation); 5 P95.11 3a; *sealte sæwegas* 1 Dan 383a. *Sealt*( ) alliterates with *sæ* (± cmpd) in 1 Exo 442, 1 Exo 473; 5 P77.15 1; 5 P79.11 2.

4b: dryhtnes cempa[3]
   *d*ryhtnes X x (x) or
   X (x) cempa   [examples limited to nouns]

dryhtnes cempa	3 Glc 727b, 901b; 3 Phx 452b
drihtnes ærist	6 Mnl 58a
drihtenes are	6 LP2 98a
drihtnes hælu	5 P95.2 3b
drihtnes handa	1 Gen 2671b
drihtnes domes/e/as	3 Chr 1021a; 3 Phx 48a ¦ 1 Gen 2573a/ 4 Bwf 441a/ 1 Gen 2584a ¦ 1 Dan 32a, 744a; 1 Xst 505a, 553a
dryhtnes dreamas	3 Glc 123a
dryhtnes duguþe	3 OrW 48a ¦ 1 Gen 1205a
drihtnes egesan	5 P134.22 1b
drihtnes geongran	1 Gen 450b
dryhtnes geryno/e/u	2 Ele 280b/ 3 Chr 41b; 3 Glc 1121b/ 6 SFt 117b
drihtnes gesceafta	5 MB20 213a
dryhtnes lare	6 SFt 139b
dryhtnes mines	3 Glc 1067a
dryhtnes meahta/um	6 SnS 229b ¦ 6 Pra 53b/ 3 Phx 499b ¦ 1 Gen 218b; 1 Xst 230b; 5 MB20 209b; 5 MB29 35b
drihtnes modor	6 Mnl 169a
dryhtnes onsien	3 Chr 1650b
dryhtnes ðecelan	6 SnS 420b
drihtnes stefne	5 P94.8 1b
drihtnes spræce	5 P106.10 1b
dryhtnes swyðre	5 P117.16 1b
drihtnes þænne	6 Jg2 124b
drihtnes þances/as	6 MCh1 38b/ InC 174a
dryhtnes welle	6 PCE 24b
dryhtnes willan	3 Jln 602a ¦ 1 Gen 142b; 5 P94.8 3b
Cristes cempa/n	2 And 991a; 3 Glc 153a/ 6 SnS 139a
wuldres cempa/n	3 Glc 324b/ 558b, 688b
Geata cempa	4 Bwf 1551b
deofla cempan	3 Chr 563b
meotudes cempan	3 Glc 576a; 3 Phx 471b ¦ 3 Jln 383b
cyninges cempan	5 MB20 73a

[3] Of the many formulae with *dryhtnes* + noun, twice as many are b-lines as a-lines.

7a: þurh sefan snyttro
    x sefan snyttro

þurh sefan snyttro	3 Chr 442a
on sefan snyttro	2 And 1165a; 2 Ele 382a[4]

See also:

þurh snyttro cræft	2 Ele 374a ¦ 1 Dan 594b
þurh snyttro geþeaht	2 Ele 1059a
on sefan gehygdum	3 Glc 473a

9a: rodra wearde[5]
    rod( )ra weard(e, as, es)

rod( )ra weardes/e/as	3 R13 7b/ 1 Gen 169b/ 6 Jg2 300b

2 LINES WITH HIGH LEXICAL CONGRUENCE

With repeated word in first stressed position

2b: suðan brohte   [both stressed]
    suðan X (x) or
    X x (x) brohte

suþan bliceð	3 Phx 186b
suþan scineð	4 Bwf 606b
suþan cymene	6 SFt 87b
[þæt þe suþan com	6 SFt 92b, type B]
modor brohte	1 Gen 1213b, 2771b
liðend brohte	1 Gen 1472b
wæstmas brohte	1 Gen 1560b
idese brohte	1 Gen 1720b
eowic brohte	2 And 259b
cwene brohte	2 Ele 1129a
Gabriel brohte	3 Chr 336b
dumba brohte	3 R59 8b
sona brohte	6 P50 120b

3b: swa hit ær fore
    x x *ær* X x   or
    x x X fore

[4] Verses in which *sefa*( ) appears with *snyttr*( ): 1 Dan 84a, 485; 2 And 554; 3 Glc 473; 4 Bwf 1726.

[5] *Rodera* (*rodora*) + *weard* are part of numerous b-lines (e.g. *nu is rodera weard* (3 Chr 134b). To my knowledge, *wearde sygora* (6 InC 110a) is the only other a-line. Gen. noun + *wearde* is most common in b-lines.

With ær as first stress and alliterating syllable

With noun as second stress:

ond þær ær fela	3 Glc 143b
þeah þu ær fela	3 Jln 192b

See also:

forðon he ær fela	4 Bwf 2349b
ðe hit ær dwæsca	InC 234b

With verb as second stress:

þe we ær cuðon	1 Gen 357b; 3 Jln 75b
þæt we ær drugon	1 Xst 253a
þe we ær drugon	3 Chr 615b
þe hie ær drugon	4 Bwf 15a, 831b, 1858b
swa he ær dyde	1 Gen 1840b; 1 Xst 116b, 278b, 523b; 4 Bwf 1891b
þæt hio ær dyde	5 MB13 79b
swa ic ær dyde	4 Bwf 1381b
þæs ðe ær dyde	1 Gen 2266b
þe hi ær dydon	5 P72.15 3b
swa þu ær dydest	4 Bwf 1676b; 6 ECL 63b
þonne þu ær dydest	3 Jln 542b
þe me ær lærdon	5 P118.99 1b
swa þu ær myntest	1 Xst 688b (double alliteration)
ðe we ær nemdon	1 Xst 382b; 5 MB20 196b
hu þu ær wære	3 Chr 216a (double alliteration)
se þu ær wære	5 P101.24 1b
þa þe ær wæran	6 EgD 6b
þeah hie ær wæron	2 Ele 1117b
þe hit ær wisson	5 MB28 19b
þær hi ær wiston	3 DHl 12b
þe hi ær worhtan	5 P134.20 1b
þe mec ær wrugon	3 R2 15b

See also:

swa heo mec ær dyde	3 Jln 634b
swa hie oft ær dydon	4 Bwf 1238b
þe he þe ær dyde	5 P102.2 2b ¦ 6 F102.2 3b
bute him ær *cume*	5 MB18 10b
butan ðu ær cyme	2 And 188b
þe ic ðe ær nemde	5 MB25 62b
þe ic ðe ær sæde	5 MB25 60b

oððe her ær swefan	6 Wld1 31b
þæt he ær þon wæs	3 Phx 379b

With fore *as the second stress*

þær him [*r*une] fore	2 Ele 1261b
þe us *b*ec fore	3 Glc 528b
ond no *m*earn fore	4 Bwf 136b
gif him *w*an fore	5 MB5 4a
See also:	
þe ic a*d*reag fore þe	3 Chr 1475b
þæt his *s*oð fore us	3 Glc 764b
and him *w*epan fore	5 P94.6 3a

Collocation of *æ*r *and* fore

þara þe he sið oððe ær fore		6 MPD 26a
and him wepan fore	ðe us worhte ær	5 P94.6 3
þe ic ær fore sægde		3 Pnt 34b

While there are many instances of a system x x æ **X** x or x x **X** fore, it is clear that there is no other formula of that type in the canon. Further, in the instances of the system x x ær **X** x, the second stress is usually on a verb. With *fore* as second stress, the first stress is usually a noun. Alfred's half-line has neither, but combines two systems. Do we applaud his 'flexible use' of formulae or condemn him as incompetent for being unable to use what was to hand?

8a: forðæm he monncynnes
    x (x) he *m*oncynnes

ac he mancynnes	4 Bwf 2181a
þæt he moncynnes	1 Gen 1631a

8b: mæst gestriende[6]
    *m*æst x **X** x or
    X gestriende/s

mæste hæfde	1 Gen 1631b
mæste cræfte	4 Bwf 2181b
worn gestrynde	1 Gen 1220b
ær gestryndes	6 ECL 23b

---

[6] Judging from the 79 instances of *mæst* (with all its homographs), it is fairly unusual to have *mæst* (acc. n.) separated from its genitive by the caesura.

Note the collocation in two highly 'traditional' poems:

ac he mancynnes	mæste cræfte	4 Bwf 2181
þæt he moncynnes	mæste hæfde	1 Gen 1631

9b: romwara betest [both stresses]
 *r*omwara X (x)
 X (x) x x betst

romwara cyning	2 Ele 62a, 129b; 5 MB9 3a
romwara bearn	5MB1 34a
lastworda betst	3 Sfr 73b
beaduscruda betst	4 Bwf 453a
magistra betst	5 MB30 4b

10a: monna modwelegost
 *m*onna X x x x

monna ærest	1 Gen 1085b
monna leofost	1 Gen 1328b, 1749a ¦ 3 Jln 84a
manna mildost	1 Exo 550a
manna swiðost	5 MB26 55a[7]

13a: sende suð and norð
 x x *s*uð x (x) norð (Pope's B10c)

simle suð oþþe norð	3 Wds 138a
þætte suð ne norð	4 Bwf 858a
þæt eow suð *oððe norð*	5 MB10 24b

Compare (with *sendan*):

eastan sende	4 Jud 190b[8]

14a: brengan bi ðære bisene
 X x x x (x) X (x) x

broht from his bysene	1 Gen 680a

See also:

ealra þara bisena	3 Glc 528a
brohte to ðys burnan	6 PCE 28a

15a: sendan meahte
 *s*endan X x or
 X x meahte

---

[7] Note that none of these formulae is a d-line. *Modwelegost* (in all degrees) is unique.

[8] For the collocation of *suð* and *norð* see also: 1 Gen 807a, 1988b; 1 Dan 52b; 3 Chr 884b; 3 Phx 324b; 6 Sns 261b.

sendan wolde	3 Chr 129b; 3 DHl 27b
sendan wylle	3 Rsg 24b
sendan þence	5 P107.8 4a[9]

With repeated word in second stressed position

1a: þis ærendgewrit
    x X x x X   (Pope's type B2, 32)

sende ærendgewrit	5 MB1 63a
þurh fyrngewrito	2 Ele 155a
þa þe fyrngewritu	2 Ele 373b
ymb fyrngewritu	2 Ele 560b
þætte fyrngewritu	3 Prc 67b
?forð fyrngewritu	3 Prc 73a [a useful emendation from fyrn forð gewri tu!]

Compare:
    frod fyrngewritu   2 Ele 431a

See also in various formulae:

ærendbec	1 Dan 734a
ærendgast	1 Gen 2298a
ærendraca/n	6 Crd 12b/ 1 Gen 2436a; 6 Jg2 287a
ærendspræce	3 R60 15b
ærendsecg	1 Gen 658a

3a: iegbuendum
    X x -buend -um
                -ra

ceasterbuendum	4 Bwf 768a
egbuendra	6 EdD 37a
eorðbuendum	1 Gen 1636a, 1685a; 1 Dan 564b; 1 Xst 1b; 3 R29 8b; 5 P118.130 3b; 5 MB26 94a, MB29 71b; 6 Crd 21a
eorðbugende	2 instances
eorðbuendra	10 instances
eorðbuende	8 instances
feorbuende	6 SnS 280b

---

[9] Infinitive + *mihte, mehte, meahte*: 1 Gen 270b; 1 Exo 189b; 1 Dan 84b, 168b; 2 And 477b; 4 Bwf 207a, 511b, 571b, 656b, 1140b, 2954b; 5 P72.13 2a; 5 P91.3 2a; 6 Mld 14b; 6 SFt 164b; 6 MCh3 16b; 2 And 929b; 4 Bwf 1496b; 1 Gen 417b, 608b, 2343b; 2 And 272b; 2 DrR 18b; 2 Ele 160b, 1158b; 3 Glc 486a, 1159b; 3 Jln 570b; 3 Wan 26b; 3 R5 11b; 4 Bwf 542a, 780b, 1078b, 1561b, 1919b, 2770b, 2870b; 5 MB7 10b.

foldbuendum	3 Aza 24b; 4 Bwf 309b; 5 MB8 4b; 6 Crd 22b; 6 PCE 2b + 9 instances in other cases
grundbuendra	4 Bwf 1006a; 6 Sns 289b
herbuendum	5 MB29 60b + 2 instances in gen pl.
igbuende	6 Mnl 185a
landbuendum	4 Bwf 95b + 1 instance in np
londbuendum	3 GfM 29b; 3 Wds 132b; 4 Jud 314a
londbuende	3 OrW 80b
londbuendra	3 R95 11a
sundbuendum	3 Chr 221b
sundbuende	5 MB8 13b, MB 24 21b, MB26 48b
þeodbuendum	3 Chr 616b, 1371b
þeodbuendra	3 Chr 1172b
weoruldbuendum	5 MB27 27b
weoruldbuende	5 MB8 35b
woruldbuendra	4 Jud 82a; 5 MB29 81b[10]

5b: ryhtspell monig
    X x monig

leofspell monig	2 Ele 1016b

See also:

ealdspell reahte	5MBP 1b
wilspella mæst	2 Ele 983b[11]

7b: searoðonca hord
    searoðonca/um X or
    X x x (x) x hord

searoþoncum slog	3 Jln 494a
searoþoncum gleaw	3 R35 13b
hreþerlocena hord	3 Chr 1055a
balaniða hord	6 P50 151b

11b: Ælfred kyning
    X (x) x cyning

Neron *cynincg*	5 MB15 2a
Hiorogar cyning	4 Bwf 2158b
Hreðel cyning	4 Bwf 2430b

---

[10] Of all these half-lines, the most prominent is *eorðbuendum*, with 9 + 20 members. Note that *eorðbuendum* is the variant in T.

[11] Other examples of dissyllabic compounds with *monig* are: 1 Gen 1766a; 3 Mx1 15a; 3 Pnt 50b; 3 Rui 23a; 4 Bwf 776a, 838b, 1510b; 5 MB1 3b.

[Her] Æþelstan cyning	6 Brb 1a[12]
[Her] Eadmund cyning	6 CFB 1a
Eadmund cyning	6 CFB 13b

16a: ða ðe lædenspræce
    x x X x spræce

on glypspræce	4 Bwf 981a
on teosuspræce	5 P139.11 1b
ne to tweospræce	3 Prc 90b

Compare:

sohte hetespræce	1 Gen 263b
æfenspræce	4 Bwf 759a
ærendspræce	3 R60 15b
edwitspræce	2 And 81a; 5 P88.44 1b
fyl nu frumspræce	1 Dan 325a
fyl nu þa frumspræce	3 Aza 42a

16b: læste cuðon
    X (x) x cuðon   or
    læs (x) X (x) x

ealle cuþan	3 Chr 422b
wise cuðan	5 P118.79 3b
fæderas cuðon	2 And 752b; 2 Ele 398b
?minne cuþon	4 Bwf 418b
læs gefremede	4 Bwf 1946b

3 LINES WITH LOW LEXICAL CONGRUENCE

1b: Agustinus

Agustinus	6 Mln 97b

5a: Rome papa
    X x X x

Rome bisceop	2 Ele 1051b
godne papan	5 MB1 42b
[swa hie gebrefde us beorn on Rome	
Gregorius gumena papa	6 SFt 45–46]
[from Romana rices hyrde	
Gregoriæ gumena papa	6 SFt 93–94]

---

[12] *Her* is metrically irrelevant. See J. C. Pope, *Seven Old English Poems*, 2nd ed. (New York and London, 1981), p. 58.

6a: Gregorius
   Gregorius/æ   6 SFt 46a/ 94a

6b: gleawmod gindwod
   X x (x) X x
   gleawmod gongan   3 Glc 1002a
   gleawmode guman   1 Dan 439a

See also:
   gieddade gleawmod   3 Phx 571a[13]

10b: mærðum gefrægost
    *mæ*rþum x X x   or
    X (x) x gefrægost
    mærþum gefræ*ge*   5 MB20 2b
    mærðum gemeted   2 Ele 870a
    hæleðum gefrægost   1 Exo 394b

11a: siððan min on englisc
    siþþan x x (x) X (x) x
    {with resolution after short syllable – like Pope's A7 with alliteration on
    second stress}

    siðþan me on hreþre   3 R61 5a
    siððan he on fære   1 Gen 2380a
    siððan he mid wuldre   1 Exo 86a
    siþþan he for wlence   3 Glc 208a
    siþþan he on westenne   3 Glc 935a
    siþþan he me fore eagum   3 Glc 1254a
    siþþan heo of lichoman   3 SB2 21a
    siþþan ic þurh hylles   3 R15 27a
    siþþan he me of sidan   3 R77 6a
    siðþan he under segne   4 Bwf 1204a
    syðþan he on waruðe   2 And 240a
    syððan ðu mid mildse   2 And 1674a
    syððan ic ðe on worulde   2 Sb1 43a
    syððan ic ana of ðe   2 SB1 55a
    syþðan he for wlenco   4 Bwf 1206a
    syðþan he hine to guðe   4 Bwf 1472a
    syþðan he æfter deaðe   4 Bwf 1589a
    syððan ic on yrre   4 Bwf 2092a

---

[13] The three instances of *gleawmod* (other than that in the *Metrical Preface*) all alliterate with *god*, either in the other half-line or by double alliteration.

syððan ic for dugeðum	4 Bwf 2501a
syððan hi on worlde	5 P57.3 2a
syþþan hi on Selmon	5 P67.14 2a
syððan hi on fore	5 P104.33 2a[14]
{siððan hi*m* on bogum	1 Exo 499a (Irving's reading/ emendation)]

12a: awende worda gehwelc[15]
    (x) X (x) *w*orda x (x) or
    x (x) X (x) x gehwylc

spræc worda worn	2 And 904a
onwrige worda gongum	3 Glc 1161a
sægde eaforan worn	3 Prc 66b
scyle gumena gehwylc	3 Chr 820b
biþ storma gehwylc	3 Phx 185b
flyhð yfla gehwylc	3 Phx 460b
worþeð anra gehwylc	3 Phx 503b
scyle monna gehwylc	3 Sfr 111a
sceal ?þeodna gehwylc	3 Wds 11a
hæfde anra gehwy*lc*	5 MB26 95a
hafað tungena gehwylc	6 SnS 232a
hafað orda gehwylc	6 Sns 233a
ac sceal *wuhta* gehwilc	5 MB11 52a
sceal monna gehwilc	1 Gen 2319b

12b: ond me his writerum[16]
    x x x X (x) X

and me on teonan	1 Gen 892b
ond þu me mid þy heardan	2 SB1 31a

---

[14] Only seven of these contain dative or accusative pronouns, and only two (including Irving's emendation) have the pronoun in the oblique case alone. There appears to be no other instance with the genitive construction, a fact which may explain the shift to *me* in T and U. See Mitchell, *Syntax*, V. 2, item 3959, separation of elements; q.v. *Beowulf* 1703.

[15] Compare *þæt þu mec onwende / worda ðissa* (3 Jln 57) which Benson inaccurately cites. The half-line is neither semantically nor metrically appropriate.

[16] This line and 14b are poor compared to verse in *Beowulf*, in that they violate the 'rule' that in the off-verse the first of the two stressed syllables must alliterate and the second must not (Pope, *Rhythm of Beowulf*, p. 102). Three examples relevant to lines 12b and 14b (which Pope cites) are *The Battle of Maldon* 45b, 75b, 288b. *Maldon*, celebrating events of 991, is obviously a late poem.

me þæt sylfe	3 R4 10b
þas ic me on frofre	5 P118.50 1a
ac me to sange	5 P118.54 1a
and me to frofre	5 P118.76 2a
and ða me on ece	5 P118.144 2a
and me þin swyðre	5 P137.7 6a
and me on nihte	5 P138.9 3a
and me þine domas	6 F118.175.2a

13b: heht him swelcra ma
    heht hi(-m, -s) X (x) x X   or
    x x (x) X (x) (Genitive) ma

heht him fetigean to	1 Gen 2667b
heht his engel gan	2 And 365b

Compare:

heht nu sylfa þe	3 HbM 20b
þær bið wundra ma	3 Chr 988b
ond mines cnosles ma	3 R18 4b
swa hit beorna ma	3 R60 16b
þæt us andgytes ma	5 P73.8 3a

14b: ðæt he his biscepum
    x x x X x x [Pope's type A-3, 80b (which occurs only in the on-verse)

See also:

þær bisceopas	2 And 607a
to bisceope	2 Ele 1056a
to þam bisceope	2 Ele 1072a
æt þam bisceope	2 Ele 1216a

15b: forðæm hi his sume ðorfton
    x x x x X x X x   or
    forðam (þon) pronoun pronoun X x (x) X x

forðan ðu on ðrymme ricsast	6 KtH 40a
forþon he his bodan sende	3 Chr 1151a
forþon ic þas word spræce	3 Rsg 83b
forþon hi dome hlutan	6 Mnl 192b

4 LINES WITH NO KNOWN CONGRUENCE

4a: adihtode: no known analogue

5

Poems of the *Anglo-Saxon Chronicle*

The complex of texts known as the *Anglo-Saxon Chronicle* preserves in its four earliest manuscripts some six poems on royal events, though not all manuscripts transmit all six. [1] The poems' low variance in transmission and their connection with events affecting the West Saxon royal house invite comparison with the circumstances of the transmission of the *Metrical Preface* to Alfred's translation of the *Regula pastoralis*. Unlike the *Metrical Preface*, however, these poems cannot be ascribed to identifiable authors, and they offer remarkably little information on the facts of their composition. Though sharing transmission in the *Chronicle*, they share little else. Whatever their origins, these poems differ widely in quality, metrics and the circumstances of their preservation. But their preservation in four manuscripts of differing age and locale provides another perspective on techniques and habits of reading and writing Old English verse. They bear witness to the influence of residual orality on the reading and transmission of poetic works and on the development of graphic conventions for the writing and layout of Old English verse.

The poems of the *Anglo-Saxon Chronicle* survive in four manuscript records ranging in date from the mid-tenth to the late eleventh century. CCCC 173, fols. 1–56 (s. ix/x–xi^2) given, perhaps unjustly, pride of place

---

[1] I omit from consideration here MS G, the burnt BL, Cotton Otho B. xi (*Catalogue*, no. 180: Winchester, s. x^{med}–xi^1) as well as its sixteenth-century copy, BL, Add. 43703. In Ker's opinion (*Catalogue*, p. 233), the copy of the *Historia ecclesiastica* in Otho B. xi was copied by the scribe of the *Anglo-Saxon Chronicle* for the years 925–55 in CCCC 173. This is also the scribe of BL, Royal 12. D. XVII (for verse see fol. 125, a charm). Ker dates the hand of the remains of the *Chronicle* (hand 2) to xi^1. On version G, see *Die Version G der angelsächsischen Chronik*, ed. Lutz, pp. xxvii–l. The E-version (Oxford, Bodleian Library, Laud 636) supplies prose summaries for the verses of 937, 942, 973, 975 and 1065.

as A, transmits the four tenth-century poems, *The Battle of Brunanburh*, *The Capture of the Five Boroughs*, *The Coronation of Edgar* and *The Death of Edgar* (entries for the years 937, 942, 973 and 975) in two hands.[2] BL, Cotton Tiberius A. vi, fols. 1–35 + Tiberius A. iii, fol. 178 (B) (s. x^2), the earlier of the two manuscripts traditionally connected with Abingdon, transmits these same poems in one hand of s. x^2.[3] BL, Cotton Tiberius B. i, fols. 112–64 (C) (s. xi^1–xi^2), also associated with Abingdon, preserves, in addition to the four tenth-century poems, *The Death of Alfred* (1036) and *The Death of Edward* (1065), the first five poems in one hand (up to the annal for 1048, 119r–158r14) and the sixth in another.[4] The final manuscript to be considered here (D), BL, Cotton Tiberius B. iv, fols. 3–86 and 88–90 (xi^{med}–xi^2), the 'Worcester' Chronicle, transmits the poems for 937 and 942 in a single hand (Ker's hand 2) and those for 1036 and 1065 in two other hands.[5]

[2] See Ker, *Catalogue*, no. 39. The number of scribes at work on manuscript A is a matter of vigorous debate. For a convenient summary of the arguments see *ASC: MS A*, ed. Bately, pp. xxi and xxxiii. According to Ker, the first two poems are in 'a handsome fluent hand of s. x^{med}'. Dumville (*Wessex and England from Alfred to Edgar*, ch. 3) would further specify a date in the range 947 × 955/6 for the activity of the scribe of 26–27v (annals 924/5–955, his scribe 3). The second two poems are in the last hand, whose stint from 973–1001 makes x–xi^1 the terminus a quo. Dumville argues (ch. 3) that this scribe gives 'a contemporary's account of 1001' (in other words, the limits of this entry are 1001 × 1012–1013 when G was copied).

    The years marking entries in A have undergone considerable revision. The entry for *The Battle of Brunanburh* was originally copied against 938 and a minim was erased at some later stage (G reads 938). The entry for *The Capture of the Five Boroughs* was originally copied against 942, then corrected by erasure to 941, and finally augmented by a second 942 in another hand. The entry for *The Death of Edgar* was originally dated 984 and then corrected by another hand to 975. See *ASC: MS A*, ed. Bately, pp. 70, 73 and 76–7.

[3] Ker, *Catalogue*, p. 249 (no. 188), dates the writing of the *Chronicle* in Tiberius A. vi to between 977 and 979, since the *Chronicle* (all in one hand of a 'fluent Anglo-Saxon minuscule') ends in 977 and the regnal years of Edward the Martyr (*ob.* 978) are absent from the accompanying genealogy. The genealogy is now in BL, Cotton Tiberius A. iii, fol. 178. Simon Taylor (*ASC: MS B*, p. xxiii) dates B to 977 × 1000, but favours a time earlier in the period.

[4] Ker, *Catalogue*, esp. p. 253 (no. 191). An edition of C by A. Healey is in preparation as vol. 5 of *The Anglo-Saxon Chronicle: A Collaborative Edition*. At present the only printed edition is H. A. Rositzke, *The C-Text of the Old English Chronicle*, Beiträge zur englischen Philologie 34 (Bochum-Langendreer, 1940).

[5] Ker, *Catalogue*, no. 192, esp. p. 254, would date hand 2 somewhat before 1050. The verses on the death of Alfred (70r) are part of quire 9, supply leaves which Ker dates to the 1070s or 1080s. Presumably, hand 3 (whose stint is interrupted by the supply leaves) is

Until fairly recently, the provenance of each of the four manuscripts transmitting the poems of the *Anglo-Saxon Chronicle* was generally agreed upon. A was considered to have originated at Winchester and to have been at Christ Church, Canterbury at least by the late eleventh century, when the main scribe of BL, Cotton Domitian viii, fols. 30–70, made his annotations.[6] Since Plummer's edition, B and C have been associated with Abingdon, mainly on the basis of the annal entry for 977 in both manuscripts and on additional entries in C connecting that manuscript with Abingdon.[7] The close relationship between B and C has long been recognized, though the particulars of that relationship have not always been agreed upon.[8] D has been associated variously with Worcester and Evesham.[9]

In a broad assault on the received view of the provenance of the Parker Chronicle (CCCC 173), David Dumville challenged the attributed locale not only of that manuscript, but also of a chain of related manuscripts used to support the case for a Winchester origin for A.[10] While he does not

---

earlier than that. Manuscript D has a brief prose entry for 973 and short rhythmical entry for 975.

[6] Parkes, 'The Palaeography of the Parker Manuscript of the *Chronicle*', p. 171, states that the manuscript moved from Winchester to Canterbury 'at about the time when Bishop Ælfheah was translated from Winchester to Canterbury in 1005'. On the identification of the hand of Domitian viii with the interpolations in CCCC 173, see Ker, *Catalogue*, p. 187. See also F. Magoun, 'The Domitian Bilingual of the *Old English Annals*: the Latin Preface', *Speculum* 20 (1945), 65–72.

[7] Plummer, in *Two Chronicles* II, lxxxix, places *B (his gamma), the common source of B and C, at Abingdon. Taylor, *ASC: MS B*, p. xi, suggests Abingdon as the probable origin of B. Hart, 'The B Text of the *Anglo-Saxon Chronicle*', argues that the B-text was compiled probably at Ramsey between May 977 and 18 March 978 and is Byrhtferth's autograph. He further argues that Byrhtferth composed the poem for 973 and that the compiler had access to the A-text, either at Winchester or at Ramsey (pp. 288–95).

[8] Plummer, in *Two Chronicles* II, lxxxvii–lxxxix, postulated a common source for both manuscripts. A. Campbell (*Battle of Brunanburh*, pp. 1–7) argues that the entries for 925–77 represent a second continuation of the Chronicle (*Con.*[2]) and that B and C are copies of the original *Con.*[2] sent to Abingdon. D. Whitelock, however, raised the question of a more complicated relationship between B and C on the basis of the entries in C for 652–945 (*Anglo-Saxon Chronicle*, ed. Whitelock, pp. xiii–xiv). On the most recent approaches to this controversy by C. Hart and S. Taylor, see below, note 13.

[9] Plummer, in *Two Chronicles* II, lxxv–lxxvii.

[10] Dumville, *Wessex and England from Alfred to Edgar*, ch. 3, forthcoming. Dumville's argument is in direct disagreement with that of Parkes, 'Palaeography of the Parker Manuscript'. But see *ASC: MS A*, ed. Bately, p. xxxiii, for a middle position.

supply an alternative locale for the writing of the manuscript (and for the origin of either its exemplar or the so-called 'common-stock'), his critique of the Winchester case offers a refreshing view of the manuscript and its relative importance. Dissociating A from a necessary connection with Winchester effectively removes the manuscript and the version it transmits from the mythology of an Alfredian origin, which the text is unable to sustain. And Dumville's careful examination of the dating of the various hands of this manuscript of the *Anglo-Saxon Chronicle* reminds us that the case for privileging the A-version of the *Chronicle* is not easily supportable.[11] Finally, his examination of hand and dating gives interesting evidence about the development of Anglo-Saxon Square minuscule as a canonical script in the period 930–90.[12] Although Dumville does not consider it, another development may be seen in the visual distinction of a specifically English script. The *Chronicle* poems offer evidence to suggest the appearance of analogous 'canonical' punctuation and conventional formatting to accompany the development of this self-consciously Insular script.

Even if there is no longer a consensus on the Abingdon provenance of Cotton Tiberius A. vi and Cotton Tiberius B. i, the manuscripts were, nonetheless, almost certainly together at some point.[13] Although Cotton Tiberius B. i (C) is the later manuscript by some fifty to seventy years, textually the two versions are so close as to suggest that for large sections of the *Chronicle* they shared an exemplar: for the annals 945–77 they are

---

[11] For example, the copying of the verse-entries for 973 and 975 in B was done much closer to the events themselves than was the copying in A.

[12] See D. N. Dumville, 'English Square Minuscule Script: The Background and Earliest Phases', *ASE* 16 (1987), 147–79, at 163–5.

[13] In a radical departure from the consensus position, C. Hart, 'The B Text', would place B at Ramsey, where (he argues) Byrhtferth compiled the manuscript in 977/78, working, at least in part, from A (pp. 243, 294 and 295). Hart's arguments are too particular and complex to consider here in full. In summary, however, for that portion of the *Chronicle* containing the verses for 937, 942, 973, and 975, Hart claims the following: that B depends on A for the entries from 934–58; but that 'paradoxically' A depends on B for the entries for 971–5. He further argues that the scribe of C modelled his text chiefly on B, but also had available A and the Mercian Register. Hart's bold thesis rests on some delicate evidence. For the purposes of arguing habits of reading and formatting, I follow the more conservative position of Taylor (*ASC: MS B*, p. xxxvii), who argues the hypothesis that B was C's exemplar up to 652, that B and C shared an exemplar from 653 to 946, and that C once again used B as its exemplar from 956 to 977. See below, pp. 125–6.

111

especially close. The close textual affinity of B and C against A or D provides a useful control for the study of textual variation and manuscript pointing. If, for example, textual analysis urges the conclusion that at some points B and C shared an exemplar, then variations in pointing between them indicate either the individual scribe's freedom to alter punctuation or the difference in scribal convention at a given scriptorium over time. If, on the other hand, C used B as its exemplar, variations in pointing (given a relatively stable text) may suggest a shift in scribal convention. The records of the *Chronicle* in CCCC 173 (A) and in Tiberius B. iv (D), separated widely in date and probably in provenance as well, provide other sorts of information on variance and pointing early and late in the period.

These four manuscripts of the *Chronicle* poems offer an unmatched opportunity to examine the reading and writing of Old English poetry. The manuscript records of Caedmon's *Hymn* offered various sorts of evidence – scripts of different dates and provenance, a highly variant text with suggestive variations, graphic treatment of one text as adjunct to another – all of which illustrate the oral legacy of the illiterate poet's poem not quite fixed by writing. In marked contrast to the marginal existence of most of the records of Caedmon's *Hymn*, the poems of the *Anglo-Saxon Chronicle* have the same textual status as the prose entries of the *Chronicle*. The poems are the entries for their years and are formatted in precisely the same way as the prose entries. Each entry begins with an annal number[14] and a capital 'H' for *Her*, and is written in long lines across the writing space. While there is some variation in the text of these poems, we do not get the extent of variation characteristic of Caedmon's *Hymn* or *Solomon and Saturn I*. If there is a contextual reason for this lower variance, then the textual status of the poems of the *Chronicle* (in terms of the literacy it represents) is different in kind from that for Caemon's *Hymn* or *Solomon and Saturn I*, and this difference may be indicated by the level of conventional graphic cues in these verses. Certain combinations of manuscripts will be useful to examine: B and C against A and D; C against B for 937 and 942 and separately for 973 and 975; C for 1036 against its practice for the earlier four poems; C for 1036 and 1065 against the version in D. In the change of hand, scriptorium and date of copying, some sense of developing practice will emerge.

[14] On the missing annal-numbers of B, see *ASC: MS B*, ed. Taylor, p. xxxvi.

VARIANTS AND FORMULAIC READING

The four manuscripts of the *Anglo-Saxon Chronicle* just discussed present four different realizations of the *Chronicle* poems. Each one arises from a specific time and place in history; each is unique in its genesis (that is, the circumstances which gave rise to and affected its production) and unique in its effect (that is, as the realized text which is called forth, read, interpreted, altered by subsequent readers). [15] This point is especially important for the *Chronicle* poems in view of the way they have been handled by modern editors. This handling has been controlled by two complementary critical and editorial procedures, the first which effectively separates *The Battle of Brunanburh* from the other poems of the *Chronicle*, the second which bases editions on CCCC 173. The editorial privileging of the A-version, perhaps more accurately described as the selective privileging of the A-version, resulted from decisions made and repeated under the rubric of philologically scrupulous optimist editing. [16] Nonetheless, such editorial and critical decisions have serious consequences for our own idea of the *Chronicle* verses, both as poems and as cultural objects, and they have substantially affected our perception of the evidence which the *Chronicle* poems offer for the development of literacy in Anglo-Saxon England. [17]

[15] One important variable here is context, i.e. that *Brunanburh*, a poem essentially about West Saxon events, appears quite naturally in A, at least for the later years of the *Chronicle* most probably a Winchester production, but has a different political setting in D, probably a Worcester (Mercian?) manuscript with a northern interest. Along a similar line, the material surrounding the A-text of *Brunanburh* is ecclesiastical in nature. In the other versions it is more political. The A-version has been worked over in Canterbury and 'modernized' by the addition of metrical punctuation. A corrector (perhaps the punctuator) also emended what he considered to be blemishes, by making metrical alterations (the addition of 7 in 56a (7 *eft hira land*) and spelling changes (*cul bod ge hnades* has *vel cumbel* lined up over the separate syllables of *cul bod*). There is also the argument from silence: E has no entry for 937 and a prose entry for the death of Anlaf in 942. Lacking an entry for 973, D and E have a shorter version of the poem for 975.

[16] On the term 'optimist', see Boyle, 'Optimist and Recensionist', p. 264.

[17] Caedmon's *Hymn*, *Soul and Body*, and Exeter Riddle 30 have each been edited in separate editions: Caedmon's *Hymn*, because it occurs in Northumbrian and West Saxon dialects; *Soul and Body*, because its two versions occur in different manuscripts. *Solomon and Saturn* appears in both forms in Menner, *Poetical Dialogues*. This editorial treatment provides modern visual reminders of the multiplicity of these poems. The univocal edited form of the *Metrical Preface* and the poems of the *Anglo-Saxon Chronicle* hides evidence both of

Of all the *Chronicle* verse, *The Battle of Brunanburh* has been most frequently edited.[18] While the *Chronicle* poems all deal with events affecting royal persons, *The Battle of Brunanburh* seems to have attracted interest because of its subject and its epic style. Battles, it would appear, raise interest which coronations and obits do not. To understand the consequences of extracting the annal for 937 from its context in the *Anglo-Saxon Chronicle* it is necessary to examine afresh the context which modern scholarship has given to the separate work, *The Battle of Brunanburh*.

The Battle of Brunanburh was given its more or less definitive modern shape by Alistair Campbell in his 1938 edition. Campbell's thorough edition provided a philological and historical introduction, consideration of the four surviving manuscripts (A, B, C and D) and of Plummer's analysis of the genesis of the various recensions of the *Chronicle*, an edited text, a diplomatic text and a reconstruction of the readings contained in the burnt BL, Cotton Otho B. xi (G). He summarizes the basis of his editorial approach: 'in constructing a critical text of the *The Battle of Brunanburh*, we shall give the poem in the oldest form possible by following the text of A as regards spelling, while emending the lines where A is obviously corrupt. To make B or C the basis of the text, owing to their superior readings in a few places, is not to be recommended. A offers a greater number of those archaic and dialectal forms, which must go back to *Con.*[2], if not to the poet.'[19]

While Campbell's method of editing is optimist in choosing one

their individuality and of the development of literacy which they represent. Ironically, however, it is this form of editing which dominates our conceptualizing about the shape of an Old English poem, not the substantial evidence from the significant variants of Caedmon's *Hymn*, *Soul and Body* and *Solomon and Saturn*.

[18] The earliest printed edition is that of A. Wheloc in his 1643 edition of the *Historia ecclesiastica* in which he also printed selections from the *Anglo-Saxon Chronicle*. Wheloc used Cotton Otho B. xi (G) but made some corrections from A. He consistently capitalizes what he construes as proper names and rearranges the spacing of free morphemes to fit his own conception of 'word'. In Greenfield and Robinson, *A Bibliography of Publications on Old English Literature*, *The Battle of Brunanburh* occupies pp. 16–19 with its own entry; the other 'Chronicle Poems' are listed together on pp. 206–7 with a reference to *Brunanburh*'s separate entry. For a list of editions up to about 1941, see Dobbie, ASPR 6, clviii–clix.

[19] *Brunanburh*, ed. Campbell, p. 13. These sentiments are strikingly similar to W. W. Greg's dicta on accidentals and substantives in the choice of copy text for early modern editions, quoted in McGann, *Critique of Modern Textual Criticism*, pp. 25–6.

manuscript for a base text, its results are nonetheless idealist, since the end-product is the reconstruction of a version which is unlikely ever to have existed. Indeed, his removal of *Her* from 1a essentially abstracts the work from its context in the *Chronicle*, implying that the edited version of *Brunanburh* represents a state for the poem prior to its insertion in the original text of the *Chronicle* for 937. This editorial procedure 'rescues' the poem from history, while at the same time inventing an alternative history for it. Campbell chooses the A-version for archaisms and dialect and then emends to improve lexical choice or to correct copying error. An alternative editorial decision, to choose the B- or C-text on the basis of its lexical readings and then attempt a mixture of dialect forms possible around 937, would strike us as eccentric, at the least. On what basis, one might object, would an editor choose archaic or dialect forms to reproduce with any confidence a poetic koiné? The same objection might well be raised about the basis on which an editor would choose between semantically, syntacti- cally and metrically correct alternative lexical readings in a highly conventional formulaic poem. Both decisions do violence to an existing realized text in favour of producing a version more faithful to a hypothetical original. But this kind of faithfulness, in attempting an historically based reconstruction which would move us closer to an authorial text, ironically removes us from evidence documenting the reception of the surviving realized texts of that work. In lieu of presenting us with the work in the world, idealist editing delivers a remade, transcendent text, readable and clarified, but rendered silent about its context and contemporary effect.

Campbell's 1938 edition strongly influenced the edition most famil- iar to students of Old English, that of Dobbie in The Anglo-Saxon Poetic Records. Dobbie explicitly bases his choice of manuscript on Campbell's argument,[20] although he punctuates and emends at some different points.[21] Pope's practice in *Seven Old English Poems* is recensionist rather

---

[20] Dobbie, ASPR 6, xxxvii and n. 1.

[21] With three exceptions, Campbell's punctuation tends to be a bit lighter than Dobbie's up to about the middle of the poem. Then it tends to be slightly heavier. The exceptions are: Campbell prints a semi-colon after 7a, reading the following *swa* as an adverb. Dobbie prints a comma and subordinates the following clause. Campbell makes a new sentence at the beginning of 12b. Dobbie separates 12a and 12b by a comma. Campbell places a colon after 40a; Dobbie has a semi-colon. The following list records different readings in the two editions: Campbell: *om. Her*, 1a; Campbell, *dunnade*, 12b: Dobbie, *dænnede*; Campbell, *eargebland*, 26b: Dobbie, *æra gebland*; Campbell, *flotena*, 32a: Dobbie, *flotan*; Dobbie, *hilderinc*, 39a: Campbell, *hildering*; Campbell, *mecga*, 40a:

than optimist, and in this student edition, Pope makes scores of changes in normalizing the language to a form of Early West Saxon.[22] Well at the other end of the spectrum are the recent 'semi-diplomatic' editions of A and B of the *Chronicle* in David Dumville and Simon Keynes's ongoing collaborative edition of all the *Chronicle* records, which modernizes punctuation and capitalization, word division, paragraphing and layout.[23] For the verse, this has additionally involved breaking the long lines into modern verse format.

VARIATIONS AND REALIZED TEXTS

Whatever the demonstrably valuable contributions of idealist textual editing,[24] it cannot help but hide various kinds of reading activity done by those who have reproduced the poem and produced its realized texts. Certainly, scribal activity is carefully scrutinized in the course of making an edition, but generally in this process, scribes are 'good' if they are 'careful' and copy faithfully. And they are 'poor' if they are 'careless' and introduce 'errors' into the text. But once the 'errors' are identified and purged from the final edition, the scribe may be safely forgotten, and the record of his (or, indeed, her) peculiarities relegated to the foot of the page in an apparatus. Forgotten too are the numerous marks of punctuation and capitalization which may constitute evidence for separate readings of the poem in question. In the argument which follows, I deliberately turn my back on two common assumptions of modern editing of medieval verse: that the only version of a poetic work which has any claim to authority or attention is the authorial version (another way of confirming the notion that there are only two sorts of readings, correct and erroneous) and that the punctuation, capitalization and word division of the realized texts which survive have small claim to our attention.

There are several sources of variation within the copying tradition of the

Dobbie, *mæca* [both emend]; Campbell, *befylled*, 41a: Dobbie, *gefylled*; Campbell, *on Dingesmere*, 54a: Dobbie, *on Dinges mere*; Campbell, *eft Ira land*, 55a: Dobbie, *eft Iraland*; Campbell, *hremge*, 59b: Dobbie, *hremige*; Campbell, *hræ*, 60b: Dobbie, *hræw*; Campbell, *hasupadan*, 62b: Dobbie, *hasewanpadan*. (I omit to note where both editors make the same emendation.)

[22] *Seven Old English Poems*, ed. Pope, pp. 5–8 and 54–60.
[23] See *ASC: MS A*, ed. Bately, pp. 70–2 and *ASC: MS B*, ed. Taylor, pp. 51–3.
[24] For an admirable discussion of the merits of such editing, see Patterson, *Negotiating the Past*, pp. 77–113.

Chronicle poems. The simplest of these are the kind of mechanical, visual lapses in copying which produce eyeskips, homoeoteleuton, dittography and the like. Other variations occupy the shadowy territory between visual and verbal substitutions.[25] The most interesting variation, however, asks us to reconsider the notion of divergence as 'error' in copying and think, instead, of its presence as a symptom of participatory reception and reading.

Let us begin with the shadowy variations, significantly present in the late D. At 5b and 39a in the edited text, D transmits variants which are metrically acceptable, lexically defensible and, in terms of an 'authorial' version of the poem, probably wrong. These variants tell us something about the careful scribe of this portion of D, and I should argue that they also tell us something about the process of reading Old English verse which had developed by the mid-eleventh century.[26] The first of these interesting variants is in 5b, *bordweal clufan*. Both B and C read *bordweall*. A separates the free morphemes at the end of a line and reads *bord/weal*. D also separates the free morphemes at the end of the line but reads *heord/weal*. Now alliterative constraints argue that *bord-* is licit and *heord-* is not. But that does not necessarily mean that *heord* is simply the product of an unclear 'b' in the exemplar. More likely, the scribe scanned the morpheme **bord* and by a process of feature recognition registered an ascender and an 'rd' combination. The more familiar form *heord*, 'care', 'custody' or 'guard', with various ecclesiastical overtones, then appeared.[27]

The reading of D for 39a (*har hilderinc*) is difficult to explain. D reads *hal hylde rinc* with an accent over *rinc*. D regularly separates free morphemes, so the separation of *hylde* and *rinc* is probably not significant (nor is a regular pattern discernible in the use of accents in D). This spelling of **hilde* seems to have produced a compound whose meaning can only be inferred from the analogous *hyldemæg*, 'dear kinsman'.[28] But this reading is an excellent illustration of D's lack of 'formulaic' thinking. *Har hilderinc* occurs as an a-line in *Beowulf* 1307a, 3136a (*rinc* conjectured); *Maldon* 169a; and *An*

---

[25] See, for example, R. M. Ogilvie, 'Monastic Corruption', *Greece and Rome*, 2nd ser. 18 (1971), 32–4, at 33. See also Timpanaro, *The Freudian Slip*, pp. 19–28 and 155–71.

[26] Ker dates the work of scribe 2 to the mid-eleventh century, 'perhaps somewhat earlier than 1050' (*Catalogue*, p. 254).

[27] See T. N. Toller, *An Anglo-Saxon Dictionary Supplement*, rev. A. Campbell (Oxford, 1972), p. 535a, meaning IV.

[28] See Bosworth and Toller, *An Anglo-Saxon Dictionary*, p. 581b.

Exhortation to Christian Living 57a. In fact, it is the only formula with *hilderinc* in the nominative singular. *Hal* is probably not a visual error. But *hal* is found in numerous social and religious contexts (as the list in Bosworth and Toller testifies). This case, combined with the reading *heord* for *bord*, suggests that D not only did not think formulaically, but was also generally unfamiliar with heroic verse.[29] Although sense can be made of the readings at 5b and 39a, they are also, obviously, readings which came at the end of a tradition. In both cases the variant readings, though syntactically and metrically licit, are lexically inappropriate, taken rather from a daily or a religious context than from the word-hoard of heroic convention.[30] These readings must be distinguished from the record of the poem's earlier 'formulaic' variants.

Another class of variant, which editors have similarly relegated to the apparatus as having no authority, deserves careful consideration in terms of the kind of conventional variation which we have seen in Caedmon's *Hymn*. These variations appear in *Brunanburh* 13a, 18a, 26b, 40–42, 56a and 67a.

Let us begin with the variants of *Brunanburh* 13a, *secgas hwate/secga swate*. The first of these, *secgas hwate*, is the reading which appears in A. The other three manuscripts read *secga swate*. On the basis of the logic of external evidence, the agreement of BCD against A should define the reading in A as incorrect.[31] Crawford, who emends A with the reading in BCD, defends the emendation as well on the basis of internal evidence, i.e. evidence of a grammatical, lexical or metrical nature, showing that *secgas hwate* is metrically weak, although the type of line is not unprecedented.[32] In stylistic terms, the *Beowulf* poet seems to prefer *hwate* in first position, but *Beowulf* 3028a does combine *secg* with the weak adjective in a c-verse, *swa se*

---

[29] I should argue that D's reading of 20a, though not simple, is a visual error. For this half-line, A reads *werig wiges sæd*. B has *werig wiggessæd* and C *werig wigges sæd*. D provides the variant *werig wiges/ræd*. Little sense can be made of **wigesræd*, probably merely the result of a Square minuscule 's' misread as an 'r'. At 63a the scribe of D makes the same mistake and corrects it. The eyeskip at 35a suggests that the scribe of D heard *flod* as *flot* while he wrote it.

[30] Possibly D's variant, *eald inwuda* (46a) really is 'old in the wood'.

[31] See Patterson, *Negotiating the Past*, pp. 80–3.

[32] Campbell, *The Battle of Brunanburh*, pp. 99–100. In fact, *secgas hwate* conforms to Pope's short A1 type (*Rhythm of Beowulf*, p. 333), which in *Beowulf* is confined to the b-verse.

secg hwata.[33] As Janet Bately notes, the reading in A is possible, if the preceding half-line (the vexed and vexing *feld dæn'n'ede*) is understood parenthetically.[34]

In modern criticism on *The Battle of Brunanburh*, *secga swate* has been preferred by editors and scholars as a metrically and aesthetically attractive reading.[35] But the reading comes only at the price of a vexed interpretation for *dæn'n'ede/dynede/dennade/dennode*, whose meaning, generally accepted to be 'resounded', produces an odd synaesthesia.[36] In fact, it would appear that the *Chronicle* manuscripts transmit alternative versions of 13b–14a. BCD offer *feld dennade* (D: *dennode*) / *secga swate*, and A (G) another with *feld dæn'n'ede* (G: *dynede*) / *secgas hwata*. The occurrence of *secga swate* in three manuscripts (even discounting C as a copy of B or B's exemplar) argues that the scribes writing *dennade* accepted the necessity of a dative phrase following the verb in 13b. However, the only other formulaic occurrence of *swat* in the dative singular appears at *Genesis* 986b, where *swate* is the dative object of the preceding *swealh* (985b). At least at our present stage of knowledge, *dennade* (or *dennode*) is problematic, as Campbell's analysis of the modern attempts to gloss the word has shown.[37] If (as Campbell claims) *dennade* cannot be demonstrated to mean 'grew moist', then it may be emended to *dunnade* ('became dark') or *ðanode* ('became wet'). Or *dennade* may be read as a Kentish formation for *dynede*, a choice which provides the synaesthetic reading.[38]

Whatever the 'correct' reading, the surviving alternative readings indicate that the verb was rare and difficult. The original was transmitted in one of two ways: (1) *d-nede* (A and G); and (2) *d-nnade* (B and C) (D has *dennode*). The first was presumably intransitive, leading to the interpretation of 14a as appositive. The second was transitive, either governing the

33 See *Beowulf* 1601a, 2052b, 2517a, 2642a, 3005b, 3161a and *Elene* 22. On the possibility of a strong adjective in post-position, see Mitchell, *Old English Syntax* I, §126–7.

34 *ASC: MS A*, ed. Bately, p. cx.

35 F. C. Robinson, 'Lexicography and Literary Criticism: A Caveat', in *Philological Essays: Studies in Old and Middle English Language and Literature in Honour of Herbert Dean Meritt*, ed. J. L. Rosier (The Hague and Paris, 1970), pp. 99–110, at 107.

36 For an interpretation of the consensus position, see J. Harris, '"Brunanburh" 12b–13a and Some Skaldic Passages', in *Magister Regis: Studies in Honor of Robert Earl Kaske*, ed. A. Groos (New York, 1986), pp. 61–8, at 61.

37 Campbell, *The Battle of Brunanburh*, pp. 100–2.

38 C. T. Berkhout, '*Feld dennade* – Again', *ELN* 11 (1974), 161–2, at 162, n. 4.

dative or requiring a complementary instrumental phrase. The editorial choice of *secga swate* as the 'correct' phrase either requires emendation of the preceding verb or interpretation of the synaesthetic image as a Norse borrowing. Our choices are either a contorted reading with correct metre (and the appeal of an 'original' image) or a relatively accessible meaning with weak (but licit) metre.

The two other significant instances where A stands alone against BCD occur at 56a and 26b. In the first of these, BCD agree in the reading *eft ira land* (CD *yra*).[39] The scribe of A wrote *eft hira land*, a weak D4 type, and a later corrector inserted ⁊ to produce a b-line with vocalic alliteration.[40] While it seems fairly clear that this variant was influenced by a misunderstanding of *ira* in 56a, the reading of 26b, *ofer æra gebland* (B *ofer eargebland*; CD *ofer ear gebland*), shows a different source of variation.

Janet Bately has described this particular variation as an example of a tendency she sees in the A-version 'to replace poetic diction and structure by prose expressions'.[41] However, a look at the appearance of the simplices *ea- (ær-)* and *geblond* in half-lines elsewhere in the corpus suggests that her judgement is not entirely fair here. The compound *eargeblond* appears only once more, in the *Metres of Boethius* VIII.30a, *ofer eargeblond*.[42] *Andreas*, however, offers a half-line analogous to the reading in A, *aryða geblond* (532a), and Exeter Riddle 3 uses *eare geblonden* to describe a storm.[43] These instances suggest that the simplices are no less acceptable than the compound in the formulaic description of an angry sea, and that the variants on *Brunanburh* 26b show a legitimate example of formulaic reading.

In terms of consequential variation in *Brunanburh*, B stands against ACD in three suggestive instances. Two of these involve a variance in affix, the other a variant word. At 42a, B reads *forslegen ætsace*; ACD read *beslagen æt sæcce* (with some orthographic variance among them). This variant cannot be understood apart from its context in 40b–42a. A and D agree in reading *he wæs his mæga sceard*, and BC agree in reading *her wæs his maga sceard*. The

---

[39] G reads ⁊ *heora land*. See *Die Version G*, ed. Lutz, p. 86.

[40] See *Die Version G*, ed. Lutz, p. 222, who suggests that scribe A is the corrector.

[41] *ASC: MS A*, ed. Bately, p. xciii.

[42] *Beowulf* uses the compound *yðgeblond* (*yðgebland*), 1373a, 1593a, 1620a, and *sundgebland*, 1450a.

[43] Krapp and Dobbie, ASPR 3, Riddle 3, 22a; *Old English Riddles*, ed. Williamson, Riddle 1, 52a.

agreement between B and C here probably indicates that their common exemplar read *her* and *maga*. A reading with *her* requires construing *maga* as a nominative singular ('kinsman', 'son') and understanding *sceard* in an absolute sense as 'gashed' or 'mutilated', rather than 'deprived of'. In the AD version, 40b and 41a are parallel, with the participle in 42a a variant of that in 41a. But the reading of 40b in BC disturbs that parallelism. The scribe of B introduces another variant, *forslagen*, in 42a. This variant is almost certainly owing to B, given the likely assumption that B and C were copying from the same exemplar at this point. B's *forslagen* makes 42a parallel with his reading of 40b, but the lexical substitution seems less the result of editorial work and more of reflex.[44] One might usefully compare the collocation of *beslægene* and *forslegen* in *Genesis* 2010b and 2022a, examples of generative composition appearing in the poem's enthusiastic description of Abraham's war against the Sodomites.[45]

A similar appearance of a variant affix occurs at 67a: B *folces afylled*; ACD *folces gefylled*. The number of attestations of half-lines exhibiting the form, genitive + *gefylled*, suggests that this pattern describes a formulaic system.[46] And the very popularity of the pattern X x *gefylled* may explain why the awkward *gefylled* appears instead of a clearer word, *befylled*.[47] But *befylled* seems to have enjoyed little currency in the poetic corpus, being recorded only once (*Genesis* 2124b). By contrast, there are five poetic occurrences of *afylled*, two of these with a dependent dative, and two in the form genitive + *afylled*.[48] These attestations suggest the formulaic source of B's substitution.

B shows one further and telling change with the reading *garumforgrunden* at 18a (ACD *garum ageted*). Both Crawford and Dobbie attempt to understand the appearance of this word in B as an 'emendation'.[49] Indeed the word cannot be understood as a result of a simple visual mistake, and the reading in C makes it fairly certain that the common exemplar of B and C read *ageted*. Crawford observes that *ageted* must have been an unfamiliar word, since neither A, C nor D transmits a West Saxon form; and he

44 P. R. Orton, '"The Battle of Brunanburh", 40b–44a: Constantine's Bereavement', *Peritia* 4 (1985), 243–50, at 250, sees 'deliberate amendment' in these lines.

45 See J. L. Rosier, 'Generative Composition in *Beowulf*', *ES* 58 (1977), 193–203.

46 *Genesis* 209b; *Elene* 1134b; *Christ* 181a; *Judgement Day I* 12b; *Psalm* LXII.vi.1b; *Seasons for Fasting* 32b.

47 See Pope, *Seven Old English Poems*, p. 164.

48 *Christ and Satan* 99b and *Christ* 1562a.

49 See Campbell, *The Battle of Brunanburh*, p. 103 and Dobbie, ASPR 6, 148.

notes the lexical collocation of *agetan* with some form of *gar* in two other poems:

> garum agetan.   Hine god forstod
>
> *(Andreas* 1143)
>
> age(t)ton gealgmode   gara ordum
>
> *(Andreas* 32)
>
> sumne sceal gar agetan,   sumne guð abreotan
>
> *(Fortunes* 16)[50]

While forms of *agetan* and *gar* appear together in these lines, the verbs are all active, not passive, as in *Brunanburh* 18a, and the instances of combination do not compose any coherent formulaic system, for their syntax and metrics differ substantially.[51] By contrast, all five instances of *forgrunden* in the poetic corpus occur with the structure dative + *forgrunden* and are metrically identical (Pope's type A5). This system accommodates the single alliteration of b-line *bæle forgrunden* (*Phoenix* 227b) as well as the double alliteration of *gledum forgrunden* (*Beowulf* 2335a, 2677a).[52] The appearance of *forgrunden* in the B manuscript is not, I should argue, the product of a scholarly emendation. Given the context of poetic reading I have attempted to establish, this instance is, rather, a suggestive example of formulaic reading.

The Capture of the Five Boroughs is separated from *The Battle of Brunanburh* by only a brief prose entry (*ASC* 940 [941 A]) containing an obit for Athelstan and a notice of the accession of Edmund. By itself, the poem does not constitute the full entry for 942 but is followed by a short prose account of the baptisms of Anlaf and Rægnold. In A this continuation is distinguished in no way from the verse entry, but in B and C it is prefaced by *her* and separated from the body of the verse.[53]

---

[50] Campbell, *The Battle of Brunanburh*, p. 103.

[51] The appearance of the preterite singular in *hwa min fromcynn / fruman agette* (Exeter Riddle 83, 7: ASPR 3, 236; *Old English Riddles*, ed. Williamson, Riddle 79, 7) provides little help on this point, since the meaning and function of the word in context is vexed. See esp. Williamson, p. 368.

[52] The other instances are *Andreas* 413b (if the common emendation of *fore grunden* is accepted) and *The Battle of Brunanburh* 43b.

[53] On the peculiarities of layout and scribal confusion in the copying of A, see below, p. 132. In B the baptisms form a separate entry. In C there is space on the line to accommodate approximately fifteen letters. The baptisms are introduced by *Her* whose initial 'H' is red and the same size as the introductory initial 'H' in the other Chronicle entries.

The thirteen lines of *The Capture of the Five Boroughs* commemorate Edmund's recovery of the northeast midlands after the death of Olaf Guthfrithson. Lacking the heroic conventions of *The Battle of Brunanburh*, *The Capture of the Five Boroughs* is mnemonic rather than celebratory, and perhaps this restrained mode accounts for the literary obscurity it now enjoys. Despite the limited modern appeal of this little commemoration, its manuscript records are of substantial interest because of the variations in scribal reading which they witness.

Apart from various orthographic differences and probable slips of the pen, the manuscripts transmit three substantive variants for this poem.[54] Two of these are formulaic substitutions. At 2a the manuscripts provide us with three possible readings: *maga mundbora* (A); *mæcgea mund bora* (B; *mecga* C); and *mægþa mund bora* (D). In his edition, Dobbie emends his base-text A with the reading from B, defending his decision on the greater appropriateness of that reading.[55] *Mæcgea* ('of men') produces a more general reading than does *maga* (for *mæga*, 'of kinsmen'), but both are licit and are well supported in the surviving records of verse.[56] The reading in *Brunanburh* 40a, *mæga sceard*, offers some contextual support. The lurid reading in D, *mægþa mundbora* ('protector of maidens'), while offering an unusual perspective on Edmund, provokes an interesting, if unanswerable, question about scribe 2's reading background.

The second formulaic variation occurs at 9b, *nyde gebegde* (A); *nyde gebæded* (CD; *nede* B). The reading *gebæded* is supported by *Brunanburh* 33b, and the identical half-line appears as well in *Juliana* 343b and *The Husband's Message* 40b.[57] The half-line in A appears to be the *difficilior lectio*, although a metrically analogous *nearwe gebeged* appears in *Christ and Satan* 444b.

---

[54] B and C regularize the language to late West Saxon. The variant *burga gife* in D (*burga fife*, ABC) illustrates that scribe's weak sense of context. For the purposes of this argument, I do not consider B's variant at 8b *Dæne*, since it is not, strictly speaking, a formulaic substitution.

[55] Dobbie, ASPR 6, 149.

[56] The reading in B is in Pope's system a D11 line. There is one other instance of this type of formula surviving, *Andreas* 772a. The form occurs also in the genitive plural in *Fortunes of Men* 52a, *Maxims I* 151a, *Christ and Satan* 333b, though not in the same metrical type. The reading in A, *maga*, does not appear elsewhere in this precise formula, but is used in the genitive plural in *Wanderer* 51a; *Beowulf* 247a, 1079a, 1853a, 2742a.

[57] See also *niþa gebæded*, *Juliana* 203b, 462b.

The third instance of variation is actually the consequence of what initially appears to be the simple omission of an ⁊. Dobbie prints 8a as *and Deoraby*, noting that *and* is necessary for metre and sense. The missing *and* in A would produce a defective line unless the scribe (or indeed the poet) construed the half-line as *eac Deoraby*. This half-line scans acceptably and is supported by numerous examples of d-lines (and others) beginning with *eac*.[58] This adjustment in A suggests that the preceding 7b was understood as an A-line with double alliteration (*swylce Stanford*).[59]

Whatever the aesthetic response to these variations in *The Battle of Brunanburh* and *The Capture of the Five Boroughs*, their significance to this study lies in their genesis within formulaic possibility; quite simply, they are members of a special set of variants circumscribed by the constraints of oral formulaic transmission. In the context of the *Chronicle* poems, their presence is surprising, more so as the other two tenth-century poems, *The Coronation of Edgar* and *The Death of Edgar*, offer us no such variety of readings. As Janet Bately has noted of the *Chronicle* verses included in the years 924–75, 'No reading in any of the versions points conclusively to separate textual traditions ... There is indeed very little evidence to suggest that, where material is shared, all the versions did not share the same exemplar, and no evidence to prove that they did.'[60] In the light of this stability of transmission, how are we to understand the presence, style and location of the variants just examined?

The authentically formulaic variants in the transmission of the tenth-century poems occur in the records transmitted by scribe 3 of A and the scribe of B. These individuals produced their work within a fairly narrow band of time, sometime between 955 and probably 980 or so. If we look for such variants in the A and B copies of the poems for 973 and 975, however, we will be disappointed. Scribe 5 of A, working in the early eleventh century, is too distant from his material. Judging from a comparison of the full records of the *Chronicle* versions in both B and C, the relevant scribe of C probably had *B as his exemplar for 937 and 942 and B as his exemplar for 973 and 975.[61] This copyist, working in the mid-eleventh century,

---

[58] See, for example, *Elene* 1006b, *Juliana* 307b, *Christ* 1267b and several examples from the metrical Psalms, among them *Psalm* LXVI.6, line 3b; XCI.10, line 1b; CII.21, line 2b; CXVIII.82, line 1b; CXLIX.2, line 1b.

[59] For representative a-lines beginning with *swylce*, see *Beowulf* 830a, Exeter Riddle 89, 10b, *Christ and Satan* 321a, *Andreas* 1036, *Fates of the Apostles* 16a and *Christ* 80b.

[60] *ASC: MS A*, ed. Bately, p. xci.   [61] See below, p. 126 and n. 63.

produces a fairly accurate record, certainly with none of the interesting and suggestive variants of the earlier two. The scribe of D, working somewhat later, provides certain interesting variants to be sure, but they are revelatory of his unfamiliarity with the formulaic and lexical context of his material. Indeed, for the two rhythmic entries for 1036 and 1065, which C and D share, variation is limited to orthography and substitution (by D) of prose paraphrases for otherwise rhythmical lines.[62]

The variants of A and B in the verses of *ASC* 937 and 942, which arise so close to the time of composition, reveal the pressure which the old oral ways of understanding and remembering must have exerted. Their scribes are not poets but readers who see, hear and produce richly contextual variants. They must have thought they were faithful and accurate. Accurate they were not, but faithful they were, in their fashion.

GRAPHIC CUES AND THE READING OF VERSE

Examination of significant variation within the tenth-century poems of the *Anglo-Saxon Chronicle* reveals a clear distinction in appearance and type between the variants in the transmission of the earlier two poems and those of the later two. This disjunction, which coincides with the dates of the scribes' activity, is not limited to syntax and lexicon, but appears as well in the level of conventional graphic display which organizes and interprets the realized texts. The critical place to begin an examination of the graphic cues accompanying the transmission of the *Chronicle* poems is with manuscripts B and C. Of the manuscripts transmitting the tenth-century poems, B, with a date close to 977/79, is nearest in time to the coronation and death of Edgar (973 and 975 respectively). For this reason, it is unlikely that B is many copies away from the original compositions chronicling the events of 973 and 975.

In his edition of the B-text of the *Anglo-Saxon Chronicle*, Simon Taylor hypothesizes a complex relationship between Cotton Tiberius A. vi (B) and Cotton Tiberius B. i, fols. 112–64 (C). On the basis of evidence from missing annal numbers, textual features, shared letter forms and added information, Taylor infers that C had B as its exemplar for the years up to 652 and again for the years from 956 to the end of B's text, 977. For the

---

[62] See, for example, D's reduction of the version in C,

    sume hi man bende,   sume hi man blende,
    sume hamelode,   sume hættode,

to 'Sume hi man bende. ⁊ eac sume blende. ⁊ heanlic hættode.'

years 653–946, C may have used B's exemplar.[63] If Taylor's hypothesis is correct, then scribe 2 of C copied from B the poems for 973 and 975, but the scribes of B and C quite possibly copied the verse entries for 937 and 942 from a common exemplar. This information allows two sets of controlled inferences. For those poems which C copied from B, a substantial difference in formatting and pointing should indicate either scribal freedom or developing convention at Abingdon, where the manuscripts originated. The latter is indicated only if practice in pointing and capitalization can be shown to be consistent across the stint of the scribe. If, however, there is no consistency, we have no information on conventions, but only a sense of permissible scribal freedom. Consistent pointing between B and C for the verses of 937 and 942 would suggest stasis in scribal conventions as well as substantial scribal discipline, given that B and C were probably copied from the same manuscript. A difference between them could suggest several hypotheses: that B copied *B's pointing but C changed it; that both B and C altered the pointing of their hypothetical exemplar (*B); that B altered and C did not.

The Battle of Brunanburh and *The Capture of the Five Boroughs* occur in that section of the *Chronicle* (653–946) for which Taylor suggests that the scribe of C was no longer copying from B, but was, perhaps, copying B's exemplar. The evidence for this inference is strong: C has annal numbers where B has none; B has omissions which C does not; C does not share certain scribal errors with B. Yet C must have been using a manuscript very close to B, since even in this section, C is closer to B than to the text of any other manuscript extant.[64] For the sake of argument let us suppose that the scribes of B and C were, in the verses of 937 and 942, copying from the same manuscript, which we may designate *B. An immediately obvious difference between B and C, and one which affects the consideration of layout, is B's omission of annal numbers. For both 937 and 942, B's practice in this section is to begin an entry with a large capital 'H' (for *Her*) written in the same brown ink as the rest of the text and placed in the left margin of the writing space. For C, however, these entries begin as elsewhere in C, with an annal number written in the margin and extending into the ruled writing space. Numerals and a capital 'H' for each entry are in red. The effect is that the text appears organized by the annal number and indented throughout.

[63] *ASC: MS B*, ed. Taylor, pp. xxxvii and l.   [64] *Ibid.*, p. xxxvii.

While in general terms layout differs between the two manuscripts (B has 23 lines per page; C has 27 lines), they share several important graphic features.[65] In *The Battle of Brunanburh*, for example, both manuscripts capitalize the initial letters for *Her* (1a), *Swilce* (37a), *Gewiton* (53a) and *Swilce* (57a). (See pls. VII and VIII.) This practice contrasts with that in A and D.[66] Practice in abbreviation agrees as well in B and C against that in A and D. B and C write 'þ' in 8b, 48a, and 64b (with B adding 'þ' in 16b in a variant). A shares 'þ' in 8b and 48a but writes out *þæt* in 64b; the scribe of D writes out *þæt* in 8b, 48b and 64b.[67]

The scribes of all four manuscripts space free morphemes as they will. When examining these records together, one is struck by the elasticity of the concept 'word'. The writing of a space is not yet fully significant, an inference to be drawn from the lack of a graphic concept of 'word' as a fixed visual unit. This flexible practice of writing words has implications for the shift from sound stream to graphic representation. A comparison of the first four verses of all the records shows wide variation in spacing of nouns and adjectives and a common lack of spacing between 7 and the following word:

A: Her æþel stancyning. eorladryhten. beorna
beahgifa. 7 his broþor eac. eadmund æþeling. ealdor langne tir.
geslogon ætsæcce. sweorda ecgum . . .
B: Her æþelstan cing . eorladrihten . beorna beag gifa 7his
broþoreac eadmund æþeling ealdorlangne tir.
geslogan æt sake sweorda ecggum . . .
C: Heræþelstancing . eorla drihten . beornabeahgyfa
7his broðor eac eadmund æþeling . ealdor lagnetir. geslogon
ætsæcce . swurd ecgum . . .
D: Her æþelstan cyning
eorla drihten beorna beah gifa . 7hisbroþor eac
ead mund æþeling ealdor langne tyr geslogon æt
secce sweorda ecgum . . .[68]

[65] *Ibid.*, p. xviii; Ker, *Catalogue*, pp. 249 and 253.

[66] The initial 'H' in *Her* is the only capital for this entry in A. In D, 'H' has a black capital, and *Gewiton* (53a) has a large red capital initial 'G' and a small black rustic capital 'E'.

[67] The four manuscripts show unanimity in the use of 7 for *ond*, but there is much variation in the use of accent marks. See Dobbie, ASPR 6, cxxxix.

[68] 'In this year, King Æthelstan, lord of the noblemen, ring-giver of warriors, and his brother also, prince Edmund, won by the edges of swords life-long glory at battle near *Brunanburh*.'

Separation and combination of free morphemes with verbs are also common.[69]

In this preliminary examination of the graphic practices in the copying of the entry for 937 in all four manuscripts, B and C stand against A and D in two areas, capitalization and abbreviation, while spacing of morphemes varies independently. If B and C are indeed copies of the same manuscript, then we can infer from their careful copying that a capital is word-bound and a graphic feature significant for contemporary interpretation, but that spacing of words was not. Pointing remains to be considered, and it will give us some hint of the development of graphic conventions which are less specifically tied to words.

Let us begin by examining the pointing and layout of the poems for 973 and 975 in B and C, since B and C are so close that B is quite probably C's exemplar for this stint.[70] Given the other evidence for C's close affinity with B in the section from 947–77 (shared entries against the other witnesses, entries lacking in common, distinguishing linguistic features, accent marks in common, reappearance of 'k' in C), it will be useful to test to see how close C is to B in terms of graphics and format. The entries for 973 and 975 deal with two events in the West Saxon royal house, King Edgar's coronation and his death. These occurrences were sufficiently close together to suggest that the verses could have been composed by the same person. They share, at least, a fondness for circumlocution in giving the date.[71] For these two entries, B and C show a marked agreement on graphic items. Both manuscripts have capital initials in 975 for *Her* (1a), *ða* (16a; C *þa*), and *ða* (24a; C *þa*).[72] This agreement stands against the practice in A, which capitalizes the initial 'H' in 1a and initial 'ð' of *ða* in 16a.[73] For

---

[69] For example, A: *wundun fer grunden* (43b), *land eal godon* (9a); B: *feorhgenerede* (36b), *ðærlægsecg* (17b); C: *landgesohton* (27b), *gylpanneþorfte* (44b); D *neþorfte* (44b), *ofer comon* (72b), *sahtosetle* (17a). For D, 17a is the only example of combination other than *ne* + verb. Despite the various copying errors, D offers a graphically consistent record.

[70] *ASC: MS B*, ed. Taylor, pp. xlvii–l. Cf. *Two Chronicles*, ed. Plummer II, cxviii–cxix; Campbell, *The Battle of Brunanburh*, pp. 1–7. Whitelock, *Anglo-Saxon Chronicle*, p. xii, did not consider *B to be an Abingdon production.

[71] Campbell, *The Battle of Brunanburh*, p. 36, suggests that *The Death of Edgar* after line 12 is the inferior addition of the chronicler. Hart, 'The B Text', p. 295, ascribes the composition and writing of the poem to Byrhtferth.

[72] C paints these initials in red (as it does for the initial 'H' of each entry in this portion of the *Chronicle*, beginning with 894).

[73] In A, 15b is pointed by :, and the large capital of 16a begins 29r.

the entry for 973, B and C capitalize the initial 'H' in 1a, but B erroneously places a capital 'O' in the margin to begin 20a: *Onþa onðam . þrittigæþanwæs*, where the first *on* is clearly an error for *ond*. C corrects this to *7þaonþamðrittigeþan wæs*, omitting the faulty mid-line point.[74] B and C agree on three accents in the entry for 973 (against one for A) and on thirteen accents for 975.[75]

For B and C, pointing practices in both poems agree in an overwhelming number of cases. By and large, such pointing occurs at the end of the b-line. For 973, B and C concur in pointing fourteen b-lines in this twenty-line poem.[76] Points following the a-line are rare: B and C agree in only three instances of a-line pointing, but two of these mark off numerals and are probably to be discounted as metrical points.[77] Of the fourteen b-line markers, seven are unambiguously metrical.

There is similar agreement in the pointing of the entry for 975, where C follows B's practice of pointing after each b-line in the thirty-seven-line poem. In the three instances where C omits a point after the b-line (10b, 13b and 21b), the scribe avoids interrupting the flow of syntax. And the only instance where C adds a mid-line point not found in the B-version occurs at 4a, where the point is used to separate two independent clauses.[78] Of the five cases where B points a-lines, only one, at 20a, is purely metrical, although fifteen of thirty-seven b-line points are solely metrical, actually acting against grammatical sense. It appears in these cases that C adopts the pattern in B of marking off full lines of verse. In this method of pointing, a-lines receive points infrequently and not as markers of verse structure but as markers of syntax.

In the poems for 937 and 942, where the same scribes of B and C presumably shared an exemplar, the manuscripts diverge in pointing practice. In the thirteen-line poem for 942, both B and C point primarily at the end of the b-line. B and C agree in eleven instances of pointing the b-line. The two occasions where B and C diverge in pointing b-lines are not

---

[74] The point in B before *þrittigæþan* probably derives from a point before a numeral in the exemplar. A has ₇ but uses numerals, *xxx*.

[75] See Dobbie, ASPR 6, cxl, for a list of accents. For annal 973, B has six and C seven; for 975 B has twenty-one, C seventeen.

[76] In the two instances of disagreement, C marks 11b with a purely metrical point, and B marks 15b similarly.

[77] In the other instance, 5a marks off an independent clause. Both instances where C alone marks an a-line are clauses.

[78] Both scribes omit points at 21a and 33a, each at the opening of independent clauses.

significant disagreements (B points 1b; C points 12b), since they have the same syntactic function in separating appositives. In the four other instances where C points alone, all mark a-lines with clear syntactic significance, either separating parallel subjects or independent clauses. The five instances of purely metrical pointing are shared by B and C.

The divergence between scribal practice in C and B is clearer in pointing for the entry for 937. Of the seventy-three lines on *The Battle of Brunanburh*, B points at least sixty-two b-lines; C points fifty-nine.[79] They coincide in pointing fifty-four b-lines. While B points only twelve a-lines, C points thirty-three – nearly triple the number for B, and ten of these can only be construed as metrical points. In the brief entry for 942, C shows some tendency to point after the a-line, certainly to a greater extent than B. In the much longer entry for 937, it is clear that C points the a-line much more regularly than does B and does so not simply to clarify syntax, but to mark verse structure. This divergence presents a complication. While the shift in pointing practice is consonant with a shift in exemplar, the difficulty lies in the supposition that B and C share the same exemplar in just those entries where B and C diverge in pointing practice. Yet for those poems when C quite probably uses B as its exemplar, pointing practice is very close.

Scribe 2 of C was a careful copyist. He copied B's capitals in the entries for 973 and 975, and the agreement between B and C on capitals in 937 and 942 suggest that both copied from their exemplar exactly. For the entries in 973 and 975, C modelled his pointing on B's practice. While B's habit of pointing the b-line is consistent throughout the four poems, for which *B was presumably the exemplar, C's pointing changes for the poems of 937 and 942. If we suppose that B as we now have it represents the lost exemplar *B's pointing practice, then we must infer that the otherwise careful scribe of C arbitrarily changed pointing for 937 and 942 and then reverted to careful copying when he switched exemplars to B. This is a possible hypothesis, but an unlikely one. We could reverse the hypothesis and suggest that C represents *B's practice and that B diverged from the pointing of *B in 937 and 942, only to revert back to *B's practice. Then C copied B. This hypothesis is complex, even less likely, and less helpful.

---

[79] For B, the number sixty-two is conservative: the ending of 6b is now obscured by a repair; in 12b the point is on an erasure; and at the end of 16b the binding is too tight to see any possible point.

If, however, we suppose that *B was not pointed (or only very lightly pointed), then the pointing in B must have been supplied by that scribe, whose consistency in pointing the b-line is clear (and who, Taylor hypothesizes, intended a thoroughgoing revision of *B anyway). In this account, the pointing for 937 and 942 in C represents an entirely different approach to the undertaking. C is a copy made in the mid-eleventh century. For that presumably lightly pointed section of text taken from *B, scribe 2 repointed and accented according to eleventh-century practice.[80] For the section of text he took from B, he copied B's pointing relatively carefully. This account coincides rather nicely with the development of pointing practice we have already seen in the manuscripts of Caedmon's *Hymn* and Alfred's *Metrical Preface* to the *Pastoral Care*. Early records of verse do not point regularly to distinguish either line length or syntax.[81] B, copied after 977, but probably not long after, points mainly after the b-line, and this pointing is largely metrical, that is, it is designed to articulate line structure graphically. The pointing of the mid-eleventh century extends this practice to both half-lines.

The earliest and the latest records of the *Chronicle* poems, A and D, present complex evidence on pointing, which, despite its complexity, supports the account of the punctuation in B and C. Of the two, the punctuation in the verses of A is most difficult to decipher. To look at the entry for 937 by itself, one might conclude, certainly from the facsimile, that scribe 3 pointed *The Battle of Brunanburh* with a view to distinguishing half-lines.[82] To realize that such is not the case requires consideration of the history of correction of this portion of the manuscript and comparison of its pointing with that of *The Capture of the Five Boroughs*.

---

[80] Scribe 1 of the *Chronicle* in Tiberius B. i (whose work Ker, *Catalogue*, p. 253, dates to s. xi^{med}) also copied two poems, *Menologium* and *Maxims II* (112r–115v). As it now appears, the *Menologium* is pointed by punctus versus and punctus elevatus to separate half-lines. However, the virgules used to make these marks are sloppily formed, not always accurately placed and almost certainly the work of a later hand. The original points, placed at mid-point on the line of writing, set off half-lines. With few exceptions, half-lines in *Maxims* are marked by a raised point. This copy now ends with a punctus versus whose tail was added later. This style of pointing coincides with that of scribe 2 for the entries in 937 and 942.

[81] Compare, for example, the varying practices for pointing Old English verse exhibited in Leningrad, Saltykov-Schedrin Public Library, Q. v. I. 18, Oxford, Bodleian Library, Hatton 20, CCCC 12 and Cambridge, Trinity College R. 5. 22.

[82] *The Parker Chronicle and Laws: Corpus Christi College, Cambridge, MS. 173*, ed. R. Flower and A. H. Smith, EETS os 208 (London, 1941), 26r–27r.

Although colour of ink is no clear indicator here of inserted punctuation, the number of blurred or smeared points in the text of *Brunanburh* (where little else is blurred) is an early indication of another hand at work. Considered as a whole, the points are inconsistently placed: some squeezed in, others placed at the top of a minuscule letter, others in mid-line.[83] Fols. 26–7 show other evidence of correction, most particularly in the dates of the annals, which in some cases have been altered repeatedly.[84] The copyist of BL, Cotton Domitian viii, fols. 30–70, was also at work here adding references to Canterbury.

By contrast, *The Capture of the Five Boroughs*, also copied by scribe 3, shows no such regular pointing and, interestingly enough, no suspect accents.[85] The only points which occur in this poem occur before ⁊ (27r21 and 22), a normal practice in prose. The end of this poem should be *eadmundcyning*, but the scribe continued on, incorporating the predicate of the next annal into the last line of 27r, the end of his stint. *Onfeng anlafe* appears as an a-verse with vocalic alliteration, and although the following entry is in prose, these two circumstances clearly influenced the scribe to continue writing the 'verse'. There is no terminal mark here, contrary to his habit for the other entries of his stint. The terminal marks for *The Battle of Brunanburh* may, or may not, be genuine. The final 'n' of *begeaton* is an elongated majuscule 'n', clearly designed as terminal.

The punctuation now found in the entry for 937 consistently separates half-lines with a simple punctus. However, given the corrections and additions throughout this section of the *Chronicle*, the cramped and inconsistently placed points in the verses of 937, and the scarcity of pointing in the entry for 942, it is difficult to avoid the conclusion that this pointing of *The Battle of Brunanburh* is substantially the result of later alteration. Because these alterations make it impossible to reconstruct the original pointing, this entry provides little useful information on actual

[83] I see no evidence here of any alternation of the sub-distinctio, media-distinctio or distinctio used in Latin manuscripts.

[84] On the series of corrections of the dates of the entries on 26r–27r see, W. S. Angus, 'The Eighth Scribe's Dates in the Parker Manuscript of the Anglo-Saxon Chronicle', *MÆ* 10 (1941), 130–49; *Die Version G*, ed. Lutz, pp. cxxxvi–cl; *ASC: MS A*, ed. Bately, pp. xcvi–xcviii; and Dumville, *Wessex and England from Alfred to Edgar*, ch. 3.

[85] In *The Battle of Brunanburh*, accent marks lacking a flag have been added over *tir* (26r19), *hamas* (26r23), *up* (26v1), *tid* (26v1), *wiges* (26v4), *forð* (26v4), and *har* (26v15). In the entry for 942, the four accents, on *ea* (27r21), *eac* (27r23), *on* (27r24), and *onfeng* (27r26), all have characteristic flags.

pointing practice other than to provoke the suggestive inference that its version of *Brunanburh* (in addition to the entry for 942 in A and, arguably, the record in *B) was originally pointed lightly, a state which prompted a later reader to improve the reading text by heavier pointing.[86]

The Coronation of Edgar and *The Death of Edgar* in CCCC 173 were written by scribe 5, working in the early eleventh century.[87] This relatively late date encourages comparison of pointing practice with the earlier B and the later C.[88] Scribe 5 in A formats the entry for 975 in two sections. The first runs from 1a–14b and ends with heavy punctuation (:7) at the bottom of 28v. The scribe left the rest of the line blank, although there remains room for fourteen or fifteen letters on the line. Just such a division of the text is made in B, where the scribe ends line 14b (33v21) with room for several letters and begins 15a (*Ða wearð*) with a capital eth in the right margin of 33v22. Scribe 5 of A begins the rest of the entry for 975 (at 15a) with a capital eth at the top of the space ruled for narrative on 29r.[89]

The scribe points both a- and b-lines in *The Death of Edgar* with great consistency. The only a-lines lacking points are: 16a, 20a, 23a, 24a, 27a, 36a and 37a, representing a variety of syntactic situations. While 20a, 24a and 36a offer clear syntactic reasons for omitting the point (for example, a point after 24a would separate a verb from its object), the instances of omission in 16a, 23a and 36a do not. However, elsewhere this scribe points an a-line where the placement of points clearly disturbs the sense, a fact which suggests that pointing in this poem is primarily metrical.[90] For b-lines, scribe 5 omits points for the following: 16b, 19b, 27b, 34b and 35b, five of thirty-seven possible points.[91] Of these, only one, that after

---

[86] Campbell, *The Battle of Brunanburh*, pp. 82–92, prints these points as original. Bately, *ASC: MS A*, apparently accepts these points as original (p. lxiv), although she notes that in some places in the Chronicle verse, punctuation was inserted after the writing of the verse.

[87] Dumville, *Wessex and England from Alfred to Edgar*, ch. 3, suggests a date of '*c.* 1000'. Bately (*ASC: MS A*, at pp. xxxvii–xxxviii) dates this hand to the early eleventh century.

[88] On the overall manuscript pointing of what remains of G, see *Die Version G*, ed. Lutz, p. xlvi.

[89] The scribe of C uses a capital 'þ' but does not begin a new line.

[90] See 7a: but note the inconsistency in marking off 34a, *wide gefrege*, but not 16a, *mine gefraege*.

[91] At 8b and 11b points have been erased. At 16b and 34b, parenthetical phrases come to a close; 19b anticipates a subordinate clause. At 27b a point would separate parallel adverbial phrases.

35b, has a syntactic reason for omission, since a point there would separate the subject in 35b from its verb in 36a.

The points in this record of *The Death of Edgar* are unquestionably original. While there seems to be no consistent syntactic pattern underlying the omission of points in *The Death of Edgar*, there may be a psychological reason for the inconsistency. On four occasions, the scribe omits points in groups of three half-lines, where his attention may well have flagged. His intention may have been to point regularly by half-line, but either the practice did not come naturally, or he did not see the need for consistency, or his attention wavered.

The record of the *Chronicle* in D provides complex information about text and graphic cues. The manuscript was copied over time by several hands, and this fact alone makes its evidence difficult to evaluate. And, as we have seen on a textual level, the record is very different from that in B and C. The most obvious and startling example of this difference is its substitution of brief summaries for the verse entries for 973 and 975. I have suggested as well that the copying of *The Battle of Brunanburh* in the entry for 937 argues a copying procedure at some remove from that in A and B, not to mention the records of Caedmon's *Hymn*, Exeter Riddles 30a and 30b, and *Solomon and Saturn I*.

Ker describes the script of the copyist of the entries for 937 and 942 (hand 2, 19r–67r) as 'a careful, round hand of s. xi^med, perhaps somewhat earlier than 1050'.[92] Although copied by the same scribe, the text in each instance is handled differently. In the seventy-three lines of *The Battle of Brunanburh*, the scribe points six a-lines and forty-five possible b-lines. While it may appear from these numbers that the scribe preferred to point b-lines, the numbers are misleading. In three instances (10a, 32a and 41b), the scribe misplaces a point in the middle of a line, and in two further cases, a-line points precede an γ, a conventional place for pointing prose (2a and 62a). His pointing of only 60 per cent of the b-lines and his lack of pattern in doing so suggest that his pointing practice is either lax or uncertain. His practice for the 942 entry is casual as well. In this poem, he points six a- and six b-lines, though not the same half-lines. He mispoints 10b in mid-line here as well, by positioning a point between the free morphemes of *hafteclommum*. Actually, the pointing in 942 is closer to prose pointing than metrical pointing, since the majority of points separate

[92] *Catalogue*, p. 254.

items in a series. How then do we account for the peculiar pointing in 937? Given the number of variants unique to D in this record of the text, I suggest that D preserves for us evidence of late reading activity, where the reader shows little familiarity with either the formulae or the conventions of Old English verse. Indeed, those variants which might be defended as either syntactically or metrically possible, fail to fit contextually. The scribe of D is no poet, to be sure, and despite the attractiveness of his hand, he appears to be no good reader of verse either.

The Death of Alfred, the entry for 1036, is partly in prose, partly in hypermetric, often rhyming verse (lines 8, 9, 19, etc.), which occasionally does not alliterate (see lines 7, 12, 15 and 18, for example). Scribe 2 of C is responsible for copying this entry. There is no indication that he treats these poor verses as anything but prose. In Dobbie's edition, the first five 'lines' are printed as prose. The scribe of C points twice, in line 5, after *Haraldes* (i.e. before a subordinate clause) and after *wære* (to end an independent clause). Of the remaining twelve points which C makes, two mark a *sume* series (9b and 10a), three occur before ⁊ (7a, 19b and 20b), four occur before an independent clause (12b, 15b, 18b and 21b), and one before a subordinate clause (16b). There is one terminal point (25b) and one point whose function is unclear (23b). By contrast, scribe 5 in C, in the entry for 1065 (*The Death of Edward*), points metrically by half-line. Points are missing for both positions in line 7. Cropping of the margin of the manuscript at 2a and 33b obscures possible points.

The poems for 1036 and 1065 in D appear somewhat different in script.[93] By contrast with the practice in C, the pointing for D in 1065 is virtually non-existent. There is a point at 7b (before ⁊), at 14b and 20b (before an independent clause), in the middle of 18b (before *æðelredes*), in mid-line 23b (before ⁊), in 28b before ⁊, and after 34b, terminally. The two inappropriate internal points and the lack of regularity suggest that the scribe of D did not intend metrical pointing or did not recognize verse.

CONCLUSIONS

This chapter has examined two elements in the transmission and (by inference) the reading of the classical Old English verse in the *Anglo-Saxon Chronicle*: the occurrence of a special category of variance, whose members I

---

[93] Ker (*ibid.*) ascribes the difference to discontinuous writing.

have termed formulaic variants, and the distribution of those variants; and the occurrence and developing use of conventional graphic cues as visual information in the realized texts of these poems. The *Chronicle* verses and the *Metrical Preface* to Alfred's translation of the *Regula pastoralis* distinguish themselves from the verse compositions considered in chs. 2 and 3 in an important way – though among the very few poetic works surviving in multiple copies, their records are quite stable, presenting the impression of a fixity of text characteristic of later literacy. Given this overall stability, the number of formulaic variants in the tenth-century poems and their distribution are startling and suggestive, for their appearance is time-dependent. Their cluster in the work of scribe 3 in A and of the scribe of B (i.e. the poems for 937 and 942) suggests that such reading was more likely in the period before the end of the tenth century than later. The mid-eleventh-century scribe of C is quite accurate in his transmission, though accuracy is hardly a distinguishing characteristic of later copying; witness the peculiar variants which D produced. Similarly, the evidence of such formulaic variance survives in the records of the *Metrical Preface* in Cambridge, Trinity College R. 5. 22, which Ker has dated to s. x/xi. The appearance of formulaic variance attests to the pressure which the old oral habits of thought exerted on the literate transmission of verse in Old English. At this level, the presence of formulaic variance represents a tacit conservatism manifest in the participatory reception and transmission of copied verse, since this type of reception is characteristic of oral performance.

The other evidence examined in this chapter, that of the growth of conventional graphic cues, shows a developing trend toward the chirographic manipulation of the potential reader. Setting aside, for the moment, the question of the technical meaning of punctuation in manuscripts of Old English verse, these points testify to the development of new graphic significances. The use of points, and then of space, in the eighth-century manuscripts of Latin verse copied in England signal an early attempt to direct readers towards the correct division of verses. By the tenth century in England, Latin poetry was regularly copied in lines of verse, though not, apparently, always pointed at line ends. In fact, the regular placement of an essentially redundant metrical point at line ends in many tenth-century manuscripts is often due to a later reader's addition of a point. In terms of the use of graphic conventions, the writing of Old English lags significantly behind the writing of Latin. The reasons for this phenomenon, I should argue, are the difficulty of reading Latin verse, which from the outset necessitated extra-linguistic markers, and the corresponding familiarity of Old English verse, whose formulaic structure encouraged a participatory reception on the part of readers and copyists.

It is significant, therefore, that the differences in pointing which the four records of the *Chronicle* poems preserve are temporally distributed, from the earliest records in A (and, by inference, *B) with very light pointing, to those in B and the portions of C which were probably copied from B, which tend to point the b-line, to the late practice in C and D, which generally tended to mark both a- and b-lines. Further, this temporal distribution of pointing corresponds to the distribution of formulaic variants in the verses of the *Anglo-Saxon Chronicle*. This combined evidence suggests that it is to the late tenth century that we should look for the development of new visual information in the writing of Old English verse. Chs. 6 and 7, therefore, will examine the significance and appearance of non-lexical graphic cues in the four great codices of Old English verse.

6

Interpreting, pointing and reading

The previous chapters examined poetic works surviving in multiple copies in order to assess the information contained in significant variants and to gauge the meaning of punctuation and other spatial cues. I argued that the language of a realized text and its mise-en-page are an index of the degree to which an Old English poetic work has become a purely 'textual' production, and that the evidence of variants and pointing demonstrates that at least some Old English verse still retained a highly 'oral' character, even when written down.

Chs. 6 and 7 focus on somewhat finer-grained cues for the reading and reception of a text – the graphic signals of script, capitals and punctuation in the individual poetic codices: the Vercelli Book, Exeter Book, Nowell Codex and Junius Manuscript. While it is useless to hypothesize about possible variants in the exemplars for these codices, a background knowledge of the state of variants in the poems surviving in multiple copies clarifies the information that script, mise-en-page and especially pointing in these four codices offer about residual orality, reading and textual transmission in the Old English poetic corpus.[1]

The most immediate way to highlight the problems of interpreting punctuation in Old English verse is to examine pointing practice in comparable Latin and Old English poems. Aldhelm's eighth-century *enigma* 'Creatura' and its tenth-century Old English translation, Riddle 40

---

[1] K. Sisam, *The Structure of Beowulf* (Oxford, 1965), p. 70, acknowledges a 'looseness of transmission . . . rather than reproduction with ritual accuracy' in the copying of Old English verse; see also his *Studies*, pp. 31–44. The two versions of *Soul and Body* in the Exeter Book and the Vercelli Book and the relationship between *Daniel* and *Azarias* in the Junius Manuscript and in the Exeter Book illustrate the complex problems in evaluating residual orality and literate transmission. See above, p. 66, n. 58.

138

of the Exeter Book, are especially useful in this regard, given their close relationship, and illustrate the dramatic contrast in punctuation and spatial array between Old English and Latin verse.[2]

Oxford, Bodleian Library, Rawlinson C. 697, a ninth-century manuscript from northeast France, containing Prudentius's *Psychomachia* and Aldhelm's *Carmen de virginitate* and *Enigmata*, found its way to England some time before the mid-tenth century.[3] While the date of its arrival in England and the place of its English provenance are uncertain, the acrostic of the names *Adalstan* and *Iohannes* added by an English hand on 78v set the later limit for its importation into England in the second quarter of the tenth century.[4] Corrections in black ink in Anglo-Saxon Square minuscule, similar to the work of the second hand in BL, Cotton Cleopatra A. iii, suggest a connection with St Augustine's, Canterbury, the origin of the Latin–Old English glossaries of Cleopatra A. iii.[5] Rawlinson C. 697 has a further important connection – it is almost certainly the manuscript from which Riddle 40, 'Creatura', in the Exeter Book, was originally translated.[6] By this statement I do not suggest that Riddle 40 was translated directly into the Exeter Book – I should imagine that the only extant copy of the Old English 'Creatura' is at least at one remove from its first translation from the text in Rawlinson C. 697. I do suggest, however, that the connection between the two texts in these manuscripts, Latin *enigma* and Old English translation, should make us look closely at the differences in the copying of the two.

Whatever the genesis of the rest of the poetry in the Exeter Book, whether oral or literate, the written origin of Riddle 40 is beyond dispute. The closeness of the translation, the consequent pressure of the Latin periods on the structure of half-lines, the traces of manuscript peculiarities and glosses from Rawlinson C. 697 imported into Riddle 40 all argue the

---

[2] The best edition of Aldhelm's *Enigmata* is *Aldhelmi Opera*, ed. Ehwald, pp. 97–149. The Old English riddle 'Creatura' is numbered 40 in ASPR 3, 200–3.

[3] On the origin and dating of this manuscript, see B. Bischoff, 'Bannita: 1. Syllaba, 2. Littera', in *Latin Script and Letters A.D. 400–900: Festschrift Presented to Ludwig Bieler*, ed. J. J. O'Meara and B. Naumann (Leiden, 1976), pp. 207–12, at 211.

[4] M. Lapidge, 'Some Latin Poems as Evidence for the Reign of Athelstan', *ASE* 9 (1980), 61–98, at 72.

[5] Ker, *Catalogue*, no. 143 (s. x^{med}). And see T. A. M. Bishop, 'Notes on Cambridge Manuscripts, Part V: Manuscripts Connected with St Augustine's Canterbury, Continued', *TCBS* 3 (1959–63), 93–5, at 93.

[6] O'Keeffe, 'Aldhelm's *Enigma* no. c', p. 73.

literate nature of its production.[7] The Old English poem's connection with an identifiable manuscript provides a happy opportunity for a detailed examination of the physical evidence offered by both: if any Old English poem should show traces of Latin conventions of formatting, it should be this one.

Two scribes copied the *Enigmata* in Rawlinson C. 697 into the first two quires of the manuscript. The first scribe copied the Preface and *Enigmata* i–xcviii (1r–14v20); the second copied *Enigmata* xcix–c (14v25–16r).[8] Both scribes formatted the text in the same fashion. The solution to each *enigma* is written in red rustic capitals and is roughly centred on the line. Each *enigma* begins with a large capital initial. Verses are written one to a line and begin at the left margin with a smaller rustic capital initial. These initials are lined up in a column and separated slightly from the rest of the line of writing. There are two systems of pointing used in the first two quires. Up to 6r, scribe 1 points rarely but most commonly uses a high terminal point to mark the end of an *enigma*.[9] From 6v on, however, the scribe changes practice and ends each line of verse with a high terminal point. This method of pointing verse is consistently practised throughout the rest of the first two quires despite the change of hand. The shift to a new method of pointing is accompanied as well by a shift to numbering the riddles, beginning at 6v1, with *Enigma* xlix, 'Cacabus', and these practices continue throughout.

If I am correct in my identification of Rawlinson C. 697 as the version of *Enigma* c from which the translation of Riddle 40 was made, then the Old English translator of 'Creatura' had as a model a work which began with a number and title in capitals at the head of 15v, whose verses were consistently arranged by line, each begun with a capital initial and concluded with a terminal point, and whose final line was marked by a punctus versus. The points in question here are, most probably, redundant line markers. While it is true that the Latin poem is constructed primarily

---

[7] *Ibid.*

[8] The ink of the second scribe is a lighter brown than that on 1r–14v20. The hand of the first scribe is small and neat. This scribe tends to angle the shoulder of the 'r' and to make 'e' slightly taller than the other small letters. Both 'f' and 's' extend below the line. In the second hand, ascenders of 'b', 'd', 'h' and 'l' are taller than those in the first hand. The shoulder of 'r' has greater extension and the descender of 'f' extends well below the line.

[9] On rare occasions, he places a terminal point at the end of a line when it concludes an independent clause. There has been some later pointing. The insertion of punctus elevati and punctus versi on 5r is certainly not the work of the original scribe.

in pairs of antitheses and that the ends of most verses in *Enigma* c coincide with the ends of clauses, there are groups of verses with enjambed clauses: lines 13–16, 36–9 and 59–60. In these cases, a point at the end of the verse can only be a formal line marker, since the point actually interrupts the flow of the syntax across the lines of verse. The formatting of *Enigma* c in Rawlinson C. 697 is typical for Latin verse copied in the ninth and tenth centuries. To highlight the line of verse as a unit of meaning, it conservatively maintains the older markers of verse length – capitals and end-points – as redundant information. There is no use of internal points here to mark syntax.

The formatting of Riddle 40 in the Exeter Book is a very different matter. The poem begins on 110r at the left margin with a large decorated capital 'E' followed by a smaller capital 'c'. There is neither number nor title. The only separation between the previous riddle and Riddle 40 is the heavy terminal punctuation for the last line of Riddle 39 (. :7) and a fresh line. The Old English verses are characteristically run across the writing space. Except for tall 'i', which occurs throughout the text, the only small capitals in the riddle are 'M' in *Mara* (92a and 105a), and 'A' in *Ac* (101a).[10] The text breaks off after 111v, presumably where there has been a loss in the manuscript.

Some thirty-four points mark the 107 remaining lines of Riddle 40. Of these, twenty-nine follow a b-line, four an a-line, and one point occurs mid-half-line, coincident with the end of the page (111r).[11] The numbers here do not speak persuasively for a metrical significance to these points. Were these points to mark verses visually in the array of long lines, we should expect to find an identifiable pattern in their arrangement and use. That points occur at the b-line more frequently than at the a-line is clear. But just as clear is the fact that only 27 per cent of the b-lines are pointed at

---

[10] Krapp and Dobbie, ASPR 3, lxxvi–lxxxi, list small capitals in the manuscript, although there are difficulties with their procedure in defining these capitals. As they point out, small capitals are often distinguishable from small letters only by size. There are, as a result, many instances where they define a capital where I saw none, and where I identify a capital which they omit. Further, they include tall 'i' as a capital, but it is not at all clear that its use in the Exeter Book is similar to the use of other enlarged letters. For this reason, tall 'i' is best omitted from a list of small capitals unless preceded by a point or, arguably, when introducing a clause.

[11] These are: 9b, 15b, 19b, 22b, 28b, 32b, 39b, 41b, 43b, 45b, 47b, 51b, 52a, 59b, 67b, 69b, 73b (with an additional point mid-half-line), 75b, 77a, 77b, 79b, 81b, 83b, 85a, 85b, 87b, 91b, 94a, 94b, 97b, 100b, 104b and 105b.

all. Neither are the points evenly distributed. Points are irregular until line 39, after which there are two groups of lines (39–47 and 73–87) where every other line is pointed. But these brief and wide-spaced instances are as close a fit to metrical patterning as can be made.[12]

The occurrence of a point at the end of a b-line is probably only metrical by coincidence. In this poem, independent clauses commonly conclude at the end of the b-line.[13] Knowing this information, one may well inquire whether pointing in this poem more accurately marks syntax than metre, since syntax is the other of the two traditional categories for analysing pointing. Here, too, numbers are not encouraging. The scribe marks thirty-three independent clauses (counting the points after 85a, 77a and

[12] Although the Leiden Riddle was copied by a continental, probably French, scribe, and one who was clearly unfamiliar with Old English, its peculiarities of layout should be addressed here, since J. Gerritsen ('The Text of the Leiden Riddle', *ES* 50 (1969), 529–44) has suggested that the scribe of the riddle attempted to follow his exemplar in the layout of the text. The riddle is laid out in nine lines of writing, with lines 1–3 and 7–8 begun with a capital at the vertical bounding line and lines 4–6 and 9 slightly inset and begun with a lower-case letter. The poor condition of the manuscript, which is rubbed and has been degraded by use of a reagent, obscures any possible marks of punctuation at the end of the present lines. However, there are two visible points reported by M. B. Parkes ('The Manuscript of the Leiden Riddle', *ASE* 1 (1972), 207–17, at 208 and 214) occurring precisely at the end of b-lines. The capitals in the text of the Leiden Riddle occur at the beginning of modern edited lines 1, 3, 5, 7, 9, 11 and 13, or put another way, coincide with the beginning of each Latin line from which the Old English riddle was translated. Whether or not the scribe copied these lines from his exemplar, these occurrences of points and capitals do not indicate that the riddle's Old English exemplar was formatted in lines of verse. It seems, instead, that the foreign scribe interpreted a capital as the beginning of a line of verse (as in Latin poetry), and wherever he could, began such a 'line' at the margin. His spacing of words and his otherwise unhelpful pointing indicate that the scribe knew no Old English. His formatting, which Parkes argues accommodated pen-trials already found on 25v, thus copied Latin style. The capitals may be very early, perhaps owing to the original translator, and they call attention to the translator's faithful attempt to match each of Aldhelm's Latin lines by two Old English lines. One might note, however, that Exeter Riddle 35 has only an initial capital and points after 4b, 11b (both independent clauses) and 9a. See Parkes's argument *ibid.*, pp. 214–15 and Gerritsen's counter-argument, 'Leiden Revisited: Further Thoughts on the Text of the Leiden Riddle', in *Medieval Studies Conference, Aachen 1983*, ed. W.-D. Bald and H. Weinstock, Bamberger Beiträge zur englischen Sprachwissenschaft 15 (Frankfurt-am-Main, 1984), 51–9.

[13] K. O'B. O'Keeffe, 'Exeter Riddle 40: The Art of an Old English Translator', *Proceedings of the Patristic, Mediaeval and Renaissance Conference* 5 (1980), 107–17, at 115.

105b), but leaves twenty-five others unpointed.[14] Given that 57 per cent of possible independent clauses are so marked (double that for metrical pointing), syntax might seem a more attractive explanation than metre as the aim of pointing. But the fact still remains, that if the marking of syntax for reading was the goal of such pointing, the scribe (or his predecessor) did only slightly more than half the job.

Several issues have been raised by considering the manuscript states of these two poems side by side. The first issue is the question of common practice in the pointing of Latin verse. The second is its inevitable cognate, the common practice of pointing in Old English. Comparison of these manuscripts suggests that the two practices differ substantially and that the nature and implications of that difference want examination. The third issue is delicate, encompassing the limits of what can be inferred from a perceived pattern in pointing a manuscript copy. Is it possible to place the practice of a scribe on a continuum from conventional to idiosyncratic? All of these considerations point to the simplest and most notoriously difficult question of all: what does pointing in Old English do?

THE POINTING OF LATIN VERSE

Manuscripts of Latin verse copied in England from the eighth century onwards exhibit the following broad development in the conventions of formatting. Early on in the period, manuscripts of verse are still copied in long lines,[15] but the practice is clearly giving way to a newer, graphic technique of distinguishing verses, probably borrowed from the formatting of scripture.[16] After this shift becomes widely conventional, initial capitals (formerly part of the system for distinguishing verses written in long lines) are retained, but terminal points are largely omitted. This new

---

[14] The remaining point from the thirty-four in the poem is 'palaeographic', though not significant, since the scribe often points at the end of a page, and here the point falls within the half-line. I include here the point after 77a although it is splayed and badly shaped. For the distinction of points in four categories, metrical, syntactic, rhetorical and palaeographical, see *Old English Riddles*, ed. Williamson, p. 15.

[15] For example, the text of Sedulius's *Carmen paschale* in CCCC 173 and Paulinus of Nola, *Carmina*, in Vatican City, Biblioteca Apostolica Vaticana, Pal. lat. 235.

[16] For example, the fragment of Aldhelm, *Enigmata*, Miskolc, Zrinyi Ilona Secondary School, s.n. and the verses preserved in the eighth-century manuscripts of the *Historia ecclesiastica* copied in England. See O'Keeffe, 'Graphic Cues', p. 144.

practice may be illustrated in numerous manuscripts from the tenth century.[17] Concomitant with the development of Caroline minuscule on the continent is the development of a hierarchical system of punctuation to mark pauses and syntactic breaks.[18] These marks use the punctus, punctus elevatus and punctus versus to clarify the meaning of the verse. The popularity of this system in England is attested not only by its use for newly copied manuscripts of Latin verse in the eleventh century, but also by the numbers of earlier manuscripts 'corrected' by the addition of marks following the new technique. While the above summary sketches the larger outline of the development of formatting Latin verse in England, it overlooks two interconnected issues crucial to understanding the significance of the invention and use of such formatting as a system: (1) the very separate practices of formatting and pointing verse and prose in Latin and the purpose behind such a separation; and (2) the aim of pointing practice (whether performative or analytic).

Systematic pointing in Latin is usually traced to St Jerome's adaptation of the pointing of the manuscripts of Demosthenes and Cicero to divide scripture into phrases (the comma and colon) for reading aloud.[19] Such a system, which began each phrase at the left margin, both marked off a unit of meaning and allowed the reader a pause for breath. Although it assumed both functions, the system was primarily performative rather than analytic.[20] Alcuin's widely cited comments on pointing are, not surprisingly, directed at the correct performance of a liturgical text.[21] Scripture by itself and in the liturgy retained a substantially oral component as the 'word' precisely because of the social context within which it was performed. When this system of marking was borrowed for secular writing, the mixture of performative and analytic elements changed.

---

[17] For example, Edinburgh, National Library of Scotland, Advocates 18. 7. 7 (Gneuss, 'Preliminary List', no. 253; Thorney (s. x^ex): Caelius Sedulius, *Carmen paschale*) and Oxford, Bodleian Library, Auct. F. 1. 15 (*ibid.*, no. 533; Canterbury (s. x²): Boethius, *De consolatione Philosophiae*).

[18] Brown, 'Punctuation', p. 275. For an overview of ancient and medieval systems of pointing, see J. Moreau-Maréchal, 'Recherches sur la ponctuation', *Scriptorium* 22 (1968), 56–66.

[19] Brown, 'Punctuation', p. 274.

[20] See Parkes, 'Punctuation, or Pause and Effect', p. 135, for a discussion of the ways in which pointing may change the *sensus* of a text.

[21] *Carmen* lxvii.7–10, cited in L. C. Hector, *The Handwriting of English Documents* (London, 1958), p. 44.

Isidore of Seville is helpful here because he aims to be exhaustive in his compiling of information. There are two sets of arbitrary symbols which Isidore discusses in his section on grammar in the *Etymologiae* – accents and positurae.[22] His choice of information reveals both the literate bias of his thinking and the strong residually oral element in conceptualizing the function and working of written language. The accent, he writes, is so called from the combination of *ad* and *cantus*. Its name indicates its dependence on song, just as the adverb's name indicates its dependence on the verb ('sicut adverbium [*scil.* dictum est] quia iuxta uerbum est': I.xviii.2). The accent mark is connected to performance in its function as an indicator of pronunciation. Much of Isidore's account of accents deals with their shape and the connection of shape to the direction for the rising or falling pitch of the voice. But Isidore is aware that the accent's major function is visually to disambiguate combinations of words or cases which would be clear if spoken. Thus his example, 'uiridique in litore conspicitur sus' (I.xviii.6), illustrates that a correctly placed accent on *sus* would prevent a visual mistake (because of inconsistent spacing in the copy?) and subsequent misreading *conspicit ursus*. Accents also disambiguate case, as in the possible visual confusion of the nominative and ablative singular of the first declension. Such marks are, therefore, visual substitutes for the inflections of the voice.

Initially, at least, Isidore defines *positurae* as markers of units of meaning ('figura[e] ad distinguendos sensus'). By contrast with the melodic (hence aural/oral) source of accents, *positurae* receive their name from a form of *pono*: either because the sign for pause comes from the positioning of a point or because the voice is lowered at the place where the point indicates ('Dictae autem positurae uel quia punctis positis adnotantur, uel quia ibi uox pro interuallo distinctionis deponitur': I.xx.1). Isidore emphasizes, however, that a point is a visual phenomenon. Meaning is marked off in

---

[22] Isidore *Etymologiae* I.xviii–xx. One further sort of arbitrary sign used in literary texts, the *nota*, is discussed in I.xxi. Gneuss, 'Preliminary List', lists eight Anglo-Saxon manuscripts of the *Etymologiae*: BL, Royal 6. C. I (no. 469; St Augustine's, s. xi); Oxford, Bodleian Library, Bodley 239 (no. 561; Exeter, s. xi/xii); Oxford, Queen's College 320 (no.682; s. x[med]); Salisbury, Cathedral Library, 112 (no. 719; Salisbury, s. xi[x]); Dusseldorf, Staatsarchiv Fragm. 28 (no. 821; Northumbria, s. viii[2]); Paris, Bibliothèque Nationale, lat. 4871 (no. 885;? Northumbria, s. viii/ix [a fragment]); and lat. 7585 (no. 889; France, s. ix[1] [later at St Augustine's?]). The chronological range of these manuscripts, from the eighth century to the eleventh, suggests that the *Etymologiae* was a work familiar to and popular with the Anglo-Saxons.

units of increasing length by *comma*, the smallest portion of the overall *sententia*; *colon*, which Isidore describes as a 'limb' (*membrum*) of the *sententia* and which is itself composed of *commata*; and finally, *periodus*, which composes the full *sententia*. Each portion of the *sententia* is marked off by the appropriate placement of a point, either at the base of the line of writing (for *comma*), in the middle of the line of writing (*colon*), or at the top of a letter (for the *periodus*).

Although units of meaning coincide with syntax, the marking of *cola*, *commata* and *periodus* is not the marking of syntax. Isidore does not define the limit of *cola* or *commata* in syntactic terms, but in terms of pronunciation: 'Periodus autem longior esse non debet quam ut uno spiritu proferatur' (I.xviii.2).[23] The system, though potentially analytic, is orally based, interpretative in its function and applicable only to prose. (In a concluding remark, Isidore describes the system he has outlined as that in use 'apud oratores'.) For poetry, a much more mechanically precise system sets off units of verse, and such a system marks off scansion first and only coincidentally meaning. Here *comma* and *colon* are defined by the number of feet in a line. The *periodus* is the whole verse. In the system Isidore describes, pointing marks off verse graphically not for sense, but for metre. Such a system antedates the introduction of spatial format as an element of punctuation for verse.[24] When Latin verse is regularly written in lines of verse, format then frees pointing to express meaning beyond the distinction of metre.

POINTING IN OLD ENGLISH VERSE

To my knowledge, no contemporary description of pointing practice in Old English has survived to modern times. It is probable that no such description ever existed and even more likely that none was ever written down. Accordingly, the various statements which editors of Old English poetic works have made about pointing in the manuscripts have often been wary, and just as often, conflicting. Most of these discussions take for granted that a scribe pointed mostly for the same reasons a modern writer punctuates – to direct readers and simplify their task. But this assumption, based on a modern, literate model of reading, requires examining. Another

---

[23] 'However, the period ought not to be longer than what may be spoken in one breath.'

[24] On space as a form of punctuation see Parkes, 'Punctuation, or Pause and Effect', p. 130, n. 14.

tacit assumption about Old English punctuation construes pointing as more or less conventional, that is, that usage is regular and that symbols have fixed meaning. Such an assumption arises naturally from the more modern practice of reading, which requires considerable conventional visual information from formatting.[25]

There is another difficulty in the current state of our knowledge of Old English pointing of verse. The significance of pointing has been systematically analysed in only a limited number of poetic texts.[26] General studies have not been helpful. On slender evidence Förster pronounced pointing in the Exeter Book metrical, and the label seems to have stuck.[27] Editors, perhaps encouraged by the 'merely' metrical significance of points, generally overlook scribal indications of stops and firmly distinguish independent and dependent clauses even in cases where the Old English text is clearly ambiguous.[28] A further difficulty, at root palaeographical, lies in the freedom which medieval readers felt in marking texts. The consequence of this freedom is what amounts to layers of points – a difficult and frustrating task to puzzle out and one not always assured of success. In fact, pointing practice has been so difficult to make sense of, that the most thorough of the editors who describe punctuation in the Exeter Book calls it 'not systematic nor . . . random'.[29]

The description 'not systematic' and 'not random' is a difficult coupling. If we focus on the latter term 'not random' we can only conclude that the occurrence of points fits some recognizable pattern, that the marks are meaningful. But the 'not systematic' virtually denies us this comfort. The middle ground between 'systematic' and 'random' describes an area in which the use of marks is meaningful but inconsistent. Opinion on the nature of their meaning has varied between metrical and syntactic significance, and in the latter case among several types of marking. A recent approach applies Malcolm Parkes's observation about pointing in Latin to Old English poetic texts. In this view the scribe would point a type

[25] See above, p. 18, n. 58.

[26] See *The Wanderer*, ed. Dunning and Bliss, pp. 4–11; *Old English Riddles*, ed. Williamson, pp. 12–19 and Appendix C.

[27] *The Exeter Book of Old English Poetry*, ed. Chambers, Förster and Flowers, pp. 61–2.

[28] See Mitchell, 'Dangers of Disguise', pp. 385–413, who warns about ignoring scribal punctuation and substituting modern marks. See also his remarks on modern editorial punctuation for the complex sentence in *Old English Syntax* I, § 769–72.

[29] *Old English Riddles*, ed. Williamson, p. 18, citing Dunning and Bliss, *Wanderer*, p. 11, with approval.

of passage as a guide and leave the next similar one alone.[30] In Parkes's
reading of the evidence of Latin manuscripts, pointing functions analogously to construe-marks, and scribes, like testy school masters, push
their readers to work at a text. In the analyses of Dunning and Bliss and of
Williamson, scribes try valiantly to extend a limited number of marks to
indicate the subtlety of verse. There is an attractiveness to these
approaches, but an insurmountable difficulty as well. Parkes's scribe had to
copy critically, know the text in advance of reading it, and have a system to
draw on. Dunning and Bliss's scribe must clearly have worked in a
vacuum, ignorant of practices used in pointing Latin verse. But manuscripts of Latin verse in England already in the late tenth century were
pointed, often with the punctus versus and punctus elevatus, and these
seem not to have been used regularly for Old English verse. Why was there
no borrowing if the scribes wished to help a reader through difficult syntax
or meaning? Four interrelated questions present themselves: (1) What is
the origin of the points? (2) What is the relationship of points to the text in
which they appear? (3) Do these points articulate a set of coherent
conventions? (4) What are these points supposed to mark? Answers to
these questions should help to resolve not only the issue of the functional
significance of the points in context, but also the larger question of the
evidence such pointing practice provides about the sort of literacy behind
these poetic texts.

The first of the four is a simple question with a difficult answer.
Questioning the origin of the points seeks nothing more esoteric than to
know how the points got there. For any extant manuscript, two dia-
metrically opposed answers on the origin of points are possible. The first
answer is that the scribe himself is responsible for all points. This simple
approach implies that either the scribe had exemplars before him which
were unpointed, or that he chose to ignore the pointing before him and do
his own. It is not impossible that his exemplars lacked points if they were
sufficiently early, but it is unlikely. Most Old English verse survives in
manuscripts which post-date 970. The earliest manuscript transmitting
Old English verse, Caedmon's *Hymn* in Leningrad, Saltykov-Schedrin
Public Library, Q. v. I. 18 (mid-eighth century), uses only a terminal point
at the end of the verses. CUL, Kk. 5. 16 lacks the terminal point and places

30 McGovern, 'Unnoticed Punctuation', pp. 85–6, uses Parkes's comments in 'Punctuation, or Pause and Effect', pp. 137–9. Parkes's comments are cited with approval by
Mitchell, *Old English Syntax* I, § 711.

its only point after 6b to mark, it would seem, an independent clause. The next in age, the *Metrical Preface* and *Epilogue* to Alfred's translation of the *Regula pastoralis* in Oxford, Bodleian Library, Hatton 20 (written 890–7), place some points in the text to mark statements. Assuming that Hatton 20 illustrates contemporary practice and was neither retrograde nor ahead of its time, the presence of such points suggests that an unpointed poetic exemplar would have to have been written much earlier. Alternatively, the pointing in the A, B and C records of the *Chronicle* verses, as we saw in ch. 5, suggests that the last quarter of the tenth century saw change in the practice of pointing verse and considerable variety in that practice. Whatever may be the dates and provenances of the exemplars for the four codices of Old English verse, their use of points was an expression of a cultural moment in literacy and is understandable only within the context of English scribal practice of the late tenth and early eleventh centuries.

We are left with the other possible answer to the first question, that the scribe ignored previous pointing and did his own. The differences between the pointing of Caedmon's *Hymn* in CUL, Kk. 3. 18 and in its probable exemplar, Oxford, Corpus Christi College 279, as well as the changes the scribe of the C-version of the *Chronicle* made when pointing the entry for 937, indicate that such alterations certainly occurred. The attraction of this answer is that it allows a clear analysis of pointing by choice. However, this approach to the question also requires that pointing practice be more or less consistently applied throughout the book to avoid charging the scribe with whimsical practice – a charge which unfortunately obviates any analysis of systematic pointing. In fact, pointing is not consistent in the Exeter Book or the Vercelli Book, and this fact may be connected either to the circumstances of their copying or to the nature of the books as miscellanies.[31]

Even if it were possible to get around these difficulties, there are other serious problems with assigning the scribe responsibility for all points. This view of the scribe's task makes it impossible to explain the assortment of bizarre, non-metrical, non-syntactic, non-palaeographical points sprinkled throughout the Exeter Book, the Vercelli Book and the Nowell Codex. If the scribe intended them, they can only be ascribed to whim,

---

[31] On the argument that the Exeter Book may have been copied in three booklets (basically three stints by the same scribe, though over time), see Conner, 'Structure of the Exeter Book', pp. 237–8.

incompetence or malice. Equally serious is the problem that scribal origin for pointing is sharply at odds with the very probable conclusion that the copying of these books was relatively mechanical, given tell-tale errors in transmission.[32] Mechanical copying and intentional pointing are an unlikely mix. Intentional pointing, if it is intelligent, requires the copyist to perform some analysis – metrical, syntactic or otherwise – while writing, or to have known the text in advance.

The opposite position to the previous one is that the scribe simply copied all points as he saw them. This position nicely fits Sisam's conclusion, that textual errors are the result of mechanical copying. On this hypothesis, the scribe is an occasionally unsuccessful xerox machine. This view of the scribe's activity also makes explicable the appearance of bizarre mid-word or mid-half-line points – he copied these from exemplars which pointed at the end of a page or folio, and these are 'palaeographical' points rendered meaningless away from their purely spatial context. But this view begs the question. At what point in the copying were the points deliberately put in? A compromise position, that the scribe copied some points and added others, is similarly unrewarding, begging the question of which points were copied and which added. The choice among answers to question 1 is virtually impossible to resolve here and may depend on answers to the other three.

The second question, about the relationship between points and text, requires certain fine distinctions. It requires us to look away from the scribe, the reader and the manuscript, and to focus on an abstraction, the text. I ask the question despite my discomfort with its premise, since an 'abstract' text is only a speculative idea apart from the reality which the transmitting manuscript assures it. However, the framing of the question focuses attention on the issue of logical priority for text or points. For example, a statement that pointing is independent of the 'abstract' text implies both the existence of a coherent set of conventions for distinguishing either metre or syntax, and well-trained scribes, schooled to interpret a text by adding points. The scribe would know, for example, that a point goes before a subordinate clause or after a b-line, or at the end of a poem.

---

[32] On the copying of the Exeter Book, see Sisam, *Studies*, pp. 97–8. On the copying of the Vercelli Book, see *ibid.*, pp. 110–13 and Scragg, 'Accent Marks', p. 704. Boyle, 'Nowell Codex', p. 26, argues that the scribes copied closely from an identically lineated exemplar.

The major difficulty in entertaining the independence of pointing from 'abstract' text is the nature of most of the extant pointing. Except for Liber I of Oxford, Bodleian Library, Junius 11, whose pointing is consistent and metrical, and for which pointing only one scribe (and possibly a corrector) was responsible, the major codices and most other Old English verse copied before the eleventh century appear to have been pointed sporadically. While it is possible to make sense of the great majority of these points, such sense is made after the fact, and it is difficult to infer systematic pointing when the absence of points carries no predictive value.

The opposite statement, that pointing is text-specific, implies that the 'abstract' text itself is logically prior to the pointing and, in fact, determines the placement of a point and its significance. This approach to the relationship between points and text suggests that pointing is primarily a response to a reading of a text, rather than an objective articulation of a system of meaning. For any textual transmission, text-specific pointing may have two different implications. In an idealist reading of 'text', it means that the pointing of a text is fixed and travels with that text like a gloss, and in a materialist reading of 'text', it means that pointing changes (varies with the scribe who 'reads' the text) but is in each instance unique to that particular text. Text-specific pointing does not contradict the existence of a system of pointing; neither does it require it. In this approach to the significance of points in text, a point need mean no more than 'pause here'. Text-specific pointing is more likely a product of a rhetorical understanding of a text than a syntactic one, because syntax requires a system and rhetoric allows latitude in interpretation.

The question on the existence of conventions focuses not on the nature of the relationship of points to text but on the meaning of the points themselves. Even a cursory look at the manuscripts suggests that conventions differed at different times. A comparison of the pointing of Old English verse in Junius 11, Leningrad Q. v. I. 18, BL, Cotton Tiberius A. vi and Cotton Tiberius B. i necessitates the conclusion that either there were conventions unique to the eighth, tenth and eleventh centuries, or that pointing varied with the class of the text (whether liturgical, historical, secular, etc.).[33] However, variations among manuscripts and our still preliminary knowledge of provenance make it difficult to generalize

[33] See Ker, *Catalogue*, no. 334 (s. x/xi, xi[1]); Gneuss, 'Preliminary List', no. 846 (s. viii[med]); Ker, *Catalogue*, no. 188 (s. x[2]); and *ibid.*, no. 192 (s. xi[1]–xi[2]), respectively.

about the degree to which conventions (if indeed they existed) were followed.

A statement of the notion of conventional pointing would explain points as dependent on the scribe's application of general principles (for example, 'a point means pause. Use whenever necessary'.) In other words, points appeal to some general conventions for meaning, but their presence or absence is determined by considerations other than either metre or syntax, possibly by rhetoric, perceived 'importance' of the poetic work, or interpretation.

The nature of such conventions remains to be explored. Before the eleventh century, at any rate, pointing of Old English poetry does not resemble that for Latin verse. For Latin, pointing was hierarchical and generally used a two-position system at medial and high position to mark divisions of sense. Later, the punctus elevatus and the punctus versus would distinguish heavier or lighter stops. For verse in Latin, points marked the limits of lines. In Old English, heavy punctuation (some combination of commas and dots or dashes and dots) marked the end of a poem or (less regularly) the end of a textual division. Otherwise, the only mark used before the eleventh century (when Latin usage appears in Old English verse manuscripts) was a medial point.

The final question of the four asks what the points are supposed to mark. Without immediately referring to practice in the manuscripts, it will be useful to explore the conditions under which certain answers to the question would be possible. Traditionally, studies of the pointing of Old English verse have considered metrical and syntactic possibilities.

Metrical pointing has as its object the visual delineation of verses within the physical line of writing. This was certainly the case with pointing of Latin verse up to the eighth century; and to the extent that any pointing in an Old English manuscript is metrical by intention, it is related in this way to the earlier Latin system. The difficulty in assigning metrical significance to pointing in Old English is twofold. The first results from the general stylistic feature of Old English verse which relies on apposition and variation by half-line.[34] Generally, the half-line tends to be a syntactic unit. In such cases, a point after the half-line will appear to have more than one significance. The second difficulty lies in apparent inconsistency in the use of points. While for many manuscripts it is possible to estimate the percentage of lines pointed, such information is often misleading. A 20 per

[34] F. C. Robinson, *Beowulf and the Appositive Style* (Knoxville, TN, 1985), p. 60.

cent rate of marking does not mean that every fifth line is pointed, for one often finds clusters of points separated by large stretches of unpointed lines. Were pointing to have primarily metrical significance, we should expect a regular frequency and a high ratio of lines pointed to total number of lines. An especially important indicator of metrical pointing is pointing which interrupts the flow of syntax, whether at a- or b-line. A further indication of metrical pointing would be an only rare occurrence of anomalous points in mid-half-line (excluding, that is, points for monosyllables, numerals and runes).

Syntactic pointing has as its goal the visual delineation of meaning rather than form. In this approach to pointing, meaning is segmented formally in units of syntax, rather than rhythmic units, and thus analysis of pointing by syntactic units concentrates on the extent to which points mark off clauses, modifiers, series or apposition rather than verses. Depending on the level at which one aims a syntactic analysis, a ratio of points to possible syntactic units usually looks better than the ratio of points to actual metrical units. For one thing, there are more half-lines than syntactic units in any given poem. Most obviously there are many fewer independent clauses than lines of verse, since independent clauses (or coordinate or subordinate clauses) are composed of aggregates of smaller units. But even conceding the simple problem of numbers, syntax at least appears to have the advantage over metre as the goal of most pointing, because a syntactic hypothesis accommodates a greater number of points than a metrical one.

A point is a complex sign which is non-verbal in nature. It differs from a letter in that it does not signal the articulation of a sound, and it differs from a word in that it does not signify an utterance. Representing neither sound nor word, it is, nonetheless, a sign which predicates a relationship, indicates an operation or gives a direction to the reader. In a study of the ways in which Old English poetry is accommodated by and assimilated within the literate frameworks of the transmission of information, the presence and distribution of points directly measures a need for increased visual information in the reading of the verse. The relative economy in its use before the early eleventh century and its appreciable lag behind the use of points in Latin verse suggest that the early need for such pointing was small. As I read the evidence, the early paucity of pointing speaks to a tacit understanding that a reader of verse brought the necessary interpretative information to the text, aided by memory and by a deep familiarity with the formulaic conventions of Old English verse. Increasingly consistent pointing in the manuscripts of Old English verse indexes the growing textuality of the verse and the distance of the reader from vital oral tradition. In ch. 7 which follows, I shall attempt to apply this theoretical discussion to an understanding of the pointing of the four great poetic codices.

7

Reading and pointing in the major poetic codices

The greatest portion of surviving Old English verse is transmitted in four unique codices. Three of these, the Exeter Book, the Vercelli Book and the Nowell Codex, were probably copied in the last quarter of the tenth century. The fourth, the Junius Manuscript, is somewhat later, perhaps datable to the early years of the eleventh century. Because they preserve so much of the verse we value, their evidence about copying and reading and their witness to the development of graphic information for directing reading, are crucially important. Their use of space and their varieties of pointing confirm the suggestive evidence of the *Chronicle* manuscripts. Pointing in the three earlier codices is both individual and expressive. Its appearance suggests a transitional phase between the low visual information offered in the earliest manuscript records and the full pointing of the later eleventh century. This transition can best be examined through the trends common to the four codices and the divergencies among them.

THE EXETER BOOK

Exeter, Cathedral Library, 3501, the poetic miscellany known as the Exeter Book, was probably copied some time between the years 970 and 1000.[1] Beyond that general statement and the knowledge that this is the *mycel englisc boc* mentioned by Leofric in his donation to Exeter Cathedral, little is actually known about the book.[2] While the scribe of the Exeter

---

[1] Ker, *Catalogue*, no. 116 (s. x²); Sisam, *Studies*, p. 99, suggests 970–1000. References to edited poems in the Exeter Book are to *The Exeter Book*, ed. Krapp and Dobbie, ASPR 3, unless otherwise specified.

[2] On the donation list see E. M. Drage, 'Bishop Leofric and Exeter Cathedral Chapter (1050–1072): a Reassessment of the Manuscript Evidence' (unpubl. DPhil dissertation, Oxford Univ., 1978).

Book probably also copied London, Lambeth Palace Library, 149 (fols. 1–138) and Oxford, Bodleian Library, Bodley 319, the provenance of none of these manuscripts is certain.[3] The script of the book is a deliberate Anglo-Saxon Square minuscule with careful attention to hair strokes on 't' and 'g' and finishing strokes on 'a'.[4] The poetry is copied in long lines whose only relief is the distinction the scribe makes between individual poems. Between the end of one poem and the beginning of another the scribe leaves the remainder of the line of writing blank and often skips a line between texts.

The scribe employs both large and small capital initials in the Exeter Book. His large ornamented capital initials mark major divisions in the writing, either between what we recognize as individual poems or between major divisions of a poem. His usual practice in signalling a beginning is to write the initial letter as a very large capital, several lines tall, and to write the rest of the word, or sometimes the rest of the line, in smaller, square capitals. In *Christ II* 440, for example, *Nuðugeornlice gæst/gerynum* is written with a large, ornamented capital 'N' and with the rest of the letters up to *gæst* in large square capitals. *Guthlac B* 819 also capitalizes a portion of its first verse line (*Ðæt is wide cuð welra cneorissum*), where initial 'Ð' is a large decorated capital, the rest of 819a is in square capital letters, and *we-* is in smaller capitals. By contrast, *Judgement Day I* begins with a large decorated 'Ð' alone, and *Wulf and Eadwacer* with a single capital 'L', to mention just a few examples. In general, the two collections of Riddles in the Exeter Book begin either with a capital *IC* or with a single initial capital.

While small capitals appear in most of the longer poems, the rationale behind their use is not often clear, and it seems as if their use varies with the poem in which they appear.[5] As textual markers, capitals are supplemen-

---

[3] Ker, *Catalogue*, nos. 275 and 308. N. F. Blake, 'The Scribe of the Exeter Book', p. 319, arguing from the identification of Old English glosses in Oxford, Bodleian Library, Bodley 319 as being in the hand of the scribe of the Exeter Book, concludes that this scribe could not have been responsible for standardizing the language of the collection in the codex.

[4] On the script of the book, see the introductory chapter by R. Flower in *The Exeter Book of Old English Poetry*, ed. Chambers, Förster and Flower, pp. 83–90. Flower's belief (p. 83) that several scribes had been at work on the manuscript has not been widely accepted. See Ker, *Catalogue*, p. 153.

[5] *Exeter Book*, ed. Krapp and Dobbie, ASPR 3, lxxvi–lxxxi, prints a list of small capitals in the manuscript. However, their identification of a large number of long 'i's as small

ted by two other marking strategies: points and spacing. The scribe at times leaves one or two lines blank between poems, for example, between Christ I and Christ II, between Guthlac A and Guthlac B, and between Wanderer and Gifts.[6] As a rule, within the two collections of Riddles, the scribe does not space between riddles, but does begin each riddle on a new line at the margin.[7] Empty lines are not only devices for separating what we acknowledge as discrete works. Within longer poems which are undoubtedly intact, the written text is, on a few occasions, broken up by some combination of space, capital and heavy punctuation.[8] Such divisions are often referred to as 'sections', and varying levels of significance have been assigned to them.[9]

capitals is misleading. These long 'i's' at times are used internally within a line to distinguish them particularly from the initial minim of 'n'. Most long 'i's' are not small capitals. Krapp and Dobbie are also unfortunately inconsistent in distinguishing large 'ð's as small capitals or lower case letters. The discussion which follows identifies small capitals (usually other than 'i') by size rather than shape in selected texts from the Exeter Book.

[6] The definition of discrete poems can, of course, be problematic, especially when part of the criteria used to determine the limits of a poem is the array of capitals. See, for example, the question over the opening lines of *Guthlac A*.

[7] See *Old English Riddles*, ed. Williamson, pp. 12–13.

[8] For example, the scribe uses heavy punctuation, a blank line and a capital in *Guthlac A* after 92b, 169b, 261b, 403b, 529b, 617b, 721b; in *Guthlac B* after 893b, 975b, 1059b, 1133b, 1223b, 1304b. *Phoenix* has heavy punctuation, space and capital after 84b, 181b, 264b, 423b, 517b, 588b (heavy punctuation and capital at 349b, before a new folio). *Juliana* has heavy punctuation, space and capital after 104b, 224b, 344b, 453b; heavy punctuation and a capital alone at 606b.

[9] In Oxford, Bodleian Library, Junius 11, BL, Cotton Vitellius A. xv, and in *Elene* (Vercelli, Biblioteca Capitolare, CXVII), 'sectional' divisions are marked by roman numerals. In the other poetic works of the Vercelli Book and in the longer poems of the Exeter Book, textual divisions are marked only by heavy punctuation and spacing. Argument on the meaning of textual divisions in the major codices has focused on two origins for the divisions, authorial and scribal. H. Bradley ('The Numbered Sections in Old English Poetical MSS', *PBA* 7 (1915–16), 165–87, at 180–1) argued that numbered sections in *Genesis A*, *Genesis B*, *Exodus* and *Elene* correspond to separate sheets in the 'archtypal MSS'. B. J. Timmer ('Sectional Divisions of Poems in Old English Manuscripts', *MLR* 47 (1952), 319–22) views the divisions as authorial 'psychological units'. In a similar vein, E. R. Anderson (*Cynewulf: Structure, Style, and Theme in his Poetry* (Rutherford, NJ, 1983), p. 104) argues that the fifteen 'fitts' in *Elene* reflect poetic structure and that the division is authorial. P. Cavill ('Sectional Divisions in Old English Poetic Manuscripts', *Neophilologus* 69 (1985), 156–9, at 156) makes a similar argument.

Booklet II and the Problem with Pointing in the Exeter Book

The lack of agreement among scholars on the use and purpose of graphic markers in the Exeter Book is an indication of the complexity of the problem before us.[10] Except for the general remarks by Förster and by Krapp and Dobbie, who addressed themselves to the book as a whole, commentary on pointing in the Exeter Book has, by and large, been focused on individual poems. This fact is a helpful reminder that pointing differs from work to work in the Exeter Book. That difference and the reasons behind it will become clearer by concentrating first on one portion of the Exeter Book – that section which Patrick Conner has defined as Booklet II.[11]

There are seventeen discrete poems in Booklet II, as indicated by the scribe's arrangement of blocks of texts and their separation by heavy terminal punctuation and large, decorated capital initials.[12] These written texts differ markedly in their number of points and in the environment in which points appear. A crude indication of this difference is the ratio of points to lines for each text. Across the seventeen texts the ratios vary from a high of .72 points per line (*Widsith*) to a low of .15 (*Vainglory*), the

[10] Förster (*Exeter Book*, ed. Chambers, Förster and Flower, p. 61), considers the mark of punctuation a 'metrical point'. Krapp and Dobbie, on the basis of its sporadic nature, conclude that the pointing is neither metrical nor structural (ASPR 3, xxii). R. Woolf (*Juliana*, ed. R. Woolf (London, 1966), p. 2) considers the pointing metrical not grammatical. Dunning and Bliss (*Wanderer*, p. 11), in a detailed discussion of the problem, suggest that scribal pointing performed three functions: to mark sections in the development of the poem; to mark off parallel clauses; to elucidate difficult points of syntax. Williamson's discussion of the pointing of the riddles of the Exeter Book (*Old English Riddles*, pp. 12–19 and Appendix C) is an exemplary treatment of the subject. His conclusions about metrical pointing are significant, since he observes that pointing is infrequently solely metrical (*ibid.*, p. 16). With Dunning and Bliss, he concludes that pointing is not systematic and not random (*ibid.*, p. 18). In the most recent examination of pointing in the Exeter Book, McGovern ('Unnoticed Punctuation') discusses dry-point marks, most of which occur in *Christ II* and *Guthlac A*. He infers a date before 1200 and suggests that their purpose 'appears to have been a preparation of the text for more effective reading, either private or public' (at p. 95).

[11] That is, 53r–97v (*Azarias–Partridge* 1–2a). See Conner, 'Structure of the Exeter Book', p. 233.

[12] I have counted *Maxims* as three separate texts. The scribe ends *Maxims I* with ':~:7' and begins *Maxims II* with a large decorated capital 'F' and smaller capitals for 'ORST'. He ends *Maxims II* with ':7' and begins *Maxims III* with a large decorated capital 'R' and 'ÆD' in smaller capitals.

difference a factor of almost five.[13] In themselves, these ratios mean nothing; their significance lies solely in their indication of differences in practice.

We may start by examining *Widsith*, which offers itself to our attention by its extraordinary number of points. In 143 lines, *Widsith* has 103 points. Of these, only five occur before internal small capitals. By far the largest number of points (54) separate parallel clauses. In poetic catalogues of heroes and tribes (18a–34b) there are twenty-seven points (12 a-line, 15 b-line). In the account of tribes from 57a–69b, there are fourteen points (1 a-line, 1 mid-half-line, 12 b-lines). There are many points within hypermetric a-lines and narrative stretches with no points at all, particularly between 1a–13b and between 135a–44b. From *Widsith* one might reasonably conclude that pointing is used to separate items in a catalogue in the Exeter Book. But if we look at other catalogues elsewhere in the book, we are forced to revise this judgement. Two types of catalogues are prominent in this portion of the Exeter Book, the *sum-* catalogue and the *ne-* catalogue. A look at the arrangement and pointing of these catalogues will necessitate revising any larger conclusions on catalogues drawn from *Widsith*.

The Wanderer and *The Seafarer* are both elegiac poems mourning exile and the loss of home and companions. They are very much companion pieces in their stoic approach to anguish and pain, in the conventions of such expressions, in the use of hypermetric lines and in the rhetorically emotional use of catalogues. *Ne-* catalogues are used in each poem. In *The Wanderer* 65b–69b, this catalogue describes the attributes a man needs to endure:

Wita scealge þyldig. Ne sceal no to hat heort netohræd
wyrde. neto wac wiga neto wan hydig. neto forht. neto fægen. neto
feoh gifre. nenæfre gielpes togeorn ær he geare cun/ne.[14]

The statement begins on a new page (77v1–4), and a point after *geþyldig* (at the end of a b-verse) sets off the catalogue. The individual items are not separated by points except for those at 68a and 68b. The scribe points 68a twice, within the half-line (that is, between the two *ne-* statements) and at

13 See the Appendix (below, pp. 193–4) on the pointing of the Exeter Book poems.
14 'A wise man must be patient: he must not be too angry, nor too hasty of speech, nor too weak in battle, nor too foolhardy, nor too timid, nor too cheerful, nor too greedy for wealth, nor too quick with a boast, before he is well experienced.'

159

the end of the half-line – an unusual strategy. The points in this passage are all genuine, in my judgement, although the point between *fægen* and *ne to* is somewhat crowded. The phrase *ne to fægen* is written in an erasure, and if it is a correction, that may explain the compression of space between *fægen* and the following *to*. In a similar passage of description, *The Seafarer* describes the qualities of a *modwlanc* man:

eard gesece forþon nis þæs mod wlonc mon ofer eorþan ne
his gifena þæs god neingeoguþe toþæs hwæt ne inhis dædū
to þæs deor ne him his dryhten toþæs hold. þ he ahis sæfo
re sorge næbbe to hwon hine dryhten gedon wille nebiþ
him to hearpan hyge. neto hring þege. neto wife wyn. neto
worulde hyht neymbe owiht elles nefne ymb yða gewealc.
Ac ahafað longunge seþe onlagu fundað. bearwas blost.   (82r3–9)[15]

The point after *hold* (41b) probably marks a subordinate clause. There are a few points in 44a–46b which appear to separate items in the catalogue (after *hyge* 44a and *hringþege* 44b, after *wyn* 45a and *gewealc* 46b), but no consistent run of points separates items in the catalogue. In the brief *ne*-catalogue in 94a–96b (82r17–19), there are no points whatsoever.

The Phoenix, in part a paraphrase of Lactantius's Latin poem, has not been linked with any specific antecedent Latin manuscripts, though there has been much speculation on its Latin sources.[16] Despite the poem's clear debt to Latin verse and prose, its graphic display in Exeter Book is far from that for contemporary Latin verse. *The Phoenix* is among the most sparely pointed poems in the entire collection, with a rate of .16 points per line. Conventional opening signals separate it from the preceding *Azarias* by heavy punctuation and a blank line. The first half line, *Hæbbe ic gefrugnen*, is arrayed in a range of letter sizes. 'H' is a large decorated capital initial, the

[15] '(. . . that far from here I seek out a land of foreigners.) Indeed, there is no man on the earth proud in spirit to such a degree, nor so good in his gifts, nor so bold in his youth, nor so bold in his deeds, nor whose lord is loyal to him to such a degree that he will not always have distress about his sea-voyage, to what end the Lord will bring him. Nor will his thought be on the harp, nor on the receiving of rings, nor his joy in a woman, nor pleasure in the world, nor about anything else unless about the rolling of the waves, but always he will have longing, who sets out to sea. (The groves take on blooms . . .)', *Seafarer* 37b–48a.

[16] On the individuality of *The Phoenix* and its complex relationship with its possible sources, see D. G. Calder, 'The Vision of Paradise: a Symbolic Reading of "The Phoenix"', *ASE* 1 (1972), 167–81, at 167–8.

remainder of the half-line, up to 'gefrug-' is in smaller, square capitals, and the end of the participle '-nen' is in normal, minuscule letters. A medial point follows this display.

The scribe divides the text of *The Phoenix* into eight sections ranging in length from 70+ to 90+ lines by using a mixture of capitals and heavy terminal points.[17] In each of these cases, the scribe writes a large decorated capital initial and usually a following capital letter. In contrast to its light pointing, the poem shows a fairly well-developed mapping of sections onto narrative divisions in the text of the poem. The break at 84b divides an account of paradise from a description of the phoenix. The other breaks mark off in order the bird's building of its nest-pyre (181b); its renewed life (264b); a recapitulation and allegorical application of the story to the temptation and fall (350b); a general tropological application of the phoenix legend to Christians (423b); an account of the Last Judgement (517b); and further descriptions of the Last Judgement (588b). In the case of the latter two segments, the capitals actually break up a larger, coherent section, which would have otherwise been 159 lines long. Considerations of length or perhaps scribal stint, rather than conceptual structure, are responsible for the division of the last two sections.

Within the sections of *The Phoenix* are junctures marked by smaller capitals preceded by points.[18] These junctures (which account for twenty-four of the 109 points in the piece) are not as easily explained as the textual divisions marked by the large capitals and heavy punctuation. They occur irregularly, most often preceding the beginning of an independent clause. There are a further twenty-eight points which by themselves separate independent clauses. The other single largest grouping of points occurs in the concluding macaronic verses where thirteen points set off eleven macaronic lines, although the points are unevenly distributed.[19] In terms of style, *The Phoenix* contains a number of *ne*-catalogues: at 56r7–10 (14b–18b), 56v7–17 (50a–64b), 57v18–22 (134a–39b) and 64v14–16 (611a–14a), none of which is pointed. The majority of points in *The Phoenix*, however, occur at the juncture of two independent clauses. More than half of these in turn combine with spacing and capitals to divide the

---

[17] See above, n. 8.

[18] At 90a, 111a, 120a, 125a, 153a, 236b, 261b, 274b, 305a, 310a, 319a, 381a, 393a, 443a, 470a, 491a, 622a. In 261b–262a, *Se dreoseð oft | æt middre nihte*, *se* may introduce an independent or a dependent clause. See Mitchell, *Syntax* I, § 52.

[19] Four lines receive a- and b-line points, two none at all.

text in sections. While these points are part metrical, part syntactic and part 'rhetorical', their use is text-specific – that is, no one notion of system can be used to predict the appearance of a point save, perhaps, in the macaronic verses, which by their peculiarity invited pointing. Text-specificity of punctuation is a broad sign that pointing is subjective and marks a discrete reading of a text.

Juliana is approximately the same length as *The Phoenix*, follows it immediately in the manuscript, and is pointed at a similar rate, about 17 per cent. Here, too, the scribe uses capitals to highlight the opening of the text. *The Phoenix* ends with heavy terminal punctuation (:7 :- :7), and after two blank lines, *Juliana* opens with a large, decorated capital 'H'. The rest of the half-line is written in smaller square capitals followed by a medial point. From these indications, it might be expected that *Juliana* and *The Phoenix* would be formatted and pointed in a similar fashion. However, such is not the case.

In the six instances in the poem where the written text is divided by heavy terminal punctuation and capitals,[20] there is no indication of the sort of conceptual divisions which appear in *The Phoenix*. The breaks after 104b and 224b occur between speeches and actually interfere with statement and reply. The breaks after 344b and 454b occur within Juliana's debate with the devil. The last break, after 606b, separates Eleusius's decision to behead Juliana from the saint's joyous reaction to the news. A more coherent place for a break might have been following 602a, also beginning with *þa*. In addition to these divisions, there are thirty-one small capitals preceded by simple points, all of which (except those at 96a, 167a, and 540a marking direct address) separate independent clauses.[21] Additionally, forty-five further points distinguish independent clauses, for a total of seventy-nine of 126 points marking statements. Most heavy punctuation or combinations of points and capitals mark the opening and closing of formal speeches by Juliana or her tormentors. By contrast, the long *sum*- catalogue in 472a–94a (72v) within the devil's confession has no capitals and only one point. In *Juliana*, points are rarely used within a

---

[20] These are following 104b, 224b, 344b, 453b, ?558b (a folio is missing after 73v; only heavy terminal punctuation remains after 558b) and 606b. All except the break at 606b are marked as well by a blank line.

[21] These occur at 18a, 26b, 32a, 46a, 58a, 66a, 89a, 93a, 96a, 117a, 119a, 130a, 132a, 140a, 147a, 167a, 175a, 189a, 260a, 267a, 287a, 302a, 319a, 321a, 357a, 417b, 530b, 539a, 540a, 577b and 635a.

speech. When used, however, they set off direct address from the rest of the text.[22]

The pair of gnomic poems in the Exeter Book, *The Gifts of Men* and *The Fortunes of Men*, are of comparable lengths, 113 lines and 88 lines respectively. They are similar in another way, in that both use rhetorical catalogues to construct their lists of human possibilities, the first of skills, the second of fates. In *Gifts*, there are *sum-* catalogues at 30a–96b and 106a–113b. A point usually precedes *sum* in the nominative singular.[23] In the catalogue at 106a–113b, all eleven *sumum* clauses are set off by points. There are, however, no small capitals used internally in the poem. By contrast, *The Fortunes of Men* uses points without exception before *sum* in both nominative and oblique cases. Further, of twenty-five instances of *sum* (in any case), sixteen occur with small capital initials.[24] Not all of these begin independent clauses; in fact, those at 67a, 67b and 69b are datives in a series. The comparison of pointing and capitalization in these poems underscores the inconsistency of practice in supplying visual information in the Exeter Book. The generalizations about broader use of points and capitals indicate that practice is highly specific to individual written texts and not predictable by location in the Exeter Book (that is, within or across groupings of texts), length of text, genre or rhetorical trope.

At this stage we must return to the theoretical discussion of ch. 6 to apply its four questions about pointing (in altered order) to the information from the Exeter Book: (1) What do the points mark? (2) What is the relationship of points to text in which they appear? (3) Is there a system? (4) What is the origin of the points? The variety of strategies for providing visual information in the Exeter Book suggests the following answers:

(1) Points in the Exeter Book are neither syntactic nor metrical, if these terms mean that they articulate a system which is predictable. The crucial factor here is that in no text in the Exeter Book is the presence or absence of points predictable given any a priori generalization about placement of points.

(2) Were pointing independent of text, we should expect to see points used at a fairly constant rate, generally in the same way in the same

---

[22] Points also set off long monosyllables, such as *æ*, for example in *The Phoenix* and *Guthlac*, and runes, as elsewhere in the Riddles.

[23] Notable exceptions occur at 31b, 33b, 44a, 51b, 53b and 58b.

[24] That is, at 10a, 15a, 16a, 18b, 21a, 27a, 43a, 48a, 51a, 58a, 67a, 67b, 69b, 77a, 80a and 85a.

circumstances. The preceding discussion has illustrated quite the opposite case – that frequency of pointing is highly variable, and pointing, if ever predictable, is predictable only within a text, that is, after we recognize the pattern for that work. The evidence suggests that pointing in the Exeter Book is text-specific. Neither genre nor trope indicates conventional patterns of pointing, but rather the poem itself has evoked a specific arrangement of points in a reading.

(3) The answer to the question of system is less clear than the answers to questions (1) and (2). In certain situations points are used regularly and formally: they regularly appear around certain monosyllables, for example, *æ* and *o*, and around runes and Roman numerals; occasionally they mark the end of a page in the manuscript; and at times, they end a run of capitals at the beginning of a new work. Internally, by and large, points separate independent clauses from each other, or independent from subordinate clauses. Less frequently, they mark series, and in most poetic works, they are more frequent at the ends of b-lines than a-lines.[25] These trends suggest rudimentary conventions, but in conjunction with the answer to question (1), application of these conventions is individual to the scribe or realized text. The answers to questions (1), (2) and (3) together indicate that points in the Exeter Book construct an individual reading of the text by marking off units of meaning. These units, given the nature of Old English poetry, are usually coincidentally metrical in their shape.

(4) In the abstract, one could argue that the Exeter scribe is responsible for the pointing of the book throughout, but there are subtle (and not so subtle) signs that such is not the case. Among these are the numerous absurd points in mid-line and mid-word which cannot be explained other than by mechanical copying. Further, the number of mechanical errors made by the scribe throughout argues only a modest exactitude in copying.[26] Independent pointing would have required on his part considerable knowledge of the works he copied and a command of the rudiments of pointing. But the variability of pointing in the catalogues suggests that these rudiments were not being applied by the same individual. I suggest, therefore, that most of the points as they appear in the Exeter Book were copied by the scribe from his various exemplars.

[25] See the Appendix to this chapter (below, pp. 188–9).
[26] Sisam, *Studies*, pp. 97–8. See also Blake, 'The Scribe of the Exeter Book', p. 319.

THE VERCELLI BOOK

The Vercelli Book presents a number of problems to students of the major Old English poetic codices. The rationale behind its compilation (mixing six Old English poems and a number of homilies) defies analysis; the place of its copying and the date of its transportation to Vercelli are uncertain.[27] What little appears clear about the Vercelli Book is a product of inference. The consensus of the most recent editors of the book confirms Kenneth Sisam's earlier conclusion that the scribe of the Vercelli Book copied mechanically.[28] The arrangement of the homilies appears accidental, except for three separate groupings, whose texts seem to have been together in the exemplars from which the scribe copied.[29] The Vercelli scribe apparently took no interest in regularizing the dialects of his various exemplars, and likewise seems to have copied his accent marks from the exemplars before him.[30] This apparently mechanical approach to the copying of texts makes the Vercelli Book, like the Exeter Book, a useful witness to the varieties of practice contributing to the development of non-lexical visual cues for reading Old English verse.

Puzzling as it is in other ways, the Vercelli Book epitomizes the conundrum of Anglo-Saxon pointing practices. Copied by one scribe, the book nonetheless records a wide range of practice, and there are almost as many pointing practices as selections (and probably at least as many as exemplars). In its variety (certainly in dialect, orthography and kind of text), it preserves a set of attitudes toward pointing which reveals the state of non-lexical cues around the last quarter of the tenth century. It is entirely possible that here and there in the manuscript points were added later by other hands. Occasionally, for example, a virgule on a punctus elevatus appears to have been added, and some stray accent marks also

---

[27] On the physical compilation of the book, see Scragg, 'Compilation', p. 207, who would localize the compilation of the book to Kent on the basis of the addition of a number of southeastern forms and spelling. M. Halsall ('Vercelli and the *Vercelli Book*', *PMLA* 84 (1969), 1545–50, at 1550) suggests the eleventh century as the date most probable for the book's transportation to Vercelli. See also Sisam, *Studies*, pp. 110–13. R. E. Boenig ('*Andreas*, the Eucharist, and Vercelli', *JEGP* 79 (1980), 313–31, at 331) suggests that the book went to Vercelli with one of the bishops sent for the Council of 1050.

[28] P. Szarmach, 'The Scribe of the Vercelli Book', *SN* 51 (1979), 179–88, at 187; Scragg, 'Compilation', p. 196; *The Vercelli Book*, ed. C. Sisam, p. 37; and Scragg, 'Accent Marks', p. 704.

[29] Scragg, 'Compilation', p. 190.   [30] Scragg, 'Accent Marks', p. 704.

testify to later intervention. However, judging from placement, shape and colour of ink, the majority of points in the Vercelli Book are the work of the copyist of the manuscript. The varying patterns of their appearance in the six poetic works of the Vercelli Book lie at the heart of the conundrum.

Blank space and points (alone and in combination) in the Vercelli Book indicate hierarchies of importance and mark relationships at two distinct levels, the grammatical level of syntactic or metrical units, and the narrative level of large conceptual units of meaning. Of immediate interest to the question of reading are the various uses of points in the verse texts of the Vercelli Book.[31]

Perhaps the first assertion which should be made about pointing in the first verse text of the Vercelli Book, *Andreas* (and this statement holds as well for that in *Fates of the Apostles*), is that few useful generalizations can be made about it. It is, of course, possible to count and list the occurrence of points in various categories. For example, syntactic analysis of the points indicates that 34 per cent of the points in *Andreas* appear in contexts which suggest that they separate independent clauses. A counterbalancing metrical analysis produces the equally correct observation that 98 per cent of the points occur at the end of half-lines. But this statement, suggesting a metrical interpretation of the points, must be qualified as well, since of 3437 half-lines in the poem, only 1673 are pointed, that is, slightly less than 49 per cent.[32] If these statements appear to suggest an inauspicious beginning, it is, nonetheless, a liberating one, for it necessarily frees consideration of the punctuation from the weighty expectation of 'system'.[33] If counts and rates of pointing tell little about the internal significance of punctuation in a text, they can, nonetheless, be quite revealing of differences across patterning in a number of texts, as the following comparative analyses will show. The patterns of points in the

---

[31] The marking of long narrative units is a related but complex question beyond the scope of the present discussion.

[32] Krapp (ASPR 2) postulates in his edition seven missing half-lines (829a, 1036b, 1040b, 1434b, 1667b, 1668a and 1700b) although there are no gaps in the manuscript.

[33] In his consideration of the punctuation of the poems in the Vercelli Book, Krapp (ASPR 2, xxxi) concludes: 'It seems quite probable, however, that much of this inconsistency is due to the heedlessness of scribes in transmitting what may have been originally a more systematic style of punctuation, or perhaps to the editorial policy of the scribe of the Vercelli manuscript.' This view reads the punctuation in the manuscript as evidence of a devolution in practice. My argument, though not an evolutionary one, approaches the problem from the opposite assumption.

verse texts of the Vercelli Book neither indicate careless scribes nor conserve the remains of an originally systematic punctuation. Rather, they constitute in themselves discrete readings of the transmitted, realized texts and indicate developing conventions of use.

Perhaps the best way to illustrate the use of points in *Andreas* is to examine particular passages. Both of the following passages are speeches and occur close together in the manuscript (1345a–59b [47r23–47v11] and 1376a–85b [47v22–48r4]). In the first a devil speaks, in the second, Andreas.

Hearm sceapen agef

7sware fah fyrn sceaþa. 7his fæder oncwæð. NE /
magan we him lungre lað æt fæstan swilt þurh searwe. ga
þe sylfa to. þær þu gegninga. guðe findest frecne
feohtan gifðu furður dearst. to þā an hagan aldre
ge neðan:-
WEÐE magon eaðe eorla leofost ætþam secg
plegan selre gelæran. ærðu gegninga guðe freme.
wiges woman weald huðe sæle ætþam gegn slege.
Utan gangan eft. þ we bysmrigen bendum fæstne.
oðwitan him his wræc sið. Habbað word gearu
wiðþam æglæcan eall ge trahtod . . .[34]

And:

hwæt me eaðe

ælmihtig god niða neregend seðe inmedū iu gefæst
node fyrnum clommum þær ðu syððan a susle /
gebunden. In wræc wunne wuldres blunne syððan ðu for hogedes
heofon cyninges word. þær wæs yfles or ende næfre.
þines wræces weorðeð. Ðu scealt widan feorh. ecan þine yrmðu
þebið a symble. Of dæge on dæg. drohtaþ strengra.[35]

---

[34] 'The wretched one answered him, the hostile ancient fiend, and replied to his father, "We may not inflict evil on him entirely, death through our cunning. Go there yourself. There you will find war at once, a terrible battle, if you dare to venture your life further against that solitary one. Most beloved of earls, we may most easily advise you better about that sword-play, before you make war, the tumult of battle straightaway, whatever may happen to you at the exchange of blows. Let us go back so that we may insult him fast in his bonds, let us reproach him with his exile. Have ready words all prepared against that enemy."'

[35] 'Lo, almighty God will release me easily, the saviour of men, who before fastened you in bondage, in burning bonds. There you have suffered ever after in exile, bound in

Several observations may be made about the mechanics of pointing the first passage: that twice as many b-lines are pointed as a-lines (ten against five); that four of the a-line points mark independent clauses; that capitals are preceded by points. The speech of the sub-demon is interrupted by the thirteenth sectional break, marked by a combination of heavy punctuation, an empty space on the line, a skipped line, and the capitalization of *we þe* with a large, decorated capital wynn and following smaller square capital letters. Conceptually, the points mark off discrete, brief statements in phrases, the consequence of which produces in the rest of the poem a number of peculiar, hanging phrases (here, *þær þu gegninga*). Pointing in this passage presents a relatively hypotactic understanding of the progress of the speech.

The second speech illustrates the other end of the range of pointing practice in this poem. In Andreas's reply, there is no marking of what we would define as subordinate clauses, and the passage proceeds in large sweeps of statements. Despite the lengthy phrases in this passage, there are still peculiar acephalic fragments (for example, *þines wræces weorðeð, of dæge on dæg*) which prevent the judgement that this example of pointing indicates a style more paratactic in nature.

However, the pointing of this speech should not be understood strictly as syntactic. The points mark statements, frequently shaped as short, independent clauses. The pointing represents an understanding of the poem which proceeds locally and immediately. By this I mean that points are placed not according to a spatial understanding of the larger grammatical or logical relationships among elements in a sentence, but rather temporally, as the result of a process of understanding the gradual unfolding of statements in time. This process is responsible, I should argue, for producing the brief, visually hypotactic statements which the points mark and for the number of separated phrases (primarily variations) which result from placement of a point at the earliest apparent end of a statement.

I have claimed that the pointing in *Andreas* is not syntactic but phrasal, and I shall claim further that it is less metrical than rhythmical. While there is a perceptible preference for points following the b-line (a preference which coincides with the trend in the pointing of verse shown in the *Chronicle* records), the elucidation of metrical structure is not the goal of

torment, you forfeited your glory after you despised the word of the king of heaven. There was the beginning of evil; there will never be an end to your exile. You must for eternity increase your misery. Day after day forever your lot will be more miserable.'

punctuation in *Andreas*, as the rate of 49 per cent for b-line points testifies.[36] The effect of pointing the fragments at the end of Andreas's speech
above is, however, distinctly rhythmical with the separation of the temporal markers (*widan feorh, symble, of dæge on dæg*) set off in separate phrases.

Soul and Body I is the next poetic text in the Vercelli Book after *Fates of
the Apostles*, although these two verse texts are separated by some ninety-
four pages of homilies (Homilies VI to XVIII). Although both *Soul
and Body I* and *Andreas* each begin with an initial word capitalized in
approximately the same fashion, the similarity between their use of visual
cues ends there. *Soul and Body I* demonstrates an entirely different use of
internal capitals and points from that in the preceding poems.

The points in *Soul and Body I* are infrequent when compared to those in
Andreas and *Fates*. There are some sixty-two points distributed over the
surviving 166 lines of the poem (a rate of 37 per cent). Almost a third of
these (eighteen) occur before small capitals, and well over half (thirty-six)
mark either independent or subordinate clauses. Another quarter seem to
mark off variations or parallel phrases (sixteen), although these do not
appear with any regularity. The following passage, written out in the lineation of the manuscript, illustrates something of the scribe's practice in
this text.

> scealt ðu minra ge synta
> sceame þrowian onðam myclan dæge þonne eall
> manna cynn se acenneda ealle ge samnað ne eart
> ðu þon leofra nænigū lifigendra men to ge mæccan.
> ne meder ne fæder. ne nænigum ge sybban. þonnese
> swearta hrefen syððan ic ana ofðe utsiðode þurh
> þæs sylfes hand þe ic ær on sended wæs. ne mæg þe nu
> heonon adon hyrsta þe readan. ne gold ne seolfor
> ne þinra goda nan ne þinre bryde beag. ne þin
> gold wela. ne nanþara goda þe ðu iu ahtest. Ac her
> sceolon on bidan ban be reafod besliten synum. 7þe
> þin sawl sceal [7] minum unwillu oft gesecan wemman
> þe mid wordū swa ðu worhtest to me. eart ðu nu dumb

(102r12–24 [49–65a])[37]

---

[36] Such an argument might be made more comfortably for *Fates of the Apostles* where 63 per
cent of b-lines are pointed.

[37] 'On the great day of my prosperity you must suffer shame when the only-begotten one
assembles together all mankind. Nor will you be better loved as a companion for any
living being, neither mother nor father, nor any sibling, than the black raven, after I

This passage begins with an independent clause marked off by a preceding point. However, the passage neatly illustrates the relatively *ad hoc* method of pointing throughout the text and its contrast with practice in *Andreas*. Subsequent clauses, both independent and dependent, may or may not be pointed. (Compare 'ne eart...' [102r14], which is not distinguished from what precedes it, to 'ne mæg...' [102r18] which is.) For *Soul and Body I*, this passage is unusually full in its pointing, owing to the *ne*-catalogues. But even these are inconsistent.[38]

Soul and Body I divides at 126b, where the speaking voice changes, and the blessed soul begins to address its body. The Vercelli manuscript presents the matter from 127a on as if it were a separate sectional division. The rest of 103r20 is blank following the single word, *gehwam*, after which there is heavy punctuation (:7). The next line begins with a capital in the margin. This is the point where the Exeter Book record (*Soul and Body II*) stops.

Soul and Body I points verse differently from *Andreas*, although their general styles might equally be described as phrasal and rhythmical. While it is probable that the scribe derived the pointing of his poems from his exemplars, it cannot be argued that the pointing of *Soul and Body I* represents authorial practice or the practice of a hypothetical original. *Soul and Body II* in the Exeter Book is much more sparsely pointed, although at a rate of 21 per cent is about average for pointing in the Exeter Book. By contrast, *Soul and Body I* points at a rate of 37 per cent. Of the verses which these poems have in common, the Vercelli record places fifty-three points in 126 lines, while the Exeter Book record has twenty-six points in 121 lines. They share points in thirteen places, but considering their 121 lines in common, this figure is not especially impressive. Perhaps more suggestive are the five (of six) capitals which the Exeter Book record shares with the version in the Vercelli Book. However, the Vercelli record has thirteen capitals in the first part of the poem. I am tempted to argue that the pointing in the Exeter Book represents an earlier state of reading the

have travelled alone out of you by that self-same hand by which I was previously sent. Nor may the red ornaments now remove you hence, not gold nor silver, not any of your goods, neither your wife's necklace, nor your rich possessions, nor any of the things which you once owned, but here your bones must abide bereft, torn by sins, and your soul shall often seek you out, all against my will, to reproach you with words, just as you did to me.'

38 Compare 102r19–20 with 102r20–1, for example.

text, but such an argument can only be made as a product of inference from the chronology of pointing practice hypothesized in ch. 5.

The Dream of the Rood is similar in length to *Soul and Body I* and points at a slightly higher rate, 49 per cent. Unfortunately, this statement can be seriously misleading, since the poem is pointed very spasmodically. In the first twenty-one lines, for example, points are infrequent and occur primarily in conjunction with capitals. Following 21b of the poem (and coincident with a new folio on 105r where the scribe changes practice and copies thirty-two lines per page in a smaller, quite compressed hand), pointing becomes much more frequent and tends to favour the marking of b-lines.[39] But from 115a to the end of the poem (the greatest portion of 106r), the poem has only ten points, one of which is terminal.

For sheer scarcity of pointing, few Old English poems can compete with *Elene*, and this poem stands in startling contrast to *Andreas*. Its actual rate of pointing (15 per cent) confirms what is obvious upon even casual examination of the pages of the manuscript, that *Elene* is virtually unpointed. This is not to say that its use of points is without pattern. Quite the contrary: when points occur, almost 60 per cent of them occur before capitals. The contrast between rates of pointing a- and b-lines is also dramatic, with the former at 13 per cent and latter at 87 per cent.

The difference in pointing between *Elene* and *Andreas*, even without the evidence of the other poems, would argue that the Vercelli scribe was not responsible for the pointing of the verse he copied. *Elene* and *Andreas* are both verse narratives, both contain a number of speeches, use highly traditional diction and are divided into fifteen sections. Given their overall similarity as narratives and saints' lives, their different approaches to pointing suggest that their individual exemplars were the source of points. But this said, it must be allowed that the Vercelli scribe has quite probably omitted or added a few points.[40] If points travel with texts, then they do so in the way glosses do and are subject to change by accretion.

[39] On the scribe's shift in practice, see *The Vercelli Book*, ed. C. Sisam, pp. 18 and 39.

[40] There is nothing to indicate that the surviving 'signed' poems of Cynewulf – *Christ II*, *Elene*, *Fates of the Apostles* and *Juliana* – preserve among them any trace of 'authorial' punctuation. *Christ II* (Exeter Cathedral Library, 3501, 14r–20v) is most lightly pointed, although a later reader (or readers) has heavily repointed 14v–15v and 16v–20v. See Ker, *Catalogue*, p. 153. This later repointing marks off both a- and b-lines, and although it is usually identifiable, it makes confident generalizations about the scribal punctuation impossible. On the incised, dry-point marking of verse in the Exeter Book, see McGovern, 'Unnoticed Punctuation', pp. 90–3. *Fates of the Apostles*

If I am correct that both Exeter and Vercelli scribes copied more or less what they saw, and thus were not responsible for the patterns of points we see, then scarcity of points in a realized text represents an early state in the conceptualizing of visual information, and a higher number of points arranged in a coherent pattern indicates a later stage.

THE NOWELL CODEX

When compared to the other major codices with respect to the copying of Old English verse, the Nowell Codex appears quite conservative in its practice. Whether this impression is due to its having been copied in a scriptorium substantially untouched by contemporary trends in format and pointing, or whether it is due to the age of the exemplar for this record, the fact remains that the records of *Beowulf* and *Judith* which have survived in BL, Cotton Vitellius A. xv are surprisingly 'old' in the details of their presentation. The standard date for the Nowell Codex is Ker's estimate of 's. x/xi', which, as Ker notes, may only be accurate to within twenty-five years of the millennium.[41]

In recent years two widely different accounts of the codicology of the Nowell Codex have appeared with significantly different implications.[42] Kevin Kiernan has argued that on historical grounds *Beowulf* could not have been composed before the reign of Cnut and sets a terminus post quem of 1016.[43] Whatever the historical arguments may be for a relatively late

(Vercelli, Biblioteca Capitolare, CXVII, 52v–54r) is the most highly and consistently pointed of the four (at an average of one point per line) and shows a preference for pointing following the b-line. *Elene* and *Juliana* are comparable poems as narratives and are pointed at approximately the same rates (*Elene*, Biblioteca Capitolare, CXVII, 121r–133v, at 15 per cent; *Juliana*, Exeter Cathedral Library, 3501, 65v–76r, at 17 per cent). *Elene*, however, shows a marked preference for pointing before capitals not characteristic of *Juliana*. *Juliana* generally uses points to set off speeches and rarely uses points internally within a speech. *Elene* distributes the points within speeches fairly evenly.

[41] See his *Catalogue*, no. 216 and on the useful and deliberate flexibility of Ker's dating, see p. xx. See now D. Dumville, '*Beowulf* Come Lately. Some Notes on the Palaeography of the Nowell Codex', *Archiv für das Studium der neueren Sprachen und Literaturen* 225 (1988), 49–63.

[42] See Kiernan, *Beowulf*, pp. 65–169 and 219–43 and a summary article, 'Eleventh-Century Origin', p. 20. Kiernan's reading of the evidence is vigorously countered by Boyle, 'Nowell Codex', pp. 28–9.

[43] Kiernan, *Beowulf*, p. 15.

date (and these are certainly not incontestable), Kiernan's assembly of palaeographical evidence does not provide internal evidence to date or localize the two hands of the manuscript. His assembly of palaeographical and codicological data is primarily devoted to revising the standard account of the quiring, a crucial element in his argument that the record of *Beowulf* preserved in Cotton Vitellius A. xv was originally a separate codex.[44]

Perhaps the most distinctive element in Kiernan's argument about *Beowulf* is his interpretation of the damage on fol. 182 (his fol. 179 following Zupitza's foliation), which he takes to be evidence that the folio is a palimpsest.[45] The combination of revised foliation, some evidence of scribal correction elsewhere in the manuscript and interpretation of the rubbing on fol. 182 as deliberate excision led Kiernan to argue that *Beowulf* is the composite of two originally separate compositions, and that the palimpsest is the evidence of editing by scribe B, who attempted to reconcile the two poems. He concludes that 'the eleventh gathering, containing Beowulf's homecoming, is paleographically and codicologically as well as textually transitional'.[46]

Kiernan's view of the poem as we have it presents a picture of scribes A and B as highly self-conscious editors, who, having hit upon the idea of uniting two disparate poems on Beowulf, performed the following operations: numbered the fitts for the first time (B following A), deleted fitt xxiv (A in revisions of the tenth quire), composed a transitional section to mesh the two previously independent poems, Beowulf's homecoming (1888–2199) (B), washed off and rewrote fol. 182 (*Beowulf* 2207–2252) (B), and 'many years later' (p. 262) continued to revise the join made in the supposed palimpsest (B).[47] Kiernan makes several questionable assumptions about the process of writing the manuscript, two of which touch on the significance of visual cues: that the fitt numbers were added as a part of the modernization of the manuscript record and that the writing

---

[44] *Ibid.*, p. 139. In his view of the quiring, *Beowulf* began on what is now quire 6, which he construes to have been a four sheet gathering with two added leaves. This view requires the last gathering of *Alexander's Letter* to be composed of three sheets, that is, quire 5^6 (see his p. 126).

[45] Kiernan acknowledges T. Westphalen's earlier account of the possibility of a palimpsest in *Beowulf 3150–55: Textkritik und Editionsgeschichte* (Munich, 1967).

[46] Kiernan, *Beowulf*, p. 258.

[47] For a review of his argument and conclusions, see especially J. D. Niles, review of *Beowulf and the Beowulf Manuscript* by Kevin S. Kiernan, *Speculum* 58 (1983), 76–7.

of the manuscript was done late in the first quarter of the eleventh century.[48] On these two issues the punctuation in the manuscript provides telling evidence that Kiernan does not address. Given the development of the practice of pointing Old English verse which can be inferred from the texts of the earlier two codices, as well as from other, separately transmitted poems, it is quite unlikely that the pointing in *Beowulf* represents eleventh-century practice or was added by the scribes who copied this work.

Before examining the pointing of the manuscript, it would be useful, however, to present Leonard Boyle's alternate version of the copying of the manuscript. Boyle argues that scribes A and B collaborated by dividing between them a copy-text which had the same works in the same order as the current Nowell Codex. When B took over from A on 175v4 (British Library foliation), he had already written quires 12–14. In this reconstruction, quire 11 is important, not as a sign of revision, but as evidence that the copy-text of the Nowell Codex was of the same dimensions as the existing manuscript. Though ruled for 20 lines, quire 11 has 21 lines each on 177v–179r. The unobtrusive placement of these added lines on two openings argues that the scribe knew well in advance that he had to make up four lines, because, as Boyle concludes, quire 11 was 'exactly of the same size, text-frame, and ruling' as scribe B's copy text.[49] In other words, both scribes had to have been copying faithfully and carefully.[50]

Neither Boyle nor Kiernan examines the pointing of the manuscript in his argument. In itself, this omission is unsurprising, given the general editorial disinclination to engage the problem of pointing in the poetic records of the manuscript.[51] But the pointing of the verse in this manuscript, though difficult to decipher, is significant within the larger

[48] For an account of the numbering, see P. W. Conner, 'The Section Numbers in the *Beowulf* Manuscript', *ANQ* 24, nos. 3–4 (1985), 33–8.

[49] Boyle, 'Nowell Codex', p. 26. Boyle notes further that A had made similar adjustments in his quire 10 when he filled his already ruled frames with 22 instead of 20 lines to gain 32 lines in copying.

[50] Boyle argues that the 'fitt' numbers existed in the copy-text and that the scribes simply copied them (*ibid.*, p. 30).

[51] As, for example, Dobbie, ASPR 4, states, 'as in other Anglo-Saxon manuscripts, the purpose of these points is by no means clear, since it is difficult to find any structural significance in them' (p. xxx). See also *Beowulf*, ed. F. Klaeber, 3rd ed. (Boston, 1950), p. c.

context of pointing in the poetic records and contributes to the question of the copying and possible revision of the poem.

While the pointing of *Andreas*, for example, or *Widsith* is interesting and provokes speculation because it is copious, the pointing of *Beowulf* and *Judith* is problematic because it is so sparing. It is, however, significant, that the pointing of *Beowulf* is consistent across the two stints of the scribes, that the very brief instances of fuller pointing occur in both stints, and that the pointing of *Judith*, copied by scribe B, is even sparer than that in his stint in *Beowulf*.

In gross terms, the overall rate of pointing in *Beowulf* is 19.6 per cent. This figure reflects the agreement between the rates of pointing in the stints of each scribe, A at 19 per cent and B at 20 per cent.[52] Placement of points tends to be consistent as well. Both scribes avoid pointing a-lines; of 624 points only 45 occur following a-lines.[53] Nonetheless, one could hardly describe the pointing of the poem as either metrical or even rhythmic, given its sparsity. The pointing generally marks off statements, and more than half of the points are placed at the juncture of independent clauses. This is not to say, however, that the pointing is syntactic, in the main, since (as in *Andreas*) the absence of points bears no predictive value. Such pointing contrasts markedly with the pointing of the *Menologium* in BL, Cotton Tiberius B. i, but is closer to that of *Juliana* in the Exeter Book, or of *Solomon and Saturn* in CCCC 422. Its similarity to the pointing of the latter poems suggest that its approach to marking the text considerably antedates that in Oxford, Bodleian Library, Junius 11.

There are, however, two brief stretches where the pointing of the manuscript increases in density. The most extensive of these instances occurs in the stint of scribe B, and Dobbie has located this occurrence 'from l. 1963 to about l. 2500'.[54] These specifications are seriously in error and are owing to a suppressed inference that the anomalous punctuation in effect corresponds with the beginning of 'fitt' xxviii and terminates with the end of a sentence. Actually, the new punctuating style begins on 178r,

---

[52] Scribe A writes 370 points in 1926 lines; B writes 253 in 1246 lines in *Beowulf*. The modestly higher percentage in B may be owing to the brief stretches of denser pointing on 177v to 181v.

[53] Eight of these mark the end of a page or folio, and most of the rest separate independent clauses or mark off subordinate clauses. In A's stint there are twenty-eight a-line points, in B's there are seventeen.

[54] ASPR 4, xxx.

where the instances of separation of phrases (as against the distinction of independent clauses) increases radically and continues through the end of 181v.[55]

In this section, pointing still consistently avoids the a-line but becomes more frequent and, as a consequence, marks phrases more than it marks statements. This shift may best be illustrated by the practice on 178v (2062a–84b; Zupitza foliation, 175v).

> [(li) figend]e con him land geare þon[*ne* bioð]
> [(a)br]ocene onba healfe að sweorð eorla
> [syð]ðan ingelde weallað wæl niðas ⁊hī
> [(wif)l]ufan æfter cear wælmū colran
> [weor]ðað þy ic heaðo bearna hyldo ne
> [telg]e. dryht sibbe dæl denū unfæcne
> [fr]eond scipe fæstne ic sceal forð
> [spr]ecan. gen ymbe grendel. þ ðu geare
> [cun]ne sinces brytta to hwan syððan
> [we]arð. hond ræs hæleða syððan heofones
> [gi]m. glad ofer grundas gæst yrre cwō
> [ea]tol æfen grom user neosan. ðær we
> [g]esunde sæl weardodon þær wæs hond
> [s]cio hilde on sæge feorh bealu fægum
> [h]e fyr mest læg gyrded cempa him
> grendel wearð mærū magū þegne
> to muð bonan. leofes mannes lic
> eall for swealg. noðy ær ut ðagen
> [i]del hende. bona blodig toð bealewa
> gemyndig ofða gold sele gongan
> wolde. ac he mægnes rof min costode[56]

---

[55] There are instances of relatively increased pointing on 183r–186v, but these are well within the limits of passages in the stint of scribe A, specifically on fols. 139 and 141.

[56] '(The other one) escapes alive from there; he readily knows the land. Then on both sides will the oaths of warriors be broken; afterwards deadly hatreds will boil within Ingeld, and love for his wife will become cooler after the seethings of sorrow. For this I do not value the loyalty of the Heathobards, a measure of peace secure for the Danes, firm friendship. I must speak further yet about Grendel, that you may readily know, dispenser of treasure, what became of the hand-fight of warriors afterwards. After the gem of heaven had glided over the earth, the angry guest came, a terrible being enraged in the evening came seeking us where safe we guarded the building. Battle was fatal for Hondscio there, a deadly evil for the man fated to die; he lay dead first, a girded

The pointing in this passage (in which Beowulf describes his first encounter with Grendel) is slightly more than double that for the usual practice in the stint of scribe B. There is an uncharacteristic number of syntactical separations caused by the points, e.g. 'sprecan. gen', 'wearð. hondræs', 'gim. glad', 'idelhende. bona', representing placement of four of the nine points. But observing the presence of this anomalous pointing does not go very far towards explaining it. Much of this pointing occurs during Beowulf's account to Hygelac of his adventures among the Danes. However, its use is inconsistent and begins not with Beowulf's speech, but with the imagined exhortation of the old Heathobard (lines 2047–56). The occurrence of this pointing in quire 11 and its brief appearance in quire 12 provides positive information about the source of the pointing and some negative information about the date of the copying of the codex.

An examination of the spacing of 178r–181v illustrates how costly of space pointing is. That the points are not crowded but are given their own space implies (in conjunction with the colour of ink and the shape of the points, matching the dot over a 'y') that these were written by scribe B. That they are additionally costly of space and occur on those folios pressed to include twenty-one instead of twenty lines suggests that the scribe acknowledged that they were important, since he might have gained a bit of space by either crowding or omitting the points. However, their presence in a portion of the quire pressed for space suggests that the scribe took them from his exemplar, since it is unlikely that he would begin to add a practice especially costly of space at precisely the place that he was working so diligently to conserve it. Two further pieces of evidence suggest that this pointing is not original with the scribe as a consequence of some 'revision'. The first of these is the presence of identically peculiar pointing in the work of scribe A in fols. 139 and 141; the second is the dating of this style of pointing.

Had the unusual pointing of quire 11 begun on 175v4 (with the beginning of scribe B's work in that quire), one might reasonably infer that this pointing was characteristic of the approach of scribe B. However, the pointing in this part of the quire is identical to that which precedes it and continues quite normally until 178r. Even so, one might have suspected

champion; for that illustrious young retainer Grendel became a cannibal, he entirely swallowed the beloved man's body. Nor for anything did that bloody-toothed slayer, mindful of destruction, wish to leave that gold-hall empty-handed, but bold in his strength he made trial of me.'

the anomalous pointing to be the work of scribe B, were it not for its presence also early in the work of scribe A. Fols. 139 and 141 show the same propensity to point more frequently, and perhaps, as a result, to place points where they interrupt syntactic units. This style of pointing occurs early in scribe A's copying of *Beowulf*, though it does not coincide with the beginning of the text. While there does not seem a syntactic or a metrical reason for the frequency of pointing here, the points do mark off speeches, and perhaps are meant to be a rhythmical marker of heightened drama. Certainly, this argument could be defended for the old Heathobard's speech, and most of the rest of the pointing in quire 11 is part of Beowulf's own account of his adventures among the Danes.

If the anomalous pointing which appears in quire 11 were the work of scribe B and part of some revision he had made in the surviving record of *Beowulf*, it would be reasonable to suppose that this style of pointing was contemporary with the manuscript, in short, that it represented current practice in contradistinction to that pointing in the copy-text of the manuscript. The presence of similar pointing in two brief bursts in the stint of scribe A, located as they are in a portion of the manuscript never suspected of being rewritten or revised, suggests that this practice does not reflect B's unique reading of the narrative. Does it, then, suggest that this pointing is contemporary with scribes A and B? This contention is harder to demonstrate or disprove, owing to the possibility that these scribes may be working out of the mainstream of developments in current scribal practice. Nonetheless, some useful negative information may be derived from these passages.

The main style of pointing in *Beowulf*, that is, division of the text into long statements, is consonant with practice in poetic manuscripts which may be dated relatively early. *Solomon and Saturn*, as preserved in CCCC 422 is pointed in this fashion.[57] I have argued that the exemplar for the B and C versions of the Chronicle entries for 937 and 942, a manuscript which antedated 978, must have been pointed very lightly. However, the records of the verses for 973 and 975 in both B (Cotton Tiberius A. vi, s. x^2) and C (Cotton Tiberius B. i, s. xi^1–xi^2) show a clear preference to mark the b-line (that is, in passages where C is presumably copying B), and I suspect that this preference is a transitional pointing strategy of the late tenth century. Where C is almost certainly supplying his own punctuation (in the entry

---

[57] Ker, *Catalogue*, no. 70 (s. x^{med}).

for 937), he uses the eleventh-century practice of marking both half-lines. This tendency to mark both half-lines in the eleventh century can be illustrated from a number of manuscripts.[58]

Whatever the argument for the hinterland location of the scriptorium which produced the present *Beowulf* manuscript, the pointing of the manuscript does not support Kiernan's contentions either that the manuscript represents work done in the latter part of the first quarter of the eleventh century or that the work of the eleventh quire and the so-called palimpsest of fol. 179 (fol. 182) represent contemporary editing. The evidence of the pointing simply cannot sustain such a hypothesis. Rather, the relatively undeveloped punctuation, which marks an understanding of statements, suggests a pointing of the text from a time in the tenth century antedating, or at the latest, contemporary with, the copying of the B-text of the *Chronicle*. Certainly, the anomalous points in *Beowulf* imply a date for their insertion not much later than the turn of the century. And there is every sign that they were simply taken from the copy-text. Such a use of pointing cues places the manuscript of *Beowulf* and *Judith* in stark contrast with the last of the great codices, Junius 11.

THE JUNIUS MANUSCRIPT

Oxford, Bodleian Library, Junius 11, differs in virtually every respect from the earlier three codices. The Exeter Book and the Vercelli Book are miscellanies, each copied by one scribe, apparently over a period of time. The Nowell Codex is a volume produced by the collaboration of two scribes. By contrast, the Junius Manuscript, as we now have it, is a composite of a sort: Liber I was copied by one scribe; *Christ and Satan* of Liber II (on which two or three scribes worked) was added to Liber I some time later. Scholars are divided on the specific thematic unity of the composite manuscript, but generally agree that the scribe who added *Christ and Satan* attempted to 'complete' the contents of the manuscript.[59] Unlike any other

---

[58] For example, Oxford, Bodleian Library, Junius 11; CCCC 201; Oxford, Bodleian Library, Junius 121; BL, Cotton Tiberius B. i (*Menologium* and *Maxims*).

[59] J. R. Hall ('The Old English Epic of Redemption: the Theological Unity of MS Junius 11', *Traditio* 32 (1976), 185–208, at 190, and in 'On the Bibliographic Unity of Bodleian MS Junius 11', *ANQ* 24, nos. 7–8 (1986), 104–7, at 107) sees in Junius 11 an editorial arrangement designed to reflect salvation history. Finnegan (*Christ and Satan*, ed. Finnegan, p. 11), suggests that *Christ and Satan* was collected for a theme of 'ages of man', but was added to the manuscript quite a bit later. Cf. Lucas, 'Incomplete Ending

manuscript of Old English poetry, Junius 11 is illustrated. In short, Junius 11, the youngest of the four codices, presents a very different conception of book from that in the earlier poetic codices.

While there is general agreement among scholars that Liber I was written by one scribe and Liber II by two or three, there is little agreement on date, hands or provenance. Ker describes the handwriting of Liber I as 'a distinctive upright hand, s. x/xi', but dates the hands of Liber II to s. xi¹.⁶⁰ Such a dating reinforces the argument that Liber II was an afterthought and was added to the original state of the manuscript at a later time. However, Francis Wormald's dating of the manuscript's illustrations to the second quarter of the eleventh century, complicates the issue enormously. Since space was allowed throughout the manuscript for illustrations, and the present illustrations only fill blanks in the text of *Genesis* (up to p. 96), there is no way of being certain whether the illustrations were contemporary with the written text or added later.⁶¹ If both Ker and Wormald are correct, the book which Junius 11 presents was produced less by design than by accretion.

If neither the text nor the illustrations in Junius 11 provide sufficient evidence on which to judge the date or provenance for the production of the manuscript,⁶² the interplay of the two says a great deal about the making of

---

of *Daniel*', pp. 51–2, where he argues that *Christ and Satan* was originally a separate booklet and in the process of combining the booklet with what is now Liber I, *Christ and Satan* 710–29 on p. 229 was rewritten.

⁶⁰ Ker distinguished three hands in Liber II (*Catalogue*, no. 334, p. 408). Raw, 'Construction', p. 189, n. 7, maintains that only two scribes copied Liber II. Raw's arguments on binding and codicology refute Lucas's hypothesis that *Christ and Satan* was originally a folded booklet ('Incomplete Ending of *Daniel*', p. 51). However, her argument that *Christ and Satan* was written beginning on a blank leaf remaining after *Daniel* (in contrast to the separate booklet hypothesis), does not address the question whether *Christ and Satan* was added in the same scriptorium that produced Liber I.

⁶¹ F. Wormald, *English Drawings of the Tenth and Eleventh Centuries* (New York, 1953), p. 76 (no. 50). O. Pächt and J. J. G. Alexander, *Illuminated Manuscripts in the Bodleian Library Oxford*, 3 vols. (Oxford, 1966–73) III, no. 34, date Junius 11 to 1000. Temple, *Anglo-Saxon Manuscripts 900–1066*, no. 58, dates the manuscript '*c*. 1000'.

⁶² For a Christ Church provenance, see Temple, *Anglo-Saxon Manuscripts 900–1066*, no. 58. Temple has been criticized for some uncritical attributions to Christ Church. See L. L. Brownrigg, 'Manuscripts Containing English Decoration 871–1066, Catalogued and Illustrated: a Review', *ASE* 7 (1978), 239–66, at 262. T. Ohlgren suggested the New Minster on the basis of stylistic similarities to illustrations from Fleury manuscripts and Winchester's connection with that continental monastery ('Some New Light on the

Junius 11 as a book. George Henderson's examination of the disagree-ments between text and illustrations in *Genesis* leads him to conclude that text and illustrations were done some time apart, with little or no contact between scribe and illustrators.[63] His analysis implies that the book we now have was actually produced in three disconnected stints perhaps over a period of more than a quarter-century, and any coherence we may see in its construction would be due to the latest redactor of the manuscript.

However, the disagreement between text and illustrations is not necessarily due to a lapse of time between copying and drawing. Herbert Broderick has argued that the occasions where the illustrations are either inappropriate or badly placed is evidence that the artists were providing these illustrations to the text for the first time. His identification of iconographic details and motifs in common with the Utrecht Psalter draws attention to the fact that the illustrators of Junius 11 had nowhere to turn for material for their vernacular text but to Latin exemplars.[64]

Whatever the copying history of the texts of *Genesis A*, *Genesis B*, *Exodus* and *Daniel*, it appears that the individual who planned their combination in the earlier stage of the Junius Manuscript envisaged a significant departure from the usual practice for vernacular poetic manuscripts. *This* vernacular manuscript was to receive treatment previously reserved for important Latin poetic texts. And so space was left for illustrations,

---

Old English Caedmonian Genesis', *Studies in Iconography* 1 (1975), 38–73, at 64). P. J. Lucas ('MS Junius 11 and Malmesbury', *Scriptorium* 34 (1980), 197–220, at 214–15 and *Scriptorium* 35 (1981), 3–22 at 14) has argued a Malmesbury provenance for several reasons, the most important of which is the presumed identity of the second artist with the illustrator of CCCC 23, a beautiful copy of Prudentius's *Psychomachia*, demonstrably from Malmesbury. Apropos the present argument, the *Psychomachia* and *Peristephanon* are formatted in single column lines of verse. For an argument against Malmesbury and for Christ Church as an origin for Junius 11, see R. Thomson, 'Identifiable Books from the Pre-Conquest Library of Malmesbury Abbey', *ASE* 10 (1982), 1–19, at 17–18.

[63] G. Henderson, 'The Programme of Illustrations in Bodleian MS Junius XI', in *Studies in Memory of David Talbot Rice*, ed. G. Robertson and G. Henderson (Edinburgh, 1975), pp. 113–45, at 126.

[64] H. R. Broderick, 'Observations on the Method of Illustration in MS Junius 11 and the Relationship of the Drawings to the Text', *Scriptorium* 37 (1984 for 1983), 161–77, at 176. B. C. Raw ('The Probable Derivation of Most of the Illustrations in Junius 11 from an Illustrated Old Saxon *Genesis*', *ASE* 5 (1976), 133–48, at 134), on the basis of other evidence, infers that the text and illustrations were done together, copied from an Old Saxon Genesis. She follows Wormald in dating the production to the second quarter of the eleventh century.

particular attention was paid to capitals, and the scribe was instructed to point the text metrically, after the fashion of the older Latin verse manuscripts.[65] All this makes Junius 11 not simply the youngest of the four codices, but also the most 'modern'.

Although Junius 11 is unusual among the four codices of verse in regularly marking half-lines, not all its punctuation and accents are the work of the main scribe(s).[66] The scribal point is lozenge-shaped and varies slightly in its position depending on the shape of the preceding letter and its finishing stroke. The accent mark has a slight tick to the right. Accents added later lack this tick, are usually shorter, less confident in execution, and placed at different angles. A good example of later additional pointing occurs on p. 5 of the manuscript. While most half-lines on this page are originally pointed, someone else has added virgules to make punctus versus and has added many accents.[67] This is an important qualification to the punctuation, since the use of the punctus versus and punctus elevatus is a convention borrowed from Latin manuscripts and applied to manuscripts

[65] Whatever the impress of Anglo-Latin or continental models of books of verse on the production of Junius 11, the hands of the manuscript are an Anglo-Saxon minuscule, not much affected by Caroline minuscule.

[66] Krapp (ASPR 1, xxii–xxiv) is insufficiently discriminating in his acceptance of varieties of points. See below, n. 67. Recent editors of individual poems in the manuscript have been more circumspect. See *Genesis A: a New Edition*, ed. A. N. Doane (Madison, WI, 1978), pp. 14–15; *Exodus*, ed. P. J. Lucas (London, 1977), pp. 17–24; *Christ and Satan*, ed. Finnegan, pp. 8–9. G. C. Thornley ('The Accents and Points of MS. Junius 11', *TPS* 1954 (Oxford, 1955), pp. 178–205, at 188–9) notes the colours of the points in the manuscripts. He argues that the text is marked for performance, with the accents placed as a guide to liturgical recitative.

[67] Krapp (ASPR 1, xxiii) uses *Genesis* 345–353a (*Genesis B*) to discuss the pointing of Junius 11. Unfortunately, the passage is found on p. 18 of the manuscript, one of the pages which have been gone over heavily by another hand, certainly by a corrector, and possibly by someone else as well. As a result, the impression that Krapp gives about the frequency of accents and the use of punctus versus and elevatus to mark half-lines is misleading. The hyphens on lines 17–18 of the page must be later, and the virgules inserted to form punctus elevati and versi are shaped like nothing else in the original scribe's repertoire. The accent marks on this page are variously shaped. There are small ones with ticks to the right, short ones, as well as accents in the standard form. In terms of colour and placement, the points appear to be the work of the original scribe. The added mark for punctus versus, however, often resembles the shape of the corrector's caret, beneath, for example, *ænga* (p. 18, line 25). See Ker, *Catalogue*, p. 408, for further comments on additional pointing in the manuscript.

of English poetry only late in the Old English period, perhaps well into the eleventh century.[68]

The unusual regularity and frequency of pointing in Junius 11 has been widely observed. Its interest for this study lies precisely in its unambiguously metrical marking of half-lines, its relatively early date for such marking (certainly in Liber I) and the difference between scribal practice in such marking between Liber I and Liber II. I should argue that the occurrence of this method of pointing in Junius 11 is a consequence of its religious subject and of the intended status of the book. Its presence both underscores the uniqueness of the book and represents a new style in the pointing of Old English verse.

In the vast majority of cases in Liber I, the scribe used a point to separate half-lines. The location of the points on the line of writing is regular and is determined by the place where the pen has finished the previous letter. Normally, the scribe leaves plenty of room on either side of the point, though the point tends to be a bit closer to the previous, rather than the following, letter. The scribe mostly uses a simple point, although he at times provides some extra terminal marks. There are some moments when his attention lapses, as, for example, in the last three or four verses of p. 6, where points have been supplied by a later hand. The scribe of Liber I does not always divide the hypermetric verses of *Genesis B* according to 'modern' practice and makes a peculiar hash of 730b–731a: *nu hie word cwyde. his. lare for leton* (p. 34). The correct point after *his* appears an afterthought. Occasionally, he will supply extra points in the middle of a hypermetric line.

Pointing practice in Liber II differs significantly from that in Liber I. Liber II (that is, the last seventeen pages of the manuscript) was written by at least two different hands: pp. 213–15 by a rather clumsy scribe, whom Ker describes as 'incompetent'; pp. 216–28, by a second scribe; and p. 229, possibly by a third.[69] The stint of the 'incompetent' scribe (pp. 213–15) has been much corrected to compensate for careless copy-

---

[68] For manuscripts of Old English verse displaying this kind of metrical point, see below, n. 72.

[69] Ker, *Catalogue*, no. 334. Ker dates the first two hands to s. xi[1], but does not date the third. Cf. Raw, 'Construction', p. 189, n. 7, who cites a private communication from Francis Wormald to the effect that there are only two hands in Liber II.

ing.[70] Even apart from his orthography, the original scribe's perceived faults are worthy of note. When it was determined that this scribe's notion of pointing was clearly at odds with the practice of the main scribe of Liber I, the original pointing of pp. 213–15 was supplemented by another hand, apparently the corrector of pp. 1–26.

The scribe of pp. 213–15 was somewhat casual in his pointing practice. He neglected to point before internal capitals, for example, on p. 213, line 7, *Seolua* (line 13a) and p. 214, line 11, *atol* (line 61a), before which the present points have been added by the corrector. The scribe also neglected terminal points, for example, on p. 214, line 20 after *drugon* (line 74b) and p. 215, line 26 after *gelomp* (line 124b). In fact, the 'incompetent' scribe of pp. 213–15 appears to have had difficulty remembering to point. He did not have much sense of space, and if some of the crowded points are indeed his, they seem to have been afterthoughts on his part. For example, on p. 215, line 21, following *swa he aer dyde* (line 116b), either the scribe inserted a caret and squeezed in a point for consistency's sake, or he placed a punctus versus in an unusual and peculiar position. The points on p. 215 are so tiny and closely spaced that they appear in most cases to be afterthoughts, especially on the first half of the page.

Pointing is somewhat easier to assess in the stint of the second scribe of Liber II (pp. 216–28). His point is regularly dark and diamond-shaped, and though the hand is somewhat compressed, genuine points are distinct. The added pointing is faint, small and continues in the same fashion as that in the stint of the earlier scribe (for example from p. 217). Whoever copied p. 229 does not point half-lines consistently, and the corrector occasionally makes mistakes here in his pointing.

The scribes of Liber II had a different concept of pointing than did the scribe of Liber I. In *Christ and Satan*, those marks which appear to be the work of the original scribe are closer to the pointing style in the other major codices: occasional, sporadic, not easily predictable. In fact, the 'incompetent' scribe even omits the terminal point at the end of his stint. The pointing has been 'completed' by the later corrector, who squeezed in points where he thought necessary. He also provided virgules to make the

---

[70] M. D. Clubb (*Christ and Satan: an Old English Poem*, Yale Studies in English 70 (New Haven, CT 1925), xvi) notes the work of a 'corrector' who changed vowels to Late West Saxon, mostly through *Christ and Satan* 125b. This individual also has corrected separations and errors of jointure. To this scribe's work Clubb ascribes the interlinear glosses.

punctus elevatus, normally found between a- and b-lines. In this, he borrows from the practice in Latin manuscripts.[71]

The uncertain pointing of the scribes of Liber II, who were adding *Christ and Satan* to the manuscript at some time removed from the original production of the manuscript, underscores the uniqueness of the metrical pointing in Liber I (especially if Ker is correct in his dating of the manuscript to the turn of the century). To find a close analogue to this sort of verse pointing in Old English poems one has to look in some interesting places, primarily late copies of verse, all religious.[72]

The Old English verses copied closest in date to those in Junius 11 are found in Part A of CCCC 201 (written, according to Ker, in a 'delicate, unusual hand of s. xi in'.). Its poems, *Judgement Day II*, *An Exhortation to Christian Living* and *A Summons to Prayer* (pp. 161–7), use a medial point to mark half-lines, though some lines are not marked. Capital initials are preceded by a punctus versus.[73]

Another useful comparison is offered by BL, Cotton Tiberius B. i and CCCC 201. In Tiberius B. i, the work which Ker identifies as that of hand 2 (112r–118v: s. xi^{med}) begins with the *Menologium* on a new quire of 8. *Maxims* follows on fol. 115. The large difference between the present states of the pointing of the two poems is due to the work of a later reader. To 113v13, the *Menologium* is pointed metrically and a punctus elevatus appears as well, primarily at the a-line. The virgule forming the punctus elevatus, however, is by another hand, sloppily formed, and not always accurate. The original scribal points are medial and consistently mark half-lines. The following poem, *Maxims*, is marked in half-lines by medial

---

[71] The tails of the punctus versi in *Christ and Satan* are owing to the corrector.

[72] Manuscripts of Old English verse displaying this kind of metrical pointing include: BL, Cotton Tiberius B. i, 112r–115v (Ker, *Catalogue*, no. 191: s. xi^{med}); Oxford, Bodleian Library, Junius 121, 43v–52r and 53v (*ibid.*, no. 338: s. xi$^{3/4}$); CCCC 201, pp. 161–7 (*ibid.*, no. 49: s. xi^{in}) and pp. 167–9 (s. xi^{med}); and BL, Cotton Julius A. ii, 136r–137r (*ibid.*, no. 158: s. xii^{med}). It is worth noting that the poetic contents of all these manuscripts are religious.

[73] The same scribe copied a translation of the *Regularis concordia* on pp. 1–7, and took some pains to produce an attractive right-justified page. He uses both a medial point and a punctus versus to mark statements within divisions of the text. Usually the punctus versus precedes a capital. Single points are less frequent than punctus versus and are used sometimes before ⁊, around numerals, before subordinating adverbs, though infrequently. By contrast, his practice in the poems highlights his formal, metrical pointing for verse.

points. This hand continues through the annal for 491 in the C-version of the *Chronicle*. At this point the work of the hand examined in ch. 5 begins, whose practice reflects at times the practice of his exemplar and at times his own contemporary conventions.

In both cases just discussed, purely metrical pointing occurs in manuscripts later than Junius 11. It is, I believe, significant that the earliest examples of verses pointed purely for metrical reasons, that is in the 'new' fashion, are the religious verses in CCCC 201. In terms of the status or the interest of the text, one might argue that the first candidate for a newer style of pointing, one that looked to Latin modes of arraying a written text, would be overtly, theologically didactic. And it is to this connection that I believe that Liber I of Junius 11 owes its new, bookish metrical pointing.[74]

Junius 11 is a textual production different from the other three codices. It is unique among Old English verse manuscripts in its treatment of pointing, its special ornamentation of large initial capitals, and certainly in its illustrations to the text.[75] The sequence of pictures and text in *Genesis* connect Junius 11 more surely with the illustrated manuscripts of the *Psychomachia* than with any of the other three great codices of Old English verse.[76]

CONCLUSIONS

From this analysis it should be clear that Junius 11 differs markedly from the other three codices in its use of graphic cues to direct a reader's activity. It is a forward-looking text, applying as it does a system of metrical pointing independent of the specific poems it informs and elucidates. The pointing practices of the Exeter Book, the Vercelli Book and the Nowell Codex are, by contrast, conservative and backward-looking. I have suggested that the evidence of these manuscripts indicates that their pointing was copied along with the texts and not added by the scribes. This

---

[74] P. Clemoes ('Liturgical Influence on Punctuation in Late Old English and Early Middle English Manuscripts', *Occasional Papers* 1 (Cambridge, 1952), 1–22, at 16) discusses the influence of liturgical marking of positurae on the writing of Old English prose.

[75] The illustrations in Cotton Vitellius A. xv and Cotton Tiberius B. v are to prose texts.

[76] On the manuscripts of the *Psychomachia* written or owned in England before the Conquest, see G. R. Wieland, 'The Anglo-Saxon Manuscripts of Prudentius's *Psychomachia*', *ASE* 16 (1987), 213–31, at 215–17.

inference is simply the most economical way to account for the variety of punctuation practice in the manuscripts. There is, however, another possible explanation: if the scribes indeed pointed these texts themselves, then the individual texts each called forth discrete pointing. Both explanations present the state of pointing in these codices as highly individual, expressive readings. They are performances and readings, not directions for the performance of a reading. They record, in short, a transitional stage in the transmission of verse, where necessary interpretative information appears in graphic directions determined and mediated by the subjectivity characteristic of oral performance.

APPENDIX

Pointing in the Exeter Book[1]

	Lines	Points	Rate
Christ I	439	67	.152
Christ II	427	43	.10
Christ III	797	132	.165
Guthlac A	789	177	.22
Guthlac B	560	91	.16
[Subtotal Booklet I	3012	510	.169]
Azarias	191	51	.267
Phoenix	677	109	.16
Juliana	731	126	.17
Wanderer	115	43	.373
Gifts of Men	113	50	.44
Precepts	94	22	.23
Seafarer	124	20	.16
Vainglory	84	14	.16
Widsith	143	103	.72
Fortunes of Men	98	34	.346
Maxims I (A)	70	16	.228
Maxims I (B)	66	21	.318
Maxims I (C)	66	19	.287
Order of World	102	15	.147
Rhyming Poem	87	33	.38
Panther	74	17	.23
Whale	88	23	.26
[Subtotal Booklet II	2923	716	.244]

[1] I follow here Patrick Conner's division of the Exeter Book into three booklets: Booklet I (1r–52v) Booklet II (53r–97v) and Booklet III (98r–end).

188

Partridge	16	3	.187
Soul and Body	121	26	.214
Deor	42	13	.309
Wulf and Eadwacer	19	5	.263
Riddles 1–59	931	194	.208
Wife's Lament	53	9	.169
Judgment	119	21	.176
Resignation	118	14	.118
Descent into Hell	137	32	.23
Almsgiving	9	1	.11
Pharaoh	8	1	.125
Lord's Prayer	11	1	.09
Homiletic Fragment	20	10	.50
*Riddle 3*ob	9	1	.11
Riddle 60	17	4	.235
Husband's Message	53	6	.11
Ruin	49	12	.244
Riddles 61–95	409	78	.19
[Subtotal Booklet III	2141	431	.201]
TOTAL	8076	1657	.205

8

Conclusion

In its analysis of the mode of scribal literacy represented in the manuscripts of Old English verse, this book has attempted to construct a framework within which to understand the various forms of evidence that manuscript transmission offers. Such a study necessitates recognizing the material aspects of a literary text, that is, that a text exists in the world as a written object, that important elements of its meaning are fixed in the visual array by which it is presented on a page, and that each realization of the text depends on a unique act of scribal reception. For this reason, the visual array of the manuscript and the ability of the scribe as reader have been the twin focuses of this study.

The most immediate point of entry into this study of the mode of literacy behind the manuscripts of Old English verse was the difference between their visual conventions and those found in manuscripts of Latin verse. The complex use of lineation, capitalization and punctuation in the copying of Latin verse and its absence for so long in the copying of Old English verse suggest that a reader brought different kinds of knowledge to the reading of verse in the two languages. Because its manuscripts were low both in orthographic redundancy and in graphic cues, Old English verse must have required a good deal of predictive knowledge from its readers.

The amount and kind of information encoded in the visual array of a text afforded a second point of entry into the question of the mode of scribal literacy, for this information reminds us of the importance of the manuscript as a physical object. The ubiquity of books in modern life – cheap, mass-produced, apparently identical – easily effaces the significance of the medieval book as both a textual object and a textual reading, and it fosters at the same time a view of 'text' as a disembodied entity. But the differences between modern and early medieval literacy suggest that

190

classical approaches to the editing of Old English verse texts, insofar as they disregard the text's visual array, may filter out important information on the reading and transmission of Old English verse. A third point of entry into the problem of scribal literacy lay in the examination of the oral formula as a continuing mode of thought. Studies of oral formulae are generally composition- or production-oriented, but formulae are crucial also for the reception of a 'traditional' message. The present study has broadened the inquiry into formula by extending it (in an early literate situation) to the receiver of the message – in this restricted instance, the scribe.

Given these approaches to the problem, I believe that it is possible to draw a number of conclusions about the scribal literacy represented in the manuscripts under investigation. The preceding chapters have defined characteristics of what I have termed a 'transitional literacy' in the copying of Old English verse. Prominent among them is the significant variance which appears in the transmission of multiply attested works. In my view, the evidence of these variants indicates that early readers of Old English verse read by applying oral techniques for the reception of a message to the decoding of a written text. Specifically, I have argued that in the cases where variants are metrically, semantically and syntactically appropriate, the scribe has read 'formulaically' and has become a participant in and a determiner of the text. Such a view reinterprets the nature of scribal literacy and the significance of textual variance. I have argued as well for a reinterpretation of the visual cues which the Old English verse manuscripts afford. The comparatively late development of abstract visual cues as interpretative markers (e.g. space, capitals, points) suggests a rough limit for appearance of a more nearly 'modern' scribal literacy.

Chs. 2 and 3 infer the working of a transitional literacy in the reading and copying habits of the scribes who transmitted Caedmon's *Hymn* and *Solomon and Saturn I*. These poems are radically dissimilar, the first generally accepted as oral in its remote origins, the second clearly the product of a written culture. Their only shared features are the remarkable number of appropriate variants in their manuscript transmissions and the low visual information of their individual manuscript states. For Caedmon's *Hymn* I have argued that the variability of the text in the *AE version shows us a reading activity which is formula-dependent (observing metrical and alliterative constraints) and context-defined (in that the variants are semantically appropriate). Such reading uses 'oral' techniques of reception

191

in 'literate' transmission. Similarly, the numerous appropriate variants in *Solomon and Saturn I* indicate that 'formulaic' reading was a possible strategy even in the case of an almost certain composition in writing. Such instances of textual transmission, where the scribes' participation in the texts made them literate analogues to oral performers, may also be seen in the two versions of *Soul and Body* and of Exeter Riddle 30.

Chs. 4 and 5 examine poems which have been considered relatively stable in their transmission. For the *Metrical Preface* to the *Pastoral Care,* it seems clear that Alfred's method of composition was less 'literate' than has been previously thought; certainly Asser's biography is unable to sustain the image of Alfred as a writer. He was, however, a reader, and it would appear that he not only called on traditional formulae in composing his *Metrical Preface,* but also adapted and combined a number of formulae to accommodate new ideas. The variance in the 'stable' text of the *Metrical Preface* takes on a double valence: the variant *eorðbugendum* of Trinity R. 5. 22 shows the same 'oral' reading characteristic of Caedmon's *Hymn* and *Solomon and Saturn I*, while the hesitating variants in the copying of Alfred's hybrid formulae in Trinity and CUL, Ii. 2. 4 show some textual consequences of thwarted formulaic reading. Ch. 5 traces both the variance in the *Chronicle* poems (to 975) and the development of pointing in the verse texts of the *Chronicle* (to 1065). Here the pattern of variance plotted over time and across scribal stints suggests that 'formulaic' reading was more likely in the period before the end of the tenth century than later. Similarly, punctuation in the *Chronicle* poems is also time-dependent, and the appearance, in the late tenth century, of a trend toward apparently metrical punctuation at the b-line coincides with the diminishing of 'formulaic' reading in these records. Chs. 6 and 7 use this information to examine the difficulties inherent in developing a theory of punctuation for Old English verse. In my reading of the evidence, the relative economy of punctuation in manuscripts of Old English verse (especially compared to the use of points or space in Latin verse) argues that the early reader of verse brought to the text necessary interpretative information aided by an understanding of formulaic convention. The growth of visual cues as interpretative supplements in the manuscripts charts the gradual alienation of the reader from vital formulaic tradition.

While the B- and C- manuscripts of the *Chronicle* poems suggest a movement toward metrical pointing at the b-line in the late tenth century, it is an interesting shared feature of the Exeter Book and the Nowell Codex that their spare pointing is both conservative and backward-looking. The poems of the Vercelli Book are pointed in widely differing fashions, and its scribe, like the scribe of the Exeter Book, appears to have copied, in the main, the pointing of his various exemplars. The reason behind the light pointing of *Beowulf* and *Judith* is less amenable to explanation: if the pointing was not simply taken from their exemplars, the copying of the texts may well have been done in a scriptorium out of the main stream. The Junius Manuscript, however, is quite a different story. It is a forward-looking production, systematically applying a metrical pointing to the text. If the illustrated, pointed poems of Liber I look to the rule of Latin modes of arraying texts, Liber II, with its idiosyncratic pointing, reminds us of an earlier set of vernacular origins.

The evidence of scribal reading and transmission which this study has presented offers both challenges and reminders. To the extent that scribal reading and copying of verse implies scribal participation in the making of the text, the evidence of verse in multiple copies raises important questions about the conventions in which we normally present modern textual editions of Old English verse. In a participatory transmission, and in the context of an early, transitional literacy, presentation of a standard edition with modern literate spacing, capitalization and punctuation may limit the historical usefulness of such an edited text. The challenge is clear: what editorial strategies may we devise to present a multiply attested Old English poem in a form which both reflects its existence as a complex of realized texts and represents the subtle visual information contained in its graphic arrays? More generally, in scholarly editions, how may printing conventions be extended to accommodate the developing visual significances of scribal practice in order to present Old English verse in its fullest historical dimensions?

This evidence challenges as well the ways in which we read and criticize Old English verse. The material features of the texts under discussion remind us that a poetic text comes into existence within a social context. Surviving Old English verse texts, whatever the circumstances of their composition, are collaborative products whose scribes have not merely transmitted the texts but have actually taken part in shaping them. Knowledge of the circumstances of transmission should make us wary about inferring authorial intention from a text affected to an unknown degree by participatory reading and copying. Indeed, the modern, critical reflex to recover an authorial text devalues the historical significance and

193

meaning of the actual, realized texts which show us the poem working in the world.

And finally, the evidence of distinct modes of scribal literacy, at least as they are represented by multiply attested texts of Old English verse, presses us to become conscious of the cultural assumptions and historical circumstances of our own literacy. To do so is to recognize the time-bound nature of perception which, even as it divides us from the past, allows us to claim kinship with it. In that moment of recognition we affirm the past's critique of the present. The exchange is a fair one.

Bibliography

Arngart, O., ed., *The Leningrad Bede: an Eighth-Century Manuscript of the Venerable Bede's 'Historia Ecclesiastica Gentis Anglorum' in the Public Library, Leningrad*, EEMF 2 (Copenhagen, 1952)

Bately, J. M., ed., *The Anglo-Saxon Chronicle: MS A*, The Anglo-Saxon Chronicle: a Collaborative Edition 3 (Cambridge, 1986)

Bäuml, F. H., 'Varieties and Consequences of Medieval Literacy and Illiteracy', *Speculum* 55 (1980), 237–65

Benson, L. D., 'The Literary Character of Anglo-Saxon Formulaic Poetry', *PMLA* 81 (1966), 334–41

Bessinger, J. B., and P. H. Smith, *A Concordance to the Anglo-Saxon Poetic Records* (Ithaca, NY and London, 1978)

Blair, P. H., ed., *The Moore Bede: an Eighth-Century Manuscript of the Venerable Bede's 'Historia Ecclesiastica Gentis Anglorum' in Cambridge University Library (Kk. 5. 16)*, EEMF 9 (Copenhagen, 1959)

Blake, N. F., 'The Scribe of the Exeter Book', *Neophilologus* 46 (1962), 316–19

Bosworth, J., and T. N. Toller, *An Anglo-Saxon Dictionary* (London, 1898)

Boyle, L. E., 'Optimist and Recensionist: "Common Errors" or "Common Variations"?', in *Latin Script and Letters: 400–900*, ed. J. J. O'Meara and B. Naumann (Leiden, 1976), pp. 264–74

'The Nowell Codex and the Poem of *Beowulf*', in *The Dating of Beowulf*, ed. C. Chase (Toronto and London, 1981), pp. 23–32

Brown, T. J., 'Punctuation', *Encyclopaedia Brittanica*, 15th ed. (1974) XV, 274–7

Campbell, A., ed., *The Battle of Brunanburh* (London, 1938)

Chambers, R. W., M. Förster and R. Flower, ed., *The Exeter Book of Old English Poetry* (London, 1933)

Chaytor, H. J., 'The Medieval Reader and Textual Criticism', *Bulletin of the John Rylands Library* 26 (1941–2), 49–56

Clanchy, M. T., *From Memory to Written Record: England, 1066–1307* (London, 1979)

Colgrave, B., and R. A. B. Mynors, ed., *Bede's Ecclesiastical History of the English People* (Oxford, 1969)

Conner, P. W., 'The Structure of the Exeter Book Codex (Exeter, Cathedral Library, MS. 3501)', *Scriptorium* 40 (1986), 233–42

Cross, J. E., 'The Literate Anglo-Saxon – On Sources and Disseminations', *PBA* 58 (1972), 67–100

Derrida, J., *Of Grammatology*, trans. G. C. Spivak (Baltimore, MD, 1976)

Dobbie, E. V. K., *The Manuscripts of Cædmon's Hymn and Bede's Death Song* (New York, 1937)

Dobbie, E. V. K., ed., *Beowulf and Judith*, ASPR 4 (New York and London, 1953)
The Anglo-Saxon Minor Poems, ASPR 6 (New York and London, 1942)

Duggan, J. J., ed., *Oral Literature* (New York, 1975)

Dumville, D. N., *Wessex and England from Alfred to Edgar: Six Essays on Political, Cultural, and Ecclesiastical Revival* (Woodbridge, forthcoming)

Dunning, T. P., and A. J. Bliss, ed., *The Wanderer* (New York, 1969)

Ehwald, R., ed., *Aldhelmi Opera*, MGH, Auctores Antiquissimi 15 (Berlin, 1919)

Finnegan, R. E., ed., *Christ and Satan: a Critical Edition* (Waterloo, Ontario, 1977)

Fry, D. K., 'Caedmon as a Formulaic Poet', in *Oral Literature: Seven Essays*, ed. J. J. Duggan (New York, 1975), pp. 41–61
'The Memory of Cædmon', in *Oral Traditional Literature: a Festschrift for Albert Bates Lord*, ed. J. M. Foley (Columbus, OH, 1981), pp. 282–93

Gibson, E. J., and H. Levin, *The Psychology of Reading* (Cambridge, MA and London, 1975)

Glorie, F., ed., *Variae Collectiones Aenigmatum Merovingicae Aetatis I*, CCSL 133 (Turnhout, 1968)

Gneuss, H., 'A Preliminary List of Manuscripts Written or Owned in England up to 1100', *ASE* 9 (1981), 1–60

Goody, J., *The Domestication of the Savage Mind* (Cambridge, 1977)
The Interface between the Written and the Oral (Cambridge, 1987)

Greenfield, S. B., and F. C. Robinson, *A Bibliography of Publications on Old English Literature to the End of 1972* (Toronto and Buffalo, NY, 1980)

Hart, C., 'The B-Text of the *Anglo-Saxon Chronicle*', *JMH* 8 (1982), 241–99

Havet, L., *Manuel de critique verbale appliquée aux textes latins* (Paris, 1911)

Horgan, D. M., 'The Relationship between the OE MSS of King Alfred's Translation of Gregory's *Pastoral Care*', *Anglia* 91 (1973), 153–69
'The Lexical and Syntactic Variants Shared by Two of the Later Manuscripts of King Alfred's Translation of Gregory's *Cura Pastoralis*', *ASE* 9 (1981), 213–21

Jabbour, A., 'Memorial Transmission in Old English Poetry', *CR* 3 (1969), 174–90

Kellermann, G., and R. Haas, 'Magie und Mythos als Argumentationsmittel in den ae. Dialoggedichten *Salomon und Saturn*', in *Festschrift für Karl Schneider*, ed. E. S. Dick and K. R. Jankowsky (Amsterdam and Philadelphia, 1982), pp. 387–403

Ker, N. R., *Catalogue of Manuscripts Containing Anglo-Saxon* (Oxford, 1957)

Keynes, S., and M. Lapidge, *Alfred the Great: Asser's 'Life of King Alfred' and other Contemporary Sources* (Harmondsworth, 1983)

Kiernan, K. S., *Beowulf and the Beowulf Manuscript* (New Brunswick, NJ, 1981)

'The Eleventh-Century Origin of *Beowulf* and the *Beowulf* Manuscript', in *The Dating of Beowulf*, ed. C. Chase (Toronto and London, 1981), pp. 9–21

Krapp, G. P., ed., *The Junius Manuscript*, ASPR 1 (New York and London, 1931)

The Vercelli Book, ASPR 2 (New York and London, 1932)

Krapp, G. P., and E. V. K. Dobbie, ed., *The Exeter Book*, ASPR 3 (New York and London, 1936)

Lindsay, W. M., ed., *Isidori Hispalensis episcopi etymologiarum siue originum libri xx*, 2 vols. (Oxford, 1911)

Lord, A. B., *The Singer of Tales* (Cambridge, MA, 1960)

'The Merging of Two Worlds: Oral and Written Poetry as Carriers of Ancient Values', in *Oral Tradition in Literature: Interpretation in Context*, ed. J. M. Foley (Columbia, MO, 1986), pp. 19–64

Lowe, E. A., 'A Key to Bede's Scriptorium', *Scriptorium* 12 (1958), 182–90

Lucas, P. J., 'On the Incomplete Ending of *Daniel* and the Addition of *Christ and Satan* to MS Junius 11', *Anglia* 97 (1979), 46–59

Lutz, A., ed., *Die Version G der angelsächsischen Chronik: Rekonstruktion und Edition*, Texte und Untersuchungen zur englischen Philologie 11 (Munich, 1981)

McGann, J. J., *A Critique of Modern Textual Criticism* (Chicago and London, 1983)

McGovern, D. S., 'Unnoticed Punctuation in the Exeter Book', *MÆ* 52 (1983), 90–9

Menner, R. M., ed., *The Poetical Dialogues of Solomon and Saturn* (New York and London, 1941)

Meyvaert, P., 'The Bede "Signature" in the Leningrad Colophon', *RB* 71 (1961), 274–86

Miller, T., ed., *The Old English Version of Bede's Ecclesiastical History of the English People*, 4 vols., EETS, os 95–6, 110–11 (London, 1890–98)

Mitchell, B., 'The Dangers of Disguise: Old English Texts in Modern Punctuation', *RES* ns 31 (1980), 385–413

Old English Syntax, 2 vols. (Oxford, 1985)

Niles, J. D., 'Formula and Formulaic System in *Beowulf*', in *Oral Traditional Literature: a Festschrift for Albert Bates Lord*, ed. J. M. Foley (Columbus, OH, 1981), pp. 394–415

Beowulf: the Poem and its Tradition (Cambridge, MA, 1983)

O'Keeffe, K. O'B., 'The Text of Aldhelm's *Enigma* no. c in Oxford, Bodleian Library, Rawlinson C. 697 and Exeter Riddle 40', *ASE* 14 (1985), 61–73
    'Graphic Cues for Presentation of Verse in the Earliest English Manuscripts of the *Historia ecclesiastica*', *Manuscripta* 31 (1987), 139–46

Ong, W. J., *Rhetoric, Romance, and Technology* (Ithaca, NY and London, 1971)
    Orality and Literacy: the Technologizing of the Word (London and New York, 1982)

Opland, J., *Anglo-Saxon Oral Poetry: a Study of the Traditions* (New Haven, CT and London, 1980)

Page, R. I., 'A Note on the Text of MS CCCC 422 (*Solomon and Saturn*)', *MÆ* 34 (1965), 36–9

Parkes, M. B., 'The Palaeography of the Parker Manuscript of the *Chronicle*, Laws and Sedulius, and Historiography at Winchester in the Late Ninth and Tenth Centuries', *ASE* 5 (1976), 149–71
    'Punctuation, or Pause and Effect', in *Medieval Eloquence: Studies in the Theory and Practice of Medieval Rhetoric*, ed. J. J. Murphy (Berkeley, CA and London, 1978), pp. 127–42
    The Scriptorium of Wearmouth-Jarrow, Jarrow Lecture 1982 (Jarrow, 1983)

Patterson, L., *Negotiating the Past: the Historical Understanding of Medieval Literature* (Madison, WI, 1987)

Peabody, B., *The Winged Word: a Study in the Technique of Ancient Greek Oral Composition as seen principally through Hesiod's Works and Days* (Albany, NY, 1975)

Plummer, C., ed., *Venerabilis Baedae Historia ecclesiastica gentis Anglorum, Historia abbatum, Epistola ad Ecgberctum una cum Historia abbatum auctore anonymo*, 2 vols. (Oxford, 1896)
    Two of the Saxon Chronicles Parallel, 2 vols. (Oxford, 1892–9)

Pope, J. C., *The Rhythm of Beowulf* (New Haven, CT and London, 1966)

Pope, J. C., ed., *Seven Old English Poems*, 2nd ed. (New York and London, 1981)

Raw, B. C., 'The Construction of Oxford, Bodleian Library, Junius 11', *ASE* 13 (1984), 187–207

Scragg, D. G., 'Accent Marks in the Old English Vercelli Book', *NM* 72 (1971), 699–710
    'The Compilation of the Vercelli Book', *ASE* 2 (1973), 189–207

Scribner, S., and M. Cole, *The Psychology of Literacy* (Cambridge, MA and London, 1981)

Shippey, T. A., ed., *Poems of Wisdom and Learning in Old English* (Cambridge, 1976)

Sisam, C., ed., *The Vercelli Book. A Late Tenth-Century Manuscript Containing Prose and Verse: Vercelli Biblioteca Capitolare CXVII*, EEMF 19 (Copenhagen, 1976)

Sisam, K., review of Menner's *Poetical Dialogues*, *MÆ* 13 (1944), 28–36
    Studies in the History of Old English Literature (Oxford, 1953)

Bibliography

Smith, F., *Understanding Reading: a Psycholinguistic Analysis of Reading and Learning to Read*, 3rd ed. (New York, 1982)

Stanley, E. G., 'Unideal Principles of Editing Old English Verse', *PBA* 70 (1984), 231–73

Stevenson, W. H., ed., *Asser's Life of King Alfred* (Oxford, 1904)

Taylor, S., ed., *The Anglo-Saxon Chronicle: MS B*, The Anglo-Saxon Chronicle: a Collaborative Edition 4 (Cambridge, 1983)

Temple, E., *Anglo-Saxon Manuscripts 900–1066* (London, 1976)

Timpanaro, S., *The Freudian Slip: Psychoanalysis and Textual Criticism*, trans. K. Soper (London, 1976)

Treitler, L., 'Oral, Written, and Literate Process in the Transmission of Medieval Music', *Speculum* 56 (1981), 471–91

Williamson, C., ed., *The Old English Riddles of the Exeter Book* (Chapel Hill, NC, 1977)

Whitelock, D., *et al.*, ed., *The Anglo-Saxon Chronicle: a Revised Translation* (London, 1961)

Wright, D. H., review of Blair, *The Moore Bede*, *Anglia* 82 (1964), 110–17

Index

200

Index

Christ Church, Canterbury, 110, 180, n. 62
Cnut, 172
Creed, 102, 103
Cynewulf, 58, 171

Demosthenes, 144

Edgar, king, 128
Edmund, king, 122, 123
Einhard, 84 and n. 18
Eusebius, 53
Evesham, 110
Exeter Book, 59, 138 and n. 1, 139, 147, 149, 155–64, 170, 175, 179, 186, 192–3
  individual poems: *Azarias*, 60, 103, 104, 138, n. 1; *Christ*, 85, n. 22, 86, 87 and 88, n. 26, 96 and n. 1, 97, 98 and n. 4, 99, 100, 101, n. 8, 102, 103, 104, 106, 107, 121, n. 48, 124, nn. 58 and 59, 156, 171, n. 40; *Descent into Hell*, 87, 99, 102; *Fortunes of Men*, 122, 123, n. 56, 163; *Gifts of Men*, 103, 157, 163; *Guthlac*, 64, 86, 97, 98 and n. 4, 99, 100, 101, 102, n. 9, 105, 106, 156, 157, 163, n. 22; *Husband's Message*, 107, 123; *Judgement Day I*, 121, n. 46, 156; *Juliana*, 64, 65, n. 55–6, 97, 99, 101, 102, n. 9, 103, 106, n. 15, 123 and n. 57, 124, n. 58, 157, n. 8, 162–3, 171, n. 40, 175; *Lord's Prayer I*, 59; *Maxims I*, 87, n. 26, 103, n. 11, 158, n. 12; *Panther*, 87, n. 26, 100, 103, n. 11; *Phoenix*, 86, 87, 96, n. 1, 97, 98, 100, 101, n. 8, 105, 106, 122, 157, n. 8, 160–2, 163, n. 22; *Precepts*, 102, 104, 106; *Resignation*, 64, 87, 102, 107; Riddles, 156, 157, 163, n. 22; individual Riddles 2: 99; 3: 120; 4: 107; 5: 102, n. 9; 9: 64; 13: 86, n. 24, 98; 15: 105; 18: 107; 29:

102; 30a and b: 65, 79, 80, 113, n. 17, 134, 192; 35: 103; 40: 62, n. 49, 138–43; 59: 98; 60: 88, 102, 104, 107; 61: 105; 77: 105; 79: 122, n. 51; 83: 122, n. 51; 89: 124, n. 59; 95: 103; *Ruin*, 87, n. 26, 103, n. 11; *Seafarer*, 101, 106, 159–60; *Soul and Body II*, 60, 64, 65, 79, 80, 93, 105, 113, n. 17, 138, n. 1, 170, 192; *Vainglory*, 158; *Wanderer*, 65, n. 56, 102, n. 9, 123, n. 56, 157, 159–60; *Whale*, 96; *Widsith*, 87, 101, 103, 106, 158–59, 175; *Wulf and Eadwacer*, 64, n. 53, 156
Exhortation to Christian Living, 99, 100, 118, 185

Fleury, 180, n. 62
format for Latin verse, 2–3, 23, 26–7, 28–32, 140–41, 190
format for OE verse
  modern editorial, 23, 78, 89, 94, 116, 191, 193
  scribal, 1–3, 23, 34–5, 48, 68–9, 71–6, 126–8, 138–43, 156, 190; use of graphic cues in, 1, 4–5, 22, 23, 26–7, 28, 30, 35, 46, 67, 76, 80, 94, 125–8, 136–7, 138, 155, 158, 160, 186, 190; use of capitals in, 1, 23, 34, 71–3, 89–94, 112, 127–30, 141, 156–7, 160–2, 162–3, 168, 170, 171, 182, 184, 185, 186; use of punctuation in, *see* punctuation *below*
Fragments of Psalms, 99, 107

Gregory, pope, 27, n. 10, 90; *Regula Pastoralis*, 90

Instructions for Christians, 97, 99
Isidore of Seville, *Etymologiae*, 51–2, 145–6

Jerome, St, 144
Judgement Day II, 97, 98, 102, 185
Junius Manuscript, 138 and n. 1, 155, 179, 181, 193

201

Index

Plato, *Phaedrus*, 52
Plegmund, 82
Pater Noster, 48–51, 54–9, 64, 70
Pelagius, 27, n. 10
Prayer, 97
Prosper, 27, n. 10
Prudentius, *Psychomachia*, 139, 180,
    n. 62, 186; *Peristephanon*, 180, n. 62
Psalm 50, 98, 103
punctuation: in Latin verse, 136, 138–41,
    143–46, 152, 153, 182–3; in Old
    English verse, 1, 44–6, 74–6,
    89–94, 112, 126, 128–36, 138–43,
    146–54, 158–64, 165–72, 174–79,
    182–6, 192; *per cola et commata*, 144,
    146

Rægnold, 122
Ramsey, 110, n. 7, 111, n. 13
reading: entropy and, 19, n. 62, 20;
    models of modern, 14–7, 19–20;
    orthographic redundancy in, 17,
    n. 55, 19–21
Regularis concordia: OE translation of, 185,
    n. 73
runes, 51, n. 10, 58 and n. 37

St Augustine's, Canterbury, 2, 139
Satan, 57
'Sator' formula, 70 and n. 66
Saturn, 48–50, 54–5, 59, 71, 72–3
Saulus, 72
Saussure, Ferdinand de, 55
Seasons for Fasting, 97, 98, 102, n. 9, 104,
    105, 121, n. 46
Socrates, 52, 55
Solomon, 48, 50, 55, 71, 72–3
Solomon and Saturn I, 22, 47–51, 54–71,
    73–76, 79, 80, 86, 93, 97, 113,
    n. 17, 134, 175, 178, 191–92

Solomon and Saturn II, 47, 50, 68–9,
    70–4, 87, 97, 101, n. 8, 102, 103,
    106, 113, n. 17, 175, 178
Solomon and Saturn, prose dialogue, 68–9
Summons to Prayer, 185

Tatwine, 53, n. 18
Theodore, 27, n. 10, 29–30
'Tremulous' hand, 89, 91 and n. 38

Vercelli, 165
Vercelli Book, 138, 149, 155, 165–72,
    179, 186, 193
    individual poems: *Andreas*, 65, n. 55,
    85, n. 22, 86, 88, 92, n. 42, 96 and
    n. 2, 97, 98 and n. 4, 99, 102, n. 9,
    104, 105, 106, 107, 120, 122 and
    n. 52, 123, n. 56, 124, n. 59,
    166–69, 171, 175; *Dream of the
    Rood*, 102, n. 9, 171; *Elene*, 65,
    n. 55, 86, 97, 98, 99, 100, 101,
    102 and n. 9, 103, 104, 105, 107,
    119, n. 33, 121, n. 46, 124, n. 58,
    157, n. 9, 171 and n. 40; *Fates of the
    Apostles*, 124, n. 59, 166, 169, 171,
    n. 40; *Soul and Body I*, 60, 65, 79,
    80, 93, 105, 106, 113, n. 17, 138,
    n. 1, 169–71, 192
variance, 5, 14, 21, 40–41, 60–67, 93,
    108, 112, 116–25, 135–6
variants: formulaic, 39–41, 118–25, 136,
    191; 'shadowy', 117–8
Waldere I, 100
Wearmouth-Jarrow, 33, 35, 45
Werferth, teacher of Alfred, 82
Werwulf, teacher of Alfred, 82
Wheloc, Abraham, 114, n. 18
Wilfrid, 27, n. 10, 30
Winchester, 110–11, 180, n. 62
Worcester, 89, 90, 110, 113, n. 15

WITHDRAWN